J. McH. SINCLAIR

A COURSE IN SPOKEN ENGLISH: GRAMMAR

J. McH. SINCLAIR

A COURSE IN SPOKEN ENGLISH: GRAMMAR

LONDON
OXFORD UNIVERSITY PRESS
1972

Oxford University Press, Ely House, London W. 1

GLASGOW   NEW YORK   TORONTO   MELBOURNE   WELLINGTON   CAPE TOWN
IBADAN   NAIROBI   DAR ES SALAAM   LUSAKA   ADDIS ABABA   DELHI
BOMBAY   CALCUTTA   MADRAS   KARACHI   LAHORE   DACCA
KUALA LUMPUR   SINGAPORE   HONG KONG   TOKYO

ISBN 0 19 435215 3

Printed in Great Britain by
Richard Clay (The Chaucer Press) Ltd
Bungay, Suffolk

Contents

Use of this grammar

The original version of this book has been completely rewritten three times. Between each version, it has been used in a variety of teaching situations, and read by a large number of people. The many comments on it range from detailed criticism of the examples to substantial pieces of postgraduate research. It has proved useful in such courses as: advanced English Language teaching in several countries overseas; English Language courses for foreign students and teachers in this country; courses in English linguistics at universities in this country. It has already reached teachers and pupils of almost every nationality, and has been informed by most valuable feedback. This accumulated experience over eight years suggests that three types of reader may find it useful.

(a) Advanced foreign students of English. They will find it quite difficult, unless they are *very* advanced. A lot of effort has gone into the exercises and keys, and the glossary, to permit a good student to use it privately. Its functions would be to provide explanations of many features of modern English, give some practice in controlled sentence construction and to add some intellectual interest to the later stages of learning English.

(b) Foreign teachers of English. They should be able to handle the book with a little experience. It should help them to understand many aspects of the structure of English, and they will find that most of the exercises can be adapted for classroom use. The arrangement of the book is not suggested as a plan for the design of a course, however, and teachers will want to rearrange it for that purpose. Much thought has been given to its function as a work of reference for teachers, mainly in the provision of the glossary and many cross-references.

(c) Native-speaking students of English Language. University and College students can work privately or in class with this book, and it will serve both as a means of learning about English structure and as an introduction to modern linguistics. It provides tools for developing skill in textual analysis, though it does not solve every analytical problem.

Originally, the book was a set of exercises with a few grammatical notes above each exercise. The exercises are still the main feature of the book, but the notes have been expanded more and more, and are still probably too short for some readers. The presentation is usually by way of many examples, which are contrasted according to relevant criteria. From the contrasts develop systems, such as Section 1 of this book shows. A balance has to be found between the space needed to explain a point, and the importance of the point, because often the major features can be outlined in a few lines, while minor ones may take several pages. Minor points are only developed where it seems to be worthwhile in the book as a whole.

Most of the exercises can be answered by anyone with a fair command of English and an understanding of the text. Some can be answered by deduction from the text only. A few test the wider command of English that not all readers of this book will have. In these cases, the Key to the exercises will help.

A full Key with notes is supplied so that this book can be used in a variety of different ways. On a first reading, a quick reading or revision, it may not be possible to afford the time to work each exercise out; so a few examples read with the Key will suffice. On serious study or revision of one particular area, it would be necessary to read all the examples with the Key. If a distinction or a structural pattern is to be learned, or if skill is required with the analytical system or familiarity with the terminology, the exercises should be fully worked without the Key, and the answers then checked against it.

Acknowledgements

A book that has been so long in the making acquires many friends, and I cannot list them all. The debt to Angus McIntosh and Michael Halliday should be evident on every page. Particularly thorough and comprehensive criticisms came from Keith Brown, Norman McLeod and Vivian Salmon. Three colleagues in Birmingham (Vera Adamson, Tom Shippey and Malcolm Coulthard) have helped greatly on the practical side— trying to use the book as a teaching instrument to native and foreign students, and this experience has led to many changes in the manuscript. In addition, Dr Coulthard read right through the finished text and made hundreds of detailed suggestions. I am most grateful to these friends and colleagues and hope that the good qualities of this version are some recognition of their trouble and interest.

Introduction

Modern Grammars

What do you think about grammar? Do you, indeed, think about grammar? Is grammar for you something that can be bad, or good? Does it help us to speak languages? Is it something that never survives outside the classroom, and is pretty sick even inside it?

Today there is more work going on in English grammar than in any other branch of language study. Every few months brings fresh evidence, new ideas, and endless technical discussion. Linguistics is one of the enigmatic new subjects that is developing at great speed and becoming more and more difficult to understand.

Every so often it is worthwhile to pause, and consider the way in which the work in linguistics can be applied in the everyday study of languages: the learning of languages; the training of teachers of languages; the business of communication through languages. This book is a grammar of English for a wide audience. It is up to date, in the sense that it is written against the background of the most recent work in English grammar; but it is old-fashioned too, because it tries to be both comprehensive and simple. A new description of some fragment of English structure may cause a chain reaction right through the rest of the grammar, raising a whole set of problems that had not been thought of, or that had been forgotten, or put on one side because they were too difficult; or the innovations may be so detailed and complicated that they would take up far too much space in a small book.

This book is, first of all, a descriptive grammar. It tries to describe the structure of the English people use, and it pays very little attention to matters of 'correctness' in usage. It concentrates on the most common varieties of spoken and written British English, and avoids highly specialised varieties. There is rather more emphasis on informal spoken English than you commonly find in grammars. Some critics of earlier versions of this grammar asked for a classification of the examples on various scales (e.g. of formality). Certainly it would improve the book if this could be done, but it is beyond the powers of a single author. (A team of experts recently spent three years on a description of just one variety of English![1])

So the foreign reader is left with only a few scattered warnings about examples that are restricted to certain varieties of English only. The alternative—to describe just one variety of English—would have involved a long job of statistical analysis, which the Survey of English Usage is already doing.[2]

Speech and Writing

Speech and writing are different **media**. The structural differences that we notice between a lecture and a book arise partly from the contrast of medium. Pitch of the voice, for example, is used a lot in speech. If the vocal cords vibrate, they must vibrate at a certain frequency; so all the vowels of English, and about half the consonants, have pitch as one of their essential structural components. It is difficult to write down the details of pitch and length, etc. But it is easy to insert lots of small marks between letters and between words—we call them punctuation marks. In turn, it is very difficult indeed to punctuate speech. There are no word-spaces in speech, and the pauses do not occur in places where a comma might occur in writing.

Intonation does for speech something like what punctuation does for writing, and the differences between intonation and punctuation arise from the medium. Speech is continuous modification of a sound-wave; so it would be difficult to keep stopping to put in commas and so on (Victor Borge made himself famous as a comedian by punctuating speech). Writing, even handwriting, comes in separate blocks—letters or words—and it is easy to put small marks in the spaces. Of course, there are many different writing systems in the world, each with its own type of punctuation.

This is just one example of the differences caused by the medium of language. Other differences are caused by the typical situations in which we speak and write. Speech is a **two-way** activity; the **addressee**, the person being spoken to, is usually present and able to interrupt, the speaker is usually able to modify what he wants to say as he goes along; if there

[1] Huddleston *et al.*, *Sentence and Clause in Scientific English.*

[2] The Survey of English Usage is directed by Professor Randolph Quirk at University College, London. Members of the Survey team have already published a number of detailed studies which have informed this work greatly. Details of the Survey, and examples of Quirk's approach, are in his *Essays on the English Language, Medieval and Modern*; Longmans, London 1969.

are other people present the speaker may spend a lot of effort in just finding a moment to start speaking, or in keeping his speech flowing. But writing is typically composed for a remote addressee—some reader at a later date, in very different circumstances. A writer must try to keep up the level of interest for the reader, but he has no fears about being interrupted, or hurried along. He has complete control over the process of composition, while the reader has complete control over the process of understanding. Writing is not the same sort of interaction as speech.

Other speech situations are lectures and talks; the audience is expected to remain silent and listen. They allow the lecturer uninterrupted control of the process of composition. The lecturer, unless he reads out something he has previously written, has a task which is a cross between being a typical speaker and a typical writer. He does not fear interruptions, but he must keep going; he must compose in 'real time' and not at leisure in his study. However **one-way** it looks, there will be a good deal of response from the audience. Laughter, applause, nods, smiles, frowns, hisses, boos are all direct conventional responses, communications from the audience to the speaker, and different from ear-scratching, fidgeting, paper-rustling, sleeping, etc., which tell the speaker indirectly what the audience thinks of his speech but are not verbal communications.

What about two students who pass notes to each other during a lecture? Their activity is in the written medium, but two-way and in real time, so that it has some of the features of spoken conversation.

A major difference between the usual forms of speech and writing is the permanence of writing, as against the impermanence of speech. We do not remember speech accurately unless we try specially, but a writer can refer his readers back twenty pages with the greatest of ease. Our ideas of 'correct' grammar come mainly from study of the written language—speech has been very difficult to study until the present day. It is generally felt that writing should make full use of the permanence of the medium, and should leave no loose ends or ambiguities for the reader to work out.

Speech, on the other hand, is a dynamic process where strict grammatical relationships need only be made across stretches of language a few words long. We do not find only well-defined sentences and paragraphs in speech, and we find quite often that one structure can develop into another without disturbing a listener. Sentences and paragraphs as we know them in writing are divisions of the text; places where the reader can pause, where the grammatical connections are at a minimum. But speakers do not need *grammatical* stopping-places, and they tend to pause in the middle of structures rather than at the boundaries of them. A speaker who 'speaks in sentences' may have trouble in holding his audience.

This book does not attempt to describe the special characteristics of speech, the structural features that do not appear in writing. In particular it does not deal with the 'interaction' side of discourse, the way in which a number of speakers jointly construct a conversation. A lot of research is needed before a description of the real structure of speech can be made. But apart from that, the book tries to give many examples of structures that are common in speech.

Grammatical Categories and Exponents

The type of description used in this book needs a little explanation. It is now fashionable to use the words **deep** and **surface** to talk about grammars; and grammars are getting deeper and deeper. Depth in a grammar concerns the way in which the grammatical **categories** are related to the **exponents**. First of all, to explain what deep grammars are like, a word about categories and exponents.

A grammatical category is abstract—examples are *definite article, subject, transitive, morpheme*. If you want an answer to the question 'What is a transitive relationship?' you should find it defined in the grammar, because 'transitive' is a technical term. Two different grammars of English will probably have slightly different definitions. We try to make clear what we mean by the categories in two ways:

(*a*) We define each category in terms of other ones. So we say that 'the subject of a clause is a nominal group which immediately follows the first word of the predicator when the clause is interrogative'. Or we may say that 'the subject of a clause is a nominal group in number concord with the predicator'. Notice that these definitions mention a number of other categories—*clause, nominal group, predicator, mood, interrogative, number, concord*. Each of these has a definition which involves some others, probably including *subject*.

This sort of definition does not make it possible for us to recognise the subject of every clause. Not all clauses are interrogative, so the first definition relies on us being able to imagine the interrogative equivalent of a *declarative* clause—the relationship between Examples (1) and (2) below.

(1) The sparrow has flown away. (declarative)
(2) Has the sparrow flown away? (interrogative)

Number concord can be shown by comparing (1) with (3) below. But it is not present in all clauses, as Example (4) demonstrates.

(3) The sparrows have flown away.
(4) The sparrow/sparrows had flown away.

That is, we would have to change the verb *tense* from *past* to *present*, and show the difference between *singular* and *plural*. We have now used another category—that of tense.

(*b*) The second way we have of showing what we mean by grammatical categories is the use of examples. Even the four examples so far tell a lot to anyone who is familiar with English. It may not yet be clear what exactly is meant by 'predicator', or 'nominal group', but a number of such examples, along with their analysis, helps a great deal. Consider (5) and (6) with their analyses in (7) and (8).

(5) The sparrow flew away.
(6) Did the sparrow fly away.

(7) | The sparrow | flew | away |
     | subject | predicator | adjunct |

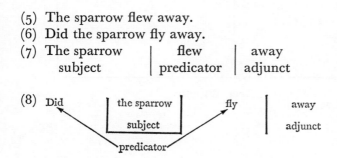

(8)

Nearly everyone would be able to analyse these, and thousands of other sentences, by following just the examples so far. Consider (9) and how it is analysed in (10)

(9) My friend has walked from London.

(10) | My friend | has walked | from London |
     | subject | predicator | adjunct |

All the words of (9) are new in these examples, but there is no difficulty in the analysis.

The examples of actual sentences—nos. (1), (2), (3), (4), (5), (6), (9), are exponents: words, letters, punctuation marks and so on that actually make up the language we write. Exponents exist, on the page or on the recording tape, or in the air as someone speaks. They are the physical events that grammars help to describe.

Deep Grammar

In the examples above, the categories and exponents are very closely related. The sort of grammar we have been doing is surface grammar. Now consider Examples (11) and (12)

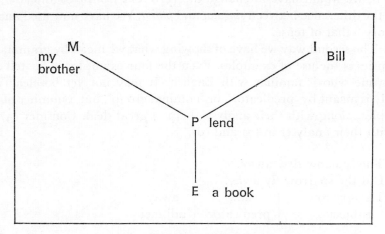

Fig. 0.1. Deep Structure

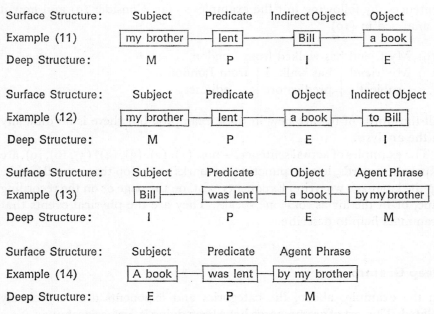

Fig. 0.2. Deep and Surface Structure Related

(11) My brother lent Bill a book.
(12) My brother lent a book to Bill.

These two sentences are nearly identical in meaning, so let us call *Bill* or *to Bill* an **Interested Party** (I) to the lending.

(13) Bill was lent a book by my brother.

The sentence has hardly changed in meaning, yet *Bill* is now the subject. We shall call *my brother* the **Prime Mover** (M), and *a book* the **Affected Entity** (E). So in (14) the subject is E.

(14) A book was lent by my brother.

If we call *lent* the **Pivot** (P) of the sentence, we can now relate examples (11)–(14) to each other by saying that they all have the same deep structure, shown in Fig. 0.1, although in each sentence the sequence of the elements is different. This deep structure develops into surface structures as shown in Fig. 0.2.

Notice how the exponent of the subject changes—*my brother, Bill, a book*. yet the deep category M always relates to *my brother*. Also the sequence of elements changes, and there is no I in (14); yet the deep structure relations do not change.

The word *underlying* is often used to describe deep structure. Here are some more examples:

(15) Bill borrowed a book from my brother.
(16) A book was borrowed from my brother.

Compare (15) and (11)—they are nearly the same in meaning. So are (16) and (14). The difference is that M and I change places. (See Fig. 0.3.)

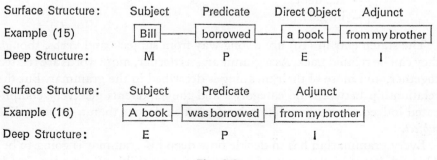

Fig. 0.3

Borrowing and lending are words for the temporary transfer of possessions, which we can symbolise:

Where x is the Prime Mover (M), the verb is *lend*; where Y is M, the verb is
borrow.

With this addition to the grammar of Fig. 0.3, sentences that do not
look a bit alike can be related, for example (17) and (18)

(17) A collection of old manuscripts was lent to the Town Hall (x = M)
     E P I.
(18) I borrowed £100 (Y = M) M P E.

There are several other pairs of verbs that seem to fit such a grammar.
Give and *take* mean a permanent transfer, that does not need the agreement
of one receiving party; *lose* and *find* show a transfer that is accidental—and
so on. The verbs do not need to be in pairs—one can *find* things that have
not been *lost*; *steal* is a verb that has no pair in English meaning *have
stolen from*; *send* adds the meaning of something else between x and Y;
receive can pair with *give, issue* and *send,* among others.

So deep grammar is an analysis of the meanings of the words at the
same time as the structure of the sentences in which they occur. Around
the general notion of 'the loss and gain of possessions' there is a cluster of
verbs. Each verb adds some details to the notion, and excludes other details.
So far we could say the following about our original verb *lend.*

(19) *lend*   [+ transfer of E]
             [+ x = M]
             [+ agreement between M and I]
             [+ temporary]
             [− accident]
             [− illegal]

The statements in (19) are a long way from subjects and verbs, though
they can be related back. As a grammar gets deeper, more words are related
together, and more of their meaning is described in the grammar. But the
relationship between the categories and the exponents gets very complicated indeed. A category like x is very much deeper than a category like
subject.

Every grammarian has to decide how deep his grammar is going to be.
This one keeps as close to surface structure as possible. Every step that it

might take in depth is measured against the amount of complication and abstraction that would be caused. *Lend* and *borrow* are different words in their sound and shape; we can only regard them as exponents of the same word if we have very strong reasons—reasons like (20) for regarding *better* and *good* as the same word.

(20) small   smaller   smallest
      good   better   best

Example: Passive voice   PASSIVE

Let us take the example of the **passive** voice in English, to see how deep and surface grammars are related. Three questions must be answered:

(*a*) What are the exponents of the passive voice?
(*b*) What is the extent of its influence over other choices?
(*c*) What can we say about its meaning?

I shall take these in turn.

(*a*) The exponent of the passive voice is a form of the verb *be* followed, usually straight away, by the *past participle* of a verb.

Example:

(21) I was lent a book.

Since past participles commonly occur as *adjectives*, and since the verb *be* has many other uses, the passive is often ambiguous.

(22) The old man was restrained.

Example (22) can be paraphrased in two ways:

(23) The old man behaved in a restrained fashion; quiet, controlling himself. i.e. he restrained himself.

(24) The old man had to be prevented from some rather violent action. i.e. someone restrained him.

Example (22) is only passive in the meaning of (24); otherwise it is similar to (25), and the participle is *complement*. (See Section 14, page 105)

(25) The old man was happy.

It is clear from this that a passive verb form must be made up of at least two words; also that there is superficial similarity with another structure of **'copula + complement'**[1]

---

[1] A recent study of the passive voice by Hasegawa (*Language*, 1968) considers the passive voice as a special type of 'copula + complement'. It should also be noted here that most of our up-to-date information about passives comes from J. Svartvik *On Voice in the English Verb* (Mouton, 1965), a highly technical book.

(*b*) The influence of the passive over other choices. It is, of course, closely related to **transitivity**; the objects and complements a verb has. Our verb *lend* can have two objects when active, but only one when passive (because one of those objects has become subject: compare (11) and (13)).

Example (26) shows that the passive allows the omission of the phrase that would have been the subject of the active clause, i.e. the person who did the lending.

(26) I was lent a book.

There are many other influences of the passive, but they do not go beyond clause structure. The basic rule to relate active and passive is as follows:

(27) Surface   Deep   Surface
      Structure   Structure   Structure

      Active   ⟵——   P   ——⟶   Passive
      Subject   ⟵——   M   ——⟶   (Agent)
      Object   ⟵——   E   ——⟶   Subject

So Example (28) changes to (29)

Surface Structure:	Subject	Predicate (Active)	Object
Example (28)	The thrush	ate	the worm
Deep Structure:	M	P	E

Surface Structure:	Subject	Predicate (Passive)	Agent Phrase
Example (29)	The worm	was eaten	by the thrush
Deep Structure:	E	P	M

Not shown how they are generated. — dependent by br. diag. Fig. 0.4

More complicated rules are needed for examples like (11)–(25).

(*c*) The meaning of the passive. Compare (28) and (29). The same event is described, but in (29) the worm is the item we are supposed to focus on; in (28), if anything, it is the thrush. The fact that M is not subject in (29) means that the prime mover of the action is not in close association with the verb.

There is one simple statement that sums up the meaning of the passive, then: its subject cannot be M. As the great majority of passives in English have no agent, no M, this statement is very important. Compare (28) and (29) with (30) and (31).

(30) John sold the car.
(31) John was sold the car.

Examples (30) and (31) do not describe the same event—their relationship is like that between past and present, or singular and plural, because the grammatical change alters the meaning in a predictable way.

There is a 'transform equivalent' of (30) and (31), as we see in (32) and (33).

(32) The car was sold by John.
(33) Someone sold the car to John.

But these are not needed to describe the meaning of the contrast between (30) and (31)—as soon as we know that *John* is not M in (31), the rest follows.

There is an interesting class of verbs which show the problem clearly. Consider (34), (35) and (36).

(34)   (i)   The baby fed.
        (ii) The baby was fed.
        (iii) Someone fed the baby.
(35)   (i)   The baby turned in its cot.
        (ii) The baby was turned in its cot.
        (iii) Someone turned the baby in its cot.
(36)   (i)   The tomatoes grew well.
        (ii) The tomatoes were grown well.
        (iii) Someone grew the tomatoes well.

In each of these trios, (i) and (iii) have M as subject; while (ii) has not; (i) and (ii) have no object, while (iii) has; (i) and (ii) also focus attention on the same item, while (iii) does not; (ii) and (iii) refer to a similar event but (i) does not.

Of the three possible pairings there are two reasons above for pairing (i) and (ii), and this is the preferred organisation in this book. The effect of pairing (i) and (ii) is that the deep structural relations are mentioned but not used in the construction of the grammar. Instead, clauses with similar surface structure are contrasted in meaning.

The verbs *feed, grow, turn,* can be transitive or not while active in voice; when **intransitive**, they can have the same subject whether active or passive. The other syntactic points are 'deeper', and this grammar only mentions them.

Systemic Grammar

Nearly all modern grammars work 'downward' from the sentence to the smaller units, and this one is no exception. The reason is that grammatical description is a way of showing how parts fit together in a whole, and the sentence is the 'whole' that we have selected for study. Each grammatical **item**—each word or each clause—has both internal and external relations. Inside a clause we find a subject, predicator, object, etc.; the clause as a whole forms all or part of a sentence. A word may be divided up into morphemes (as *sparrows* is made up of *sparrow* and *s*) or it may not; externally it forms all or part of a subject, etc. of a clause. The main emphasis in this book is on the downward, external relations, with the internal **constituency** described less fully, though not neglected. After all, a sentence that we read is nothing but a row of letters and spaces, and all the categories of clause, etc. are abstract deductions from our knowledge of the way the letters group together.

In the first instance, we arrange the **units** of description into a scale of five ranks:[1] see Fig. 0.5.

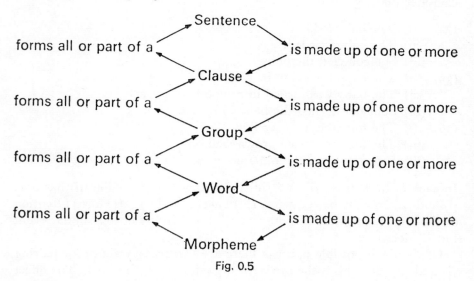

Fig. 0.5

The details of just how several words go together to make up a group form the grammar of the rank of group. The term **group** is retained in

---

[1] The originator of this form of description is Professor M. A. K. Halliday. The earliest full version is 'Categories of the Theory of Grammar', *Word*, 17, 1961, but a 'deeper' sort of grammar is developed in 'Notes on Transitivity and Theme in English', *Journal of Linguistics*, Vols. 3 and 4, 1967 and 1968. A suitable introduction to the theory is H. M. Berry, in prep. for Batsford. Another grammar on the same principles is *English Grammar*, by Scott *et al.*, Heinemann, 1968.

this grammar rather than phrase because **phrase** has so many meanings already in grammars, and could be misleading. There is an important addition to this simple picture described in Section 18, called **rankshift**, where we find structures of clause type, for example, within groups.

Each rank is described by an interlocking set of three categories— **structure, system** and **class.** Of these the most important one is system, because the distinctions of meaning arise from systemic contrast. If we say 'verbs can be active or passive' we are talking informally about the system of voice. To be more precise, we should say that the system operates at the rank of group, and only with verbal groups, and only with certain verbal groups, essentially those which appear in transitive clauses. Thus the system is related to two ranks already—group and clause.

By organising the active/passive contrast in a system, we are saying:

(*a*)   that all the specified verbal groups must show a choice between active and passive.

(*b*)   that there is evidence in the structure of verbal groups for the choice —which means that there are *exponents* of the choice. Of course there are many ambiguities in language structure—as we have already seen in discussing the passive voice (Example (22)). But evidence for each grammatical choice must appear somewhere, or it is no choice at all.

The exponents of a choice are stated in two stages. First of all, there is a structural statement. A full passive verbal group in English contains *am, is, were*, etc., followed by the past participle of a verb, and we give each of these *elements* a symbol.

am, is, are, was, were, be, being, been	have the symbol b
the past participle	has the symbol n
a 'lexical' verb	has the symbol v

So we can state the structure of a passive verbal group as containing the sequence *BVN*. An active verbal group does not have this sequence in it.

The final stage is to relate each symbol, each element of structure, to its exponents. We have just done it in reverse. This is a statement of the classes of **word** which can operate at each structural element. The element v will, of course, be restricted to the class of verbs that can occur in the passive, linking the structure once again with transitivity in the clause.

In this book the systemic choices are usually discussed with **examples** first, and then a standard diagram is presented as a summary. For voice in English, a diagram like Fig. 0.6 will be built up.

It is not always helpful to present every system in this way; and the statements of structures and classes are notes rather than exhaustive

Terms	Structures	Classes
passive	-bvn-	b : a form of the verb *be* v : any lexical verb at P (transitive) n : the past participle ending —usually -*ed* (as in *kicked*), sometimes -*en* (as in *stolen*) and (rarely) nothing at all (e.g. *hit*)
active	any other verbal group	exponents not listed

Fig. 0.6. System of the verbal group operating at P (transitive) in clause structure : Voice

NOTE : A fuller form of the voice system is set out near the end of Section 24, on page 202.

specifications. The reason for a lack of precision here is that a grammar is a very complicated network of systems which cut across each other in many different ways, and a full statement would take too much space.

The route through a network of systems is movement along a scale called *delicacy*. Each system divides up the items it operates on, so after several moves in delicacy a class may be the result of several subdivisions. The simplest way of recording this situation is by the use of superscripts—so that in Fig. 0.6 1 would be $1^{P \text{ trans}}$. But very soon the superscripts would get far too long and clumsy; in this grammar the symbols are often very much simplified.

Prominence

Some parts of a sentence are more prominent than others. The main techniques of prominence are:

(*a*) front, or early, placing.
(*b*) rear, or late, placing following a grammatical prediction, i.e. delay.
(*c*) unusual placing, where the item is not in its usual place.
(*d*) intonational pointing, or punctuation in writing.
(*e*) special effects.

Let us now have examples of these techniques. We have already had an example of (*a*), how the passive voice reorders the elements of a clause and brings what would have been the object in an active clause to the front, and makes it the focus or *theme* of the clause.

(Compare (37) and (38)).

(37) He'll come if you call.
(38) If you call, he'll come.

Notice the influence of front-placing the *if*-clause, (*a*); late-placing the other clause although it is predicted (*b*); and the comma separates the two clauses (*d*). Each clause is thus more prominent than in (37). The sequence of clauses in (38) is the less common one; (39) is certainly unusual, though still grammatical, and is an example of (*c*).

(39) He, if you call, will come.

Special effects are brought about in the spoken language by gestures, extra loud or deliberate speech, exaggeration of the normal distinctions. In writing they involve mainly typography.

(40) Provided that care is taken in loading the machine, there should be no excessive vibration.
(41) There should be no excessive vibration *provided that care is taken in loading the machine.*
(42) There should be no excessive vibration PROVIDED THAT CARE IS TAKEN IN LOADING THE MACHINE.

Example (40) both warns and then reassures the reader; (41) is a little worrying and (42) will probably make him frightened of using it.

Intonation

There is a detailed description of English intonation in Volume 2 of this series.[1] The reader is referred to it for a full explanation of the structures and systems, and the notes here are no more than a summary of the main points of intonation that affect grammatical description.

Units of English Phonology

There is a rank scale, similar to the one in grammar.

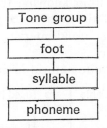

Tone group
foot
syllable
phoneme

---

[1] *A Course in Spoken English: Intonation* by M. A. K. Halliday.

Phoneme and syllable are used in the normal meanings. *Foot* is a grouping of syllables according to stress Each syllable is either stressed or not, and a foot extends from the beginning of one stressed syllable to the beginning of the next. Example (s = stressed, u = unstressed)

(43)

	Phon	eme	and	syll	a	ble	are	used	in	the	nor	mal	mean	ings
syllables	s	u	u	s	u	u	u	s	u	u	s	u	s	u
feet	1			2				3			4		5	

A *tone group* is a grouping of feet according to pitch patterns, and there are five major simple patterns, and two complex ones, as follows:

> Tone 1 : falling tone; symbol \
>
> Tone 2 : steep rising; symbol /
>
> Tone 3 : low rising; symbol ⁀
>
> Tone 4 : rise–fall–rise; symbol ∿
>
> Tone 5 : fall–rise–fall; symbol ∨∧
>
> Tone 13 : fall–low rise; symbol ∨⁀
>
> Tone 53 : fall–rise–fall–low rise; symbol ∿⁀

A typical reading of the sentence at (43) would have the intonation of (44).

(44)

		Phoneme and	syllable are	used in the	normal meanings
feet			T		T
tone groups	4			1	

The stressed syllable that carries the main pitch pattern is the *tonic* syllable, marked with a 'T' in (44). The number of the tone is given at the beginning of the group.

Between tone groups there is sometimes a special kind of pause, called a *silent stress*. We detect it from knowing that English stressed syllables occur at equal intervals of time. When a pause separates the stressed syllables by roughly twice the usual interval, it has the effect of replacing an expected stress by silence.

A silent stress would be quite natural in our example:

(45)

	Phoneme and	syllable		are	used in the	normal	meanings
		T					T
	4				1		

That is to say, an extra foot is introduced. The stressed syllable is a pause, and there is one unstressed syllable *are*. (46) picks out the stressed syllables. If you say (44) and (45) out loud, and tap rhythmically to the stresses, the taps will fall on the syllables of (46).

(46)   (i)   Pho- syll- used nor- mean-
       (ii) Pho- syll- —used nor- mean-

CHAPTER 1

Sentence Structure

SECTION 1: CONTEXTUAL TYPES

This grammar starts with the *sentence* as its largest unit. Everything that is talked about has to do with the meaning of sentences. The many ways in which sentences are connected to each other are hardly mentioned, even though some of the connections are grammatical. It is artificial, of course, to draw an imaginary line at the sentence; it suggests that each sentence is independent of all the others. Trouble starts when we find sentences that are clearly *not* independent; we must remember that to start with sentences and not with 'paragraphs' or 'conversations' is artificial, but is still worth doing.

One thing is certain—the sentence is an essential grammatical unit. A grammar tells us some of the main reasons why utterances mean what they mean and do what they do. It breaks down (or builds up) a fundamental unit of communication, and that fundamental unit is called a sentence. In speech sentences are rather different from the ones we know through writing. Other **ranks** in the grammar, like words, groups and clauses, are much the same in speech and writing, but sentences differ because of the **situations** in which we speak and write. There is a discussion of this topic in the Introduction, but in this book we describe mainly sentences that might occur in either speech or writing.

Sentences, then, are the smallest grammatical units which can *do* things. Sentences can ask questions, clauses and words cannot. (There may be one-word sentences, or one-clause sentences, but words and clauses, as they are used in this book, are **components** of sentences; units into which sentences are divided.) The distinction is important.

What can sentences do? There is a well-known list:

	statement	
response	question	exclamation
	command	

A **question** expects an answer. That is—it expects one to say something back. A **command** expects one to do something. A **statement** just expects one to listen. To each of these there is a **response**: an answer, an acknowledgement, a 'potboiler'. Responses just keep the discourse going, especially in spoken English; they do not themselves *expect* anything.

Exclamations are put into the list in case readers might wonder what had happened to them. There is no space in this book to deal with them in any detail. Many of them have a structure that is quite different from most English sentences—e.g. *Goodness gracious me!*

We will be thinking mainly, then, about *four* actions that sentences do. We could subdivide, of course, or think of many other names for sentence-actions, but we will not, for two reasons:

(*a*) The types of sentence which have been mentioned above are comprehensive and clear-cut. Every sentence that appears can be labelled with one of the four or five labels, without much trouble. If you think of another label, for example 'threat' it will become clear. A 'threat' is certainly an action that a sentence performs; but any threat can *also* be:

(i) a statement: *I'll be angry if you do this.*
or (ii) a question: *Do you think I'll let you do this without payment?*
or (iii) a command: *Sit down or I'll get very annoyed.*

'Threat' is a much more subtle action than 'question', and we cannot easily relate the idea of threatening to particular *structural* features. A great many threats have a clause in them beginning with *if* or *unless*, but such a criterion is not accurate enough—there will be many threats that do not, and many sentences with *if*-clauses that are not threats. On the other hand we can explain what a question is very simply: it is a sentence whose structure means to a listener 'this sentence expects me to say something back'. If we wanted to explain what a threat is, it would take a lot longer.

(*b*) There is an area of clause structure which has a special importance to the sentence-action. It is called the **mood-system** and it is set out in Section 10, page 62. The mood-system describes how some clauses choose their subjects and predicators.

(*a*) **Mood Declarative.** Subject comes *in front of* predicator. Clauses with this structure are very often part of statements. Example: *he is coming now.*
(*b*) **Mood Interrogative.** Subject comes *inside* predicator. Clauses with this structure are very often part of questions. Example: *is he coming now.*
(*c*) **Mood Imperative.** There is no subject. Clauses with this structure are very often part of commands. Example: *come now.*

(*d*) **Moodless.** There is no predicator. Clauses of this kind are frequent as questions (*Tomorrow?*) statements (*St. Paul's Cathedral next stop*) and commands (*Waiter, the bill please*). But they are most typical of responses.

So far, then, we have mentioned:

(*a*) that *sentences* can be labelled with one of four descriptive labels according to the *action* they perform;

(*b*) that a feature of *clause* structure which we call *mood* often tells us which label to put on the sentence.

There is one curious feature here. We are describing sentences in terms of clause structure. There can, of course, be more than one clause in

Move along a bit if you can.	command
I will go before Bill gets here.	statement
Did you say I was to switch it off?	question
Maybe on Tuesday, which suits me fine.	response

Fig. 1.1. Sentence Structure

Will you move along a bit if you can?	question
Go before Bill gets here.	command
You said I was to switch it off.	statement
It'll come on Tuesday, which suits me fine.	statement

Fig. 1.2. First Clause Changed

Move along a bit.	command
I will go, should the letter need signing.	statement
Did you say how to do it?	question
Maybe on Tuesday, as seems most likely	response

Fig. 1.3. Second Clause Changed

a sentence. Do we have to look at the structure of *all* the clauses in a sentence, or only some of them? What happens if several clauses in a sentence have different structures?

Let us look at the structure of some two-clause sentences. There are several types to choose from, and we cannot discuss them all at once. Fig. 1.1 has a selection, classified according to their **actions**.

It is already fairly clear that the *first* clause only in these sentences tells us what the action of the whole sentence is. The second clause usually does not even need to be present at all. Let us now make some changes to the clauses; if we change the mood of the first clause we will probably change the action of the sentence. If we change the second clause any way we like, we will not alter the sentence-action. Figs. 1.2 and 1.3 show the effects of mood change. The second clauses of Fig. 1.3 are not very natural, because it is difficult to alter clauses of this type.

The clauses in the examples above can be divided into two lists:

1. Clauses whose internal structure affect the whole sentence-action. We shall call these clauses *Free* clauses and we shall use the letter 'F' to refer to them in structural shorthand. In the examples so far, these are all the first clauses.

2. Clauses whose internal structure does *not* affect the whole sentence-action. They may have no subject at all, or there may be no clause at all,

Clauses at F	Clauses at B
move along a bit	if you can
I will go	before Bill gets here
did you say	I was to switch it off
maybe on Tuesday	which suits me fine
will you move along a bit	should the letter need signing
go	how to do it
you said	as seems most likely
it'll come on Tuesday	

Fig. 1.4

but the sentence-action remains the same. We shall call these clauses *Bound* clauses and we shall use the letter 'B' to refer to them in our structural shorthand.

So all the sentences that we have looked at so far have the structure FB, except for one which is F only. (Can you find it?) Fig. 1.4 shows all the F and B clauses in the examples.

Clauses

Perhaps a few of these clauses do not look like clauses at all—because they do not have a finite verb, for example. In this grammar no condition like that is laid on a clause: a clause is simply a component of a sentence.

Consider the following examples:

(1) Please return the book *when you have finished with it.*
(2) Please return the book *when finished with it.*
(3) Please return the book *at 9 p.m.*
(4) Please return the book *immediately.*

The piece in italics in (1) is clearly a clause—it has a subject, finite verb and a prepositional group. In (2) the verb is now non-finite (*finished*) and there is no subject, but there is still the conjunction *when* and the prepositional group to suggest that a clause is the correct analysis. Example (3) is different. There is no trace of 'clause grammar' in it, and it does not seem to be a shortened form of a clause with subject and verb. Example (4) is the same.

All four pieces give the same sort of meaning—they are concerned with timing. But there are two types of timing:

(*a*) timing one event by another, like (1) and (2);
(*b*) timing an event by mentioning a particular timing, like (3) and (4).

On the double basis of the structure and meaning we decide that (1) and (2) have the structure *FB*, while (3) and (4) have the simple structure *F*, with the timing built in to the clause.

The special usefulness of prepositional groups is worth mentioning here, even if it is a bit of a digression. Consider (5) and (6).

(5) Please return the book *on your next visit.*
(6) Please return the book *when you next visit us.*

The two sentences are not identical in meaning, but fairly close. The prepositional group *on your next visit* names an event, but the grammar places the event within the structure of the F clause.

So far we have used two kinds of evidence in discussion of how clauses can be defined.

(*a*) the guidance given by similar or different meanings;
(*b*) the internal details or *componence* of structures.

There is a third, which is just as important,

(*c*) the external details, or *syntax* of structures.

Clauses make up sentences, so most of this chapter describes the syntax of clauses—which clauses can occur in which positions, and so on.

A clause, then, is not defined simply according to what is inside it, although typical clauses have verbs in them. First of all, a clause is a constituent part of a sentence, and is composed of at least one group. If it contains several groups, there will be examples of the 'subject–verb–object–adjunct' relationship that are unique to clause structure. In the doubtful cases a grammarian weighs up all the evidence he can find and makes a decision—not a final decision, of course, because other evidence may crop up later on.

Exercises

Here are some more two-clause sentences, with the *F* italicized.

1. *He'll let you have it* whenever you like.
2. When it starts to boil, *let me know.*
3. *Tell me* the minute you've finished.
4. *Will you give me a ring* in case I sleep in?

Exercise 1.1

Give the structure of each of these sentences by noting each clause as *F* or *B*. Give also the sentence-action of each.

Exercise 1.2

Give the structure of each of the following sentences, using *F* and *B*, and mark the boundary between *F* and *B*. Give also the sentence-action of each.

1. It was pouring with rain when I left.
2. I dashed for the plane the minute I got my luggage through the customs.
3. Should I leave it off since you don't like it?
4. You'd better watch that fire in case the baby falls over.
5. Just pop in whenever you want to.

Exercise 1.3

Make up some more clauses with the structure *FB* from the *F*s and *B*s of the examples in this section. Note the sentence-action of each. (Not all combinations are possible; can you work out why not?)

We can now summarise this section. Sentences *do* things, and we have suggested four actions that they do, because these four actions

(*a*) cover all sentences;
(*b*) relate directly to the structure of *some* clauses.

We can then consider the structure of sentences as sequences of two structural places, F or B. Clauses which occur at F are free and relate to the sentence-action; clauses at B are bound, and do not relate to the sentence-action.

SECTION 2: CLAUSE SEQUENCE

The grammar of two-clause sentences is continued in this section. It has been shown that a sentence containing F and B may have a structure of *FB* or *BF*. The distinction in meaning between *FB* and *BF* is mentioned in the section of the Introduction entitled 'Prominence'. *FB* is the normal sequence; so *BF* will make the B clause prominent, and this sequence is called **marked.**

Exercise 2.1

Refer to the sentences of Exercise 1.2, page 23. Put the clauses into marked sequence (*BF*) and consider the difference in meaning that you have produced.

Exercise 2.2

Study the following sentences.

(*a*) Mark the boundary between F and B.
(*b*) Turn the clauses the other way round.
(*c*) Note the sentence structure of the *new* sentences.

Example: I haven't touched it since you left.
Answer: (*a*) it/since
        (*b*) Since you left, I haven't touched it
        (*c*) *BF* marked

1. Whether he'll come or not, we'll have to invite him.
2. You are entitled to this concession provided that you agree not to work for five years.
3. Don't go up to her, however much she cries.
4. He fell asleep immediately he finished his supper.
5. While I don't mind the expense, I'm a bit worried about the long delay.
6. He carried on even though he was tired out.
7. As if there was nothing at all on his mind, Mr Plumtree puffed away at his large pipe.
8. Until the plane took off I just couldn't settle myself.
9. Buy it as soon as you can.
10. We brought flowers, seeing everyone else brought sweets.
11. Since we last met, some little progress has probably been made.
12. He jumped in before you could say Jack Robinson.
13. Since it's so late, let's take a taxi.
14. No matter how long it takes, I intend to finish this tonight.
15. He came round after we finished supper.

Exercise 2.3

Make a list of all the **items** that introduce B clauses in Exercise 2.2. Here is the list for Exercise 2.1:

in case	when
since	whenever
the minute	

At the moment it doesn't matter if you write down less, or even more, than the key.

The important point is to begin to recognise these *binders*—words which join the bound clause to the free clause. Many of the actual words and groups have other syntactic functions, like prepositions and adverbs, and the main way we can see their use as binders is their position at the front of the clause. Consider the B clause of Example 4 above.

(1) immediately he finished his supper

The word *immediately* is also found as an adverb, and so can occur as a lexical *adjunct* in clause structure. (See Section 13, page 96.)

(2) he finished his supper immediately

Here *immediately* is no longer a binder, but an adjunct. Notice also the B clause of Example 15 above.

(3) After we finished supper

Compare it with (4) and (5) below.

(4) we finished supper after

(5) we finished supper after the thunderstorm

(4) is just like (2); in (5) *after* is a preposition, and again cannot be a binder.

It is quite common for words to be ambiguous in grammar, just as they are ambiguous in their lexical functions.

Summary

Many clauses can occur in either FB or BF sequences. B clauses commonly start with a binder like *when, in case*. The list of binders includes items that are exponents of other structural places in the grammar, like *after*.

Distinctr — TYPES of Beta Clause

SECTION 3: CONTINGENT AND ADDING CLAUSES

Contingent

In Section 2 we chose only some of the clauses that occur at B—namely those that could equally well occur in *FB* or *BF* structures. We need a label for these bound clauses and we will use the word *contingent*, or *cont.* for them. This term is chosen because it reminds us of the type of meaning given by cont. clauses. They may tell us of conditions, concessions, temporal and spatial settings and so on, depending usually on the choice of binder. But in every case they tell of some way in which the *generality* of an F is affected. There are some sentences in Fig. 3.1 with and without cont. clauses for comparison.

F	FB
Look in a mirror.	Look in a mirror any time you like.
I like peanuts.	I like peanuts, though I'm not hungry just now.
Can you sing?	Can you sing if we put the dog out?
He'll drive his car.	He'll drive his car wherever there's a road.

Fig. 3.1. Cont. Clauses

Cont. clauses are similar to the familiar 'adverbial clauses' of traditional grammar. But the reasons for identifying them are much more than their similar meaning to adverbs. We have three types of evidence, as set out in Section 1.

(*a*) Occurs in *BF* and *FB* structures (this is a syntactic point).
(*b*) Has initial binder, e.g. *if, when, though, since* . . . (this is a componential point).
(*c*) Expresses a contingency on the generality of F (this is a **semantic** point).

As the grammar develops, some of these points will suggest that we open the list of в clauses to let in a number of items that would not be considered 'adverbial clauses' in traditional grammar—clauses, for example, without finite verbs.

We are now going to compare cont. clauses with another class of в clauses. The new ones do *not* occur in *BF* structures. Also, they usually have quite different binders. Let us call them *adding* or *add.* clauses and look at some examples.

1. Last night we went to a performance of *Otello*—which is my favourite opera of Verdi's.
2. We had our holidays at Harrogate again, where we went last year.
3. Come and meet my new colleague, who's really an awfully nice chap.
4. I only received my passport this morning, which puts me in a spot.
5. A series of pilot experiments was planned, by which we hoped to demonstrate the precise nature of the reaction.
6. Our most successful project this year has been the drive towards economy of operation, into which we have thrown every effort.
7. Look in after ten o'clock, when we'll have plenty time for a long talk.
8. He was my father—from whom I received everything I value.
9. He said there might well be a delay, which looks fishy to me.
10. A poem was read by Mr Plumtree, whose voice is well suited to recitation.

All these sentences are written with a comma or a dash between the two clauses. The punctuation helps to distinguish add. clauses in writing from another kind of clause that looks similar. Compare the following pair:

(1) Come and see this car, which runs on tap-water.
(2) Come and see this car that runs on tap-water.

On the surface, there is little difference: the comma does not occur in (2), and the binder is *which* in (1) and *that* in (2). The binders could in fact change places without doing much damage to the grammar. Yet the meaning of the two sentences is quite different. The *which*-clause in (1) is an add. clause. It adds more detail; if it is omitted the F clause remains unchanged. *This* in (1) refers to some car near the speaker. In (2), how-ever, the *that*-clause cannot be omitted, or the sentence concerns a different car. *This* in (2) has a wider meaning than in (1); the car need not be near the speaker, and the word suggests that there has been a previous con-versation about the car.

The *which*-clause in (1) *adds*, in sentence structure.

acting as adj.

The *that*-clause in (2) *selects*, in group structure, and is not a component of sentence structure in any direct way. It is called a **rankshifted** clause. There is a section later in this book (Section 18, page 143) which deals with rankshifted clauses in greater detail.

In the spoken language, the add. clauses and the rankshifted clauses have different intonation patterns. As the comma suggests, add. clauses cannot be uttered in the same *tone group* as the clause in front of them, but must have a separate one to themselves.

Exercise 3.1

Make a list of the initial binders in the examples of add. clauses so far.

what

What-clauses

Notice that *what* is not included in the list. There are indeed clauses which might have been included as add. clauses, e.g.

(1) What's more, I don't like you.
(2) And what's a bit better than that, she can't come either.

We do *not* include these clauses for several reasons:

(*a*) they are common initially (i.e. at the start of the sentence);
(*b*) they are uncommon finally (i.e. at the end of the sentence).

These two syntactic reasons show that the add. clauses would have to be changed a lot to include *what*-clauses. Here are some more points of difference:

(*c*) Their own internal structure is very restricted. You cannot choose just any clause that starts with *what* and fit it into this pattern. On the other hand, the *which*- and *who*-clauses can be made from any clause by a few simple rules.
(*d*) Their meaning. Add. clauses supply extra details *within a sentence*. Most of them add to a particular group, but some add to a whole clause.

Let us look more closely at the meaning of add. clauses, and then return to *what*-clauses.

(*a*) Adding to the subject or object of a clause.

(3) He touched the topmost branch, which was waving violently.

(*b*) Adding to a group with a preposition group.

(4) We all went to the café on the corner opposite St. Mark's church, which has that big steeple.

Corners and cafés don't have steeples; but now consider (5) and (6).

(5) We all went to the café on the corner opposite St. Mark's church, which is a windy spot.
(6) We all went to the café on the corner opposite St. Mark's church, which started the evening well.

The add. clause in (5) could refer to church, corner or café, since each of them could be 'a windy spot'. But the add. clause in (6) doesn't seem to refer to any of the nouns. The most likely meaning is that the add. clause refers to our *visit* to the café—to the whole of the F clause. So there must be a third meaning for add. clauses:

(*c*) Adding to the whole of an F clause.

Notice that the reference of the binders cuts across the scale of ranks (see the Introduction section on 'Systemic Grammar', page 12). Reference has to be worked out according to the details of each clause and sentence, and the rank of an add. clause is not affected.

Now look back at the *what*-clauses. They do not refer to the F clause or to any part of it. Their meaning is to link one sentence to another, and they have no grammatical relationships within sentences. Later on in this chapter (Section 8) there is a discussion of *linkage* in general, because it is a relationship found all over the grammar. At present we shall label the *what*-clauses '*sentence-linkers*', and not add. clauses.

Exercise 3.2

Make a list of at least ten other items like *by, into, from* which can go in front of *which* or *whom* or *whose* at the beginning of an add. clause. They need not all be single words.

Exercise 3.3

Go back to the sentences of Exercise 3.1, and make a note of the most likely referent of the add. clause. If there is no particular referent, say so.

This section ends with a summary of the characteristics of add. clauses:

(a) they are very often introduced by the binders *which, who, whom, whose, when* and *where*;

(b) they never start a sentence;

(c) they are separated from surrounding clauses by
  (i) commas in the written language;
  (ii) a separate tone group in the spoken language;

(d) they supply extra details *within* the sentence, very often to a particular word, group or clause, which is called the *referent* or *antecedent* of the add. clause.

(margin note: ADD CLAUSES)

SECTION 4: REPORTED CLAUSES

This section deals with the third and last important type of B clause, the reported or rep. clause. It is studied first of all in comparison with cont. and add. clauses.

There is very little relationship between a cont. clause and its F clause; almost any F clause will do provided the verb tense fits. An add. clause, too, does not restrict its F grammatically. The F clause in turn does not demand very much concord with either a $B^{add.}$ or a $B^{cont.}$

On the other hand the F and B in report structures are much more dependent on each other. The F clause is called the *reporting* clause, and the B clause the *reported* clause.

Fig. 4.1 gives some examples of report structures *FB* and *BF*. Note these points:

1. The sentences in column (A) are not reversible in the speech and writing of most people.
2. Those in column (B) *are* reversible to BF, and if you turn them round you get the sentences in column (C).
3. The verbs in the F clauses are:
  said, imagine, reported, yelled, heard, insisted
  Only a small class of verbs will fit into reporting clauses, and we shall call these *reporting verbs*.
4. The difference in meaning across the table is not very great. Consider Examples A6, B6 and C6. The slight difference between A6 and B6 is mainly a difference of formality; B6 is more casual than A6. C6 shows prominence on the B reported clause (see the Introduction section on Prominence, page 14).

(A) FB	(B) FB	(C) BF
1. He said that he was going.	He said he was going.	He was going, he said.
2. I imagine that he'll come before long.	I imagine he'll come before long.	He'll come before long, I imagine.
3. The sergeant reported that a light was on in Station Headquarters.	The sergeant reported a light was on in Station Headquarters.	A light was on in Station Headquarters, the sergeant reported.
4. She yelled back that she had to rush off.	She yelled back she had to rush off.	She had to rush off, she yelled back.
5. I heard the other day that Robinson's off to Tenerife soon.	I heard the other day Robinson's off to Tenerife soon.	Robinson's off to Tenerife soon, I heard the other day.
6. I insisted that he shouldn't have done it.	I insisted he shouldn't have done it.	He shouldn't have done it, I insisted.

Fig. 4.1. Some Report Structures

5. The B clauses have the binder *that* in column (A) but no binder at all in (B) or (C). The structure *BF* can only occur in a report if the B clause has no mark of binding on it. All the B clauses in columns (B) and (C) might easily occur in other sentences as F clauses.

1. He was going no matter what we said.
2. If you invite him, he'll come before long.
3. A light was on in Station Headquarters.
4. She had to rush off, which was a great pity.
5. Robinson's off to Tenerife soon, whatever you say.
6. He shouldn't have done it, after feeling bad last night again.

Exercise 4.1

Analyse the sentences above into *FB* or *BF*, or just *F* structures, noting if the B clause is cont. or add. Compare the F clauses with the B clauses of column (B) in Fig. 4.1, page 31.

Here there is another case of ambiguous exponents—like the binders of Section 2. Many instances of report are only shown by the reporting verb and the overall meaning of a passage.

Let us bear this pattern in mind, and look for other *FB* structures which are similar. First of all, we have to widen the list of binders to include *if* and *whether*. Now *if* and *whether* cannot be omitted like *that*, since they have a more particular meaning. Therefore there is no column (B) for these clauses, and so no column (C) either. Here are some examples:

(1) I'll find out if he can manage.
(2) He'll remind us whether or not he has the space for these things.
(3) I'll just be able to see if he reaches the tape first.
(4) I always try to notice whether anyone knocks at that door or not.

If and *whether* have already appeared in this book, in the list of cont. binders. Here they are again, and so all these sentences must be ambiguous. The cont. meanings are odd in these examples but it is easy to reconstruct them just by reversing the sequence of clauses.

(5) If he can manage, I'll find out (something).
(6) Whether or not he has the space for these things, he'll remind us (of something).
(7) If he reaches the tape first, I'll just be able to see (something).
(8) Whether anyone knocks at that door or not, always try to notice (something).

We can easily construct realistic $B^{cont.}$ clauses using the *if-* and *whether-* clauses above:

(9) I'll slip off if he can manage.
(10) He'll manage somehow whether or not he has the space for these things.
(11) I'll cheer and cheer if he reaches the tape first.
(12) Keep absolutely still, whether anyone knocks at that door or not.

Exercise 4.2

Reverse the clauses in (9), (10), (11) and (12) and analyse the sentences.

Note that in converting (1) to (5), and (2) to (6), etc., there is added *something, of something*. The change from rep. to cont. reveals how closely the structure of reporting and reported clauses fits together. Traditional grammar calls rep. clauses *noun clauses*, since they seem like objects of the reporting verbs. There are quite complicated reasons for preferring to call them Brep. clauses, but they cannot be set out here.

Reversibility

Let us take a closer look at reversibility. First of all, there may be slight variations in usage in formal written English. Some people feel that sentences like the following are acceptable:

(13) That he could do it, I just couldn't believe.
(14) Whether or not he's coming he won't inform us.
       (N.B. read the B of (14) as rep. not cont.)

These show an initial *that*- and *whether*-clause. Perhaps they occur occasionally, but it is not worthwhile to learn or teach them.

Secondly, there are a number of restrictions on the F clause of a Brep.F structure, that are just mentioned here. It must be *positive*, not only in the verbs but in the clause as a whole. It must not contain a member of a class of adverb which is often called '*seminegative*', like *seldom, hardly, scarcely*. It must normally be in the dec. mood.

Fig. 4.2 shows in column (A) some examples of *FB* rep. structures where, although B has no binder, *BF* sequence does not occur. Alongside each is a sentence which is very similar in structure but which *can* be reversed to yield *BF*.

Exercise 4.3

Provide a column (c) to the two columns in Fig. 4.2. As you do that, note down the grammatical reasons why the clauses in column (A) cannot be reversed. There may be more than one reason per sentence.

(A) FB: not reversible	(B) FB: reversible
1. I never thought he would lift the thing.	1. I thought he would lift the thing.
2. No-one believed he was very rich.	2. They believed he was very rich.
3. Don't tell me you're getting married!	3. You told me you're getting married.
4. Wasn't he sure the radio could be mended?	4. He was sure the radio could be mended.
5. You needn't deny he's staying the weekend.	5. You can say he's staying the weekend.
6. I just warned him he should watch himself.	6. I warned him he should watch himself.
7. I could only assume the letter had gone astray.	7. I assumed the letter had gone astray.
8. Bill knew if he was coming.	8. Bill knew he was coming.

Fig. 4.2. Reversibility Restrictions in Report Structures

Look carefully at *just* in Example A6. There are several grammatical items which are all written down as *just*, and even a careful example can be ambiguous. The *just* that is meant here is one which is rather like *simply* and *only* in meaning. Sentence A6 could be paraphrased in this meaning as:

(15) All I did was tell him he should watch himself.

Another item *just* means approximately 'immediately before', but this *just* does not affect the reversibility of the clauses.

Exercise 4.4

Give the structure of the following sentences as *FB* or *BF*. Note the ones that can be reversed: explain those that cannot be reversed.

1. Bill was driving, I mentioned.
2. I shouted up that I'd be back in ten minutes.
3. We just didn't expect the shops would be shut.
4. Let me know whether he wants it.
5. I felt he was getting angry.
6. Mr Robinson observed that a large car had stopped beside him.
7. I merely promised I would do everything possible.
8. Bill whispered that the baby was stirring.

Exercise 4.5

Make a list of all the reporting verbs in this section. The first six are listed in note 3 to Fig. 4.1, page 30.

Exercise 4.6

Look through some pages of a novel, and make lists of

(*a*) reporting verbs;

(*b*) 'quoting verbs'—verbs which introduce quotations of actual utterances, for example (16).

(16) 'I'm just coming' he said.

There is still another class of rep. clause binder to be mentioned.
1. I explained why he was coming.
2. We all know how he managed to win.
3. Mr Plumtree mentioned who was going to talk to us.
4. You've told me what is wanted.
5. She said when it was.
6. I asked him which bus I should take for the station.
7. See where he is!

Exercise 4.7

List the binders of the B clauses in the seven examples given above.

The binders are called for convenience **wh-groups**. The same items appear in several places in the grammar. We have met most of them already as add. binders. Here they are rep. binders. They are joined by *how* and *why* which are not often used in add. clauses.

When has now appeared as a binder for cont., add. and rep. clauses. It should then be possible to construct a sentence with three meanings.

(17) She told us, that day, when it rained.

(*a*) *FB*cont.   She waited till it rained before telling us.
          BF structure is possible:
          When it rained she told us, that day.

(*b*) *FB*add.   We remember on which day it was she told us because it rained that day.
          BF structure impossible.

(*c*) *FB*rep.   That day, she told us the time of the rainfall. (In (*a*) and (*b*) we don't know what she told us.)
          BF structure impossible.

The reversibility of rep. clauses with *wh*-binders needs a word. Nearly always the structure will be *FB* rep. Very occasionally, mainly in written texts, a *BF* structure will occur, but in almost the opposite circumstances to the ones we have previously seen, in Fig. 4.1.

(18) Why he was coming, no-one explained.

(19) How he managed to win, I can only guess.

(20) Who was going to talk to us, he didn't mention.

When F is negative, or contains a 'seminegative', this *BF* structure is possible. (But not if F is a question.) — with wh-

During this section we have found four main ways in which a rep. clause may start. They are:

(*a*) no binder at all

(*b*) binder *that*

(*c*) binders *if, whether (or not)*

(*d*) binders *who, which, when, how,* etc., 'wh-groups'

There are two main distinctions between them apart from their binders.

(i) Occurrence in *BF* structures. The details are in Fig. 4.3.

(ii) We have to notice that the reporting verbs don't combine freely with all of these types. The following sequences are impossible:

(21) *I requested whether he was there.

(22) *We demanded when he had come.

(23) *John asked that he was coming.

(24) *I inquired that he caught the train.

B	binder componence	F structure	Notes
(*a*) no binder		dec. mood, no negs. or seminegs., etc.	BF unrestricted occurrence
(*b*) *that*			BF virtually impossible
(*c*) *if, whether*			BF virtually impossible
(*d*) *wh-*		neg. or semineg.	rare

Fig. 4.3. Rep. Clause BF Structure

Exercise 4.8

Consider the verbs you have in answer 4.5, along with *plead* and *inquire*. Which of them will combine with the four types of B clause above? Notice that sometimes a combination is possible only if the F clause is negative.

One footnote remains. There is an old-fashioned *FB*rep. structure that you might meet occasionally in formal written English. Here are a few examples:

I asked that he be allowed to come.
We demand that he be released immediately.
The mother begged that her son be pardoned.

The examples show that this structure allows *ask* to be followed by *that*. However, the structure is unimportant in contemporary English.

SECTION 5: B CLAUSES: SUMMARY

So far the main subject of study has been *FB* and *BF* structures. It has been necessary to distinguish three main types of B clauses:

> contingent
> adding
> reported

The reasons for this threefold division are summarised under the familiar headings of *meaning, componence* and *syntax*.

(*a*) *meaning*. Cont. clauses affect the generality of the F clause. Compare (1) and (2):

(1) All your hair will fall out.
(2) All your hair will fall out unless you use Scalpo, the wonder hormone preparation.

Add. clauses allow an extra statement to be made about a part of the F clause, or the whole of the F clause. It often reads as an afterthought. See (3).

(3) All your hair will fall out, which will be a pity.

Rep. clauses complete the meaning that starts in the reporting clauses.
   With these categories of meaning established, the grammatical features can be classified. Clauses that have little in common grammatically can be put in the same category so long as there are, ultimately, grammatical reasons. For example, the justification for some *if*-clauses being rep. is complicated and rests at times on thin evidence; but the meaning is so clearly 'report' that we select the grammatical criteria with that in mind. (See Examples (1)–(12) of Section 4, pages 32–3.)

(b) *componence*. This is the 'hard' evidence—it considers the grammatical items that are actually present in the structure. Figure 5.1 shows the typical binders of the various B clauses, noting that some rep. clauses have no binder. Notice the overlap in the three columns. The class of reporting verb is another feature of componence.

Cont. clauses	Add. clauses	Rep. clauses
after, although, as, as if, as soon as, because, before, by the time, considering, even if, even though, however, if immediately, in case, in order that, just because, no matter how, once, only, provided (that), rather than, seeing (that), since, so that, the minute, until, unless, when, whenever, whether, while, . . .	*Wh*-word (who, whom, which, when, where) (with or without preposition)	no binder at all that if, whether (or not) *wh*-word (any) (with or without preposition)

Fig. 5.1. Initial Binders

(c) *syntax*. The possibility of different sequence is the main syntactic matter that has been dealt with. Syntax describes the external relations of an item—like its concord with other items or its position.

The three types of evidence combine to give Fig. 5.2.

Syntax	Componence	Meaning
BF structure → possible →	→ when binder present →	→ CONT.
	→ when binder absent →	→ REP.
→ impossible →		→ ADD.

Fig. 5.2

Many features of two-clause structures have been left out—concord systems in the verbs; the full effect of the F-clause mood, the detailed analysis of *B*cont. clauses. But a grammar this size must select what seem to be the main points of structure.

Exercise 5.1

Check through Figs. 5.1 and 5.2, selecting a binder, a clause type and a structure, and make sure that you can construct *FB* or *BF* sentences *with the right sort of meaning* for any of them.

SECTION 6: SPLIT CLAUSES

So far in the study of sentence structure we have been talking about
sequence of clauses. The structural symbols F and B have been arranged
as either *FB* or *BF* to show the sequence. But clauses do not always follow
each other; sometimes one *splits* another. In this section the splitting is
examined.

Another convention has to be added to the structural shorthand,
since single symbols like *F* and *B* cannot be halved. Square brackets *[]*
show a splitting clause, and they follow the symbol for the clause they
split. So our two possibilities are:

$$(a) \ F \ [B] \quad \text{and} \quad (b) \ B \ [F]$$

and these mean (*a*) 'B splitting, F split' and (*b*) 'F splitting, B split'. First
we shall look at the *F [B]* clauses in more detail. Here are some examples.

I In these examples of *F [B]* sentences the F is split just after it has started;
after an initial *linker*.

1. However, when all was said and done, it wasn't much of a mess.
2. Then, if you haven't heard from Bill, open it.
3. Thus, provided no-one drops it, it should travel quite safely.
4. Therefore, the minute I heard the phone ring, I rushed downstairs.
5. But until our grant comes, how can we pay our bills?
6. Nevertheless, no matter how fast you are, this will take you a long
   time.
7. And because it rained all night, the match had to be abandoned.

Exercise 6.1

(*a*) Note all the linkers in these examples.
(*b*) What sort of B clauses occur in these sentences?

II Consider the following two sets of examples which contain initial items
or *adjuncts* in *F* clause structure.

Examples (i)

1. Later on in the day, after we had rested a little, we got moving again.
2. Tonight even if he gets angry I'll have to leave early.
3. In London, even though it's huge, you can feel very much at home.
4. Quickly, because he was in a hurry, Bill slipped down the stairs and
   out.

5. Often during the night, however tired he was, he would get up and stroll round the lake.
6. At seven-thirty, unless the children are on holiday, there's a mad rush for the bathroom always.
7. Never, whatever he says, will I give up.

Examples (ii)

1. At our newest retail store, where you can shop in the most modern and tasteful surroundings, we have opened a restaurant for your added convenience.
2. Last summer, when we had all that rain, we had to go on a camping holiday!
3. Among the guests, who had all gathered to wave off the happy couple, I could see Mrs Plumtree.
4. In this company, by which I mean the parent company and the associated concerns, our aim has always been to maintain competitive prices.
5. In Athens, where the light has exceptional clarity, the sunsets are magnificent.

Exercise 6.2

(a) List the initial items in both sets of examples above.
(b) What sorts of B clauses are there in (i) and (ii)?

The initial items in the examples above are all called *adjuncts* in clause structure. They are preposition groups and adverb groups. They must be distinguished from linkers and binders. The classification suggested can be seen in the following examples and discussion:

(1) In the morning Bill travelled to London.
(2) The Cornishman Express, which left at 11.20, was full of soldiers.
(3) When Bill travelled to London the traffic was heavy.
(4) But Bill travelled to London.
(5) Therefore Bill travelled to London.

The first example, *in the morning*, has no grammatical relations outside the clause; it is called an adjunct. The shorthand labels it just A, for *lexical adjunct*. *Which*, in (2), is both the subject of the B clause and the grammatical binder, so it is marked S^B. In the third example, *when* is the grammatical binder, and an adjunct in the B clause; so it is simply labelled A^B. In (4) *but* is A^+ for grammatical linkage. *Therefore* in (5) is a 'sentence-adverb'; it links whole complexes of clauses, but has no particular grammatical place in any of them. See also Sections 8 (page 51) and 12 (page 87) for discussion of these items—the symbol used is A^L. Fig. 6.1 shows the symbols in a diagram.

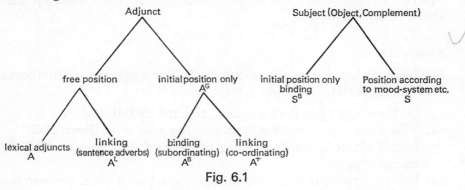

Fig. 6.1

III In the following two sets of examples of *F [B]* structure the F is split just after its subject.

Examples (i)

1. Mr Plumtree, whenever he remembered, raised his hat to ladies.
2. Bill, after he had picked himself up, cursed the cyclist softly.
3. The man across the road, before he goes out to work every morning, weeds his garden.
4. Hydrochloric acid, whether or not it is concentrated, must be kept in a locked cupboard.
5. Eggs, when they're really fresh, are delicious.
6. The men in the orchestra, the minute the curtain goes up, nip out for a drink.
7. Flowers, though they don't last long, brighten up the dingiest room.
8. Mr Plumtree, where he was sure of his audience, was quite a good speaker.

Examples (ii)

1. Modern cars, which are nearly all mass-produced, don't last as long as the earlier models.
2. The Plumtrees round the corner, who used to have those awful all-night parties, are moving to Birmingham.
3. Sheffield, where they make cutlery, is in Yorkshire.
4. This pillar, on which the whole structure is built, is made of reinforced concrete.
5. Next Thursday, when Bill arrives home, is my birthday.

Exercise 6.3

This is a revision of a point made earlier. Find the B clauses in **II** (ii) and **III** (ii) which could also occur as cont. clauses. Then make up suitable F clauses for them.

Exercise 6.4

Fit the following sentences into one of the five categories given above: **I, II** (i), **II** (ii), **III** (i), **III** (ii).

1. Or if you can't pay it all just now, give me an IOU.
2. That street, where the bus is going, takes you to the Town Hall.
3. In this old desk, which is falling to bits now, was my grandfather's manuscript.
4. Indeed, unless Bill had shouted, she might have walked out into the traffic.
5. In view of your peculiar circumstances, whether or not you have previously filled in this form we must firmly request you to fill in the enclosed.
6. Last season my friend, whenever he could, went to the races.
7. According to a friend of mine, who's an authority on sailing, this is a bad time of year for a sailing holiday.
8. Bill, although he'd never admit it, is rather fond of you.
9. In a tearing hurry, as if the end of the world was nigh, the small child recited 'The Drum'.
10. Our modern farms, where no advance is too progressive, serve your table and thousands of others.

Fig. 6.2 summarises what we have noted so far in this section.

F can be split	B-clause type		
	Cont.	Add.	Rep.
just after linker	Yes	No	No
just after lexical adjunct	Yes	Yes	No
just after subject	Yes	Yes	No

Fig. 6.2. Split Clauses *F[B]*

Consider now *B [F]* clauses, where the B is split. Here are some examples:

1. The next day, he continued, another visitor arrived.
2. Despite that, I said primly, I was not interested.
3. The man in black, Bill noticed, was walking quietly down the street.
4. Members should not, the Minister continued, accuse H.M. Government of delay in this matter.
5. All of us, he concluded cheerfully, had made a good profit on the deal.

Exercise 6.5

What are the B clauses here? Where are they split?

To summarise, rep. clauses cannot be B in *F [B]* structures; in *B [F]* structures rep. clauses alone can occur.

There are a few fixed idioms that look like reporting F clauses and make structures similar to *B [F]*, but their meaning is quite different.

1. Then, you see, he ran upstairs.
2. This dreadful cough, I mean to say, kept me in bed for weeks.
3. Tomorrow, you know, is my birthday.
4. Now the next morning, I mean, I couldn't move.
5. Madge, you understand, is very quiet.

The verbs *see, say, know, mean* and *understand* are all common reporting verbs, and there is nothing in the written shape of these sentences to suggest that they are not *B [F]*. But *you see, I mean, I mean to say* have another function in speech. They are used to keep the attention of the listeners, to keep them responding with nods and smiles. (With some speakers they become a habit.) This sort of meaning is very similar to that of the sentence-adverbs like *therefore*, and so the structural symbol A^L is used for them. Example 3 above is ambiguous: if we make a rough paraphrase it should come clear.

(*a*) 'I'm *telling* you about tomorrow—that it's my birthday.' The addressee probably does *not* know about the speaker's birthday. Sentence structure just F, with *you know* having the symbol A^L in the clause. *You know* might be replaced by *after all* without destroying the meaning of the sentence.

(*b*) 'I'm *reminding* you about tomorrow—you already know that it's my birthday'. A meaning like this relates to a *B [F]* structure; *you know* would be prominent in speech instead of just muttered.

Exercise 6.6

Describe the ambiguity of Example 1.

Exercise 6.7

This is a revision exercise for the whole section. Take each sentence in turn and note:

(*a*) its structure. Some will be *F [B]*, some *B [F]* and some just *F* (the sort of sentence we have just discussed);

(*b*) if there is a B, whether cont., add. or rep.;

(*c*) if it is *F [B]*, whether **I**, **II** or **III**—remembering the lists at the beginning of the section.

Example

Last night, after Madge had gone home, there was an awful crash.

(*a*) Structure *F [B]*

(*b*) Cont.

(*c*) **II**, i.e. following an initial lexical adjunct.

1. At ten o'clock, however difficult you find it, you must appear before the Committee.
2. Our man in Istanbul, who used to work with me here in Head Office, seems to have landed a lovely job.
3. The most important thing, he concluded triumphantly, was the support of the man in the street.
4. And in the end, you see, he fell down.
5. Therefore, whatever you say, I'm going to go ahead.
6. In all my experience, which has been very varied, I have never witnessed such an outburst.
7. We could, it seemed, cancel the contract at any time after February 1st.
8. All my friends, if they remember, send me a card at Christmas.
9. A man of his age, I mean, should know better than that.

SECTION 7: P-BOUND CLAUSES

In this section the class of clauses is widened. In Section 1 it was pointed out that a clause typically has a subject and a *finite* verb and so on, but that many clauses are not typical, and that the final decision is never made on componential evidence alone, but takes into account the syntax and the meaning.

This was said in the paragraphs on the clause in Section 1. Since then, nearly all the clauses have been typical ones, so that the main classification of clauses could be made without the strangeness of a typical clause. In this section some clauses with non-finite verbs are described—what traditional grammar might call *verbal phrases*. This term never meant very much, and is now confusing. Consider Examples (1) and (2):

(1) *Having read the book,* my friend thought the film better.
(2) *Now that he had read the book,* my friend thought the film better.

Sentences (1) and (2) have the same structure *BF*, whatever name we may call the в. The two examples of в can both occur in the same range of sentence structures, namely *FB* and *F [B]*, and the same three types of *F [B]* as shown in Section 6. In fact, our two examples of в are almost identical in syntax, and they only show some very minor differences. So it is natural to call both of them clauses, and в clauses, since they are not found at ғ. They are almost identical in meaning.

The main differences in componence are, of course, that in clauses like (1) the verbs are non-finite. A useful name for the clauses is *P-bound*, because the main exponent of в status is the predicator.

Some more examples:

1. Dashing for the train, I forgot all about my ticket.
2. Having got that off his chest, he had a stiff whisky to himself.
3. Feeling a bit worried about Bill, she stayed up for another hour, waiting for a telephone call.
4. We are considering a direct appeal, having been disappointed in all our previous requests.
5. Driven to protest to the meeting, he hardly managed to make himself heard.
6. You have to take three buses to get to that dreadful place.
7. To wash nylons to perfection, place a handful of the powder in lukewarm water.
8. I worked at this for weeks to be positive of success.

Exercise 7.1

Make a list of the predicators in the р-bound clauses above. Can you say whether these are cont., add. or rep. clauses?

The familiar idea of a finite verb is that it 'takes' a subject, with which it is in grammatical concord, in, say, number and person. There isn't much concord left in modern English, though finite verbs nearly always have subjects. The subject is identified mainly by its position (see Section 10, page 73), and the choice of finiteness is a matter for the verbal group more than for individual verbs. (See Section 23, page 181.)

Non-finite verbs do not usually *need* subjects, but they certainly can have them. Consider the following examples:

(3) John having read the book, we all discussed it.
(4) For John to read the book, someone had to find him a copy.

John is the subject of *having* in (3). If it wasn't there, as in (5), there would be no subject in the clause, and the reader would look for the subject of the F clause to understand the sentence as a whole.

(5) Having read the book, we all discussed it.

This structure is the source of many of the most famous 'howlers' of old-style English classes and examinations, for example (6).

(6) Being hot, the ice-cream pleased me.

The structure in (4) is the only type of P-bound clause where the subject is compulsory.

For also commonly occurs in English as a preposition, and this is true of several other binders, both of finite-verb clauses and of P-bound clauses. It is important to distinguish the type of structure in (4) from two similar ones, shown in (7) and (8).

(7) I am ready for him to come.

This example is all one clause, an example of *phase* that is set out in Section 16. The differences are in outline:

(*a*) The two parts of (7) cannot be reversed, so it is unlikely to be a cont. clause.
(*b*) *for him* in (7) is simply a device to introduce a new subject in a structure that is coherent without it. If removed, the subject of *come* switches to *I*. *I am ready to come.*
(*c*) The structure of (7) depends on the choice of certain adjectives just before *for*.

(8) It's dreadful for you to have all this work.

Structures starting with *it*, when *it* is not a personal pronoun like *he*, are made by different rules from the more general rules of English grammar. An introduction to the special grammar of *it* is found in Section 11.

Here are some more examples of P-bound clauses:

1. With Bill getting this rise, we can buy a new car.
2. He kept looking over his shoulder all the way home, after seeing *The Vampire*.
3. We all got bored stiff, Plumtree playing away on his flute for hours like that.
4. Before fitting the legs on, apply a first coat of varnish to the drawers.
5. For Bill to go abroad, his parents saved for months.
6. On getting home, Mr Plumtree dropped into his chair with a sigh of relief.
7. The vicar having summed up the debate in a few well-chosen words, tea was served.
8. The aircraft lost radio contact with traffic control while flying from Lagos to Cairo early this morning.
9. To become a good driver you should take regular lessons.
10. The victors marched off proudly, each of them having fought like a Hercules.
11. Many new products are now on the market for helping the housewife in her thankless task.
12. The Holder must present this document if required by a police officer.
13. Though walked off his feet, Bill managed to keep going.
14. Without Bill to help, we can't do the job in time.
15. We fixed the shelf by knocking two brackets into the wall.
16. Sunshine is essential for these plants to grow.

Exercise 7.2

(a) Make a list of the binders in the above examples. Underline those which are *not* also binders in cont. clauses with finite verbs.
(b) Compose examples of $B^{cont.}$ clauses with finite verbs, for the binders you have not underlined.

Exercise 7.3

Look back at the sixteen examples above and analyse them as follows:

(a) Note them as $+S$ if the B clause has a subject
(b) Note also the type of non-finite verb:

   (i) *to*-form (infinitive)
   (ii) *ing*-form (present participle)
   (iii) *n*-form (past participle)

There are three related grammatical features here:

S	P	A^B (a selection of exponents)	(a P-binder MUST be present)		
subject present	to-form	with (out), for			
	ing-form	with (out), for	in, on, by		
	n-form	with (out)			
subject absent	to-form		as if	so as, in order	
	ing-form	with (out), for	in, on, by	as, if	though while, when, after, before
	n-form			as, if	though . . . before

Fig. 7.1 Componence of Binders in P-bound Cont. Clauses

1. Which non-finite verb occurs.
2. Whether or not subject occurs.
3. Whether or not, and which, binder occurs.

Fig. 7.1, opposite, is a summary of the way that they combine. The presence of a subject is treated as most important here, but notice how the *infinitive* is slightly different from the *participles*.

Exercise 7.4

Check this table by choosing from each of the three columns and then composing an *FB* sentence with a P-bound B in it.

Examples

(*a*) +*S*, n-form *with*
Sentence: I went home with Bill sat on my knee
(*b*) No *S*, ing, *as*
Sentence: Mr Plumtree was called, as knowing the by-laws on this point

It has been noted that P-bound clauses of this cont. type will freely occur in *F [B]* structures. Here are some examples to show it:

1. Bill, gulping away at his dinner, was obviously in a hurry.
2. The side-board, to fit under this shelf, will have to have its legs cut short a bit.
3. Nevertheless, to keep the peace, he let it pass without comment.
4. The next morning, having been for a stroll around the grounds, Mr Plumtree admitted a liking for the college.
5. Our poor cat, caught on a breaking branch, had to jump for its life.
6. Then, seeing Bill's face, Dad changed the subject.

Exercise 7.5

Turn back to the three types of splitting that were explained in Section 6, pages 39–41. Mark these examples as **I**, **II** or **III**.

To summarise, in this section, we have extended the notion of a clause to take in non-finite verb expressions that we call P-bound clauses. All these examples are of cont. clauses.
    We have noted:

(*a*) that in the sort of detail set out in this book, there is no *syntactic* difference between P-bound and finite-verb B clauses;
(*b*) that P-bound cont. clauses may have a binder, but do not need one;

(*c*) that there are complicated subclasses of binder according to the type of verb and the presence or absence of a subject.

P-bound Reported Clauses

This is rather a restricted class. Section 4 identified three main types of reported clause:

(*a*) binder *that*, or no binder
(*b*) binder *if* or *whether*
(*c*) binder *wh*-group

Type (*c*) shows regular P-bound clauses; and *whether* in type (*b*).

1. I wonder whether to mention it or not.
2. He forgot when to salute on parade.
3. Did you say how to get hold of Bill?
4. Whisper who to ask about those things.
5. No-one told me which policy to choose for maximum profits.
6. Can't you think who to recommend?
7. I didn't know what to get Mr Plumtree on his birthday.
8. The policeman suggested how to get to Park Lane.
9. I've just remembered where to go for cheap vegetables.

Exercise 7.6

(*a*) Check the binders used here with the key to Exercise 4.7, page 220.
(*b*) Which of these examples are reversible to *BF*? The rule is given towards the end of Section 4.

There can be no subject to the rep. clause, and we understand the structures either with reference to the F-clause subject (e.g. Example 1) or assuming an entirely general subject (e.g. Example 2).

Reporting verbs are common in the structures called phase in Section 16. Compare (9), (10) and (11).

(9) I never knew how to lock the door: Report *FB*.
(10) I never knew to lock the door: phase *PP*.
(11) I never knew him to lock the door: phase with *him* as subject of *lock*.

The effect of *how* in (9) is clearly to break the connection between *I* and *lock*, without supplying a new grammatical subject for *lock*.

SECTION 8: LINKAGE AND DEPTH

This chapter has so far restricted itself to sentences with no more than two clauses in them, and no more than one F, or one B. By keeping to these short sentences we have been able to show the important *subordination* relationships in English. In this section we are going to look very briefly at two extensions of the original sentences:

1. Sentences with more than one F.
2. Sentences with more than one B.

Strings of B clauses are made from the same basic rules as FB pairs. Strings of F clauses are *co-ordinate* and need a few simple statements about them. Let us first of all look at some *FF* sentences, and the ways in which they are related. Look particularly for *linkers*, words and phrases which *show* the relationship.

F.F

1. Our sales programme is now under way, and it is likely to stimulate demand in unexpected areas.
2. He always promised to help, but he couldn't ever manage.
3. There are many difficulties in our way; nevertheless we shall not be daunted by them.
4. Come at once or you'll have to wait at least an hour.
5. He sat down at the table: therefore we could start supper.
6. We've just run out of envelopes; tomorrow I must get some more.
7. He always promised to help; he couldn't ever manage, however.
8. He gives me my pocket-money on Friday or she does on Saturday.
9. Don't go; stay.
10. He always promised to help; however, he couldn't ever manage.
11. Mr Plumtree is my uncle; he can be trusted with anything.
12. People had made all that fuss but there wasn't anything to see.
13. Mr Plumtree likes music, and we often go to concerts together.
14. We've just run out of envelopes; tomorrow, therefore, I must get some more.
15. I tried to get Mrs Plumtree along, but she was too busy today.
16. He always promised to help; he couldn't, however, manage on this occasion.
17. I wasn't in yesterday—I was out with Madge at the cinema.
18. Bill expected to be away during August; he turned up, nevertheless, on the 17th.

Exercise 8.1

Find as many linkers as you can—for example *and* in no. 1. Note the number of any example without a linker.

Exercise 8.2

Divide the list you have in answer to 8.1 into two lists headed

(a) *linker fixed initial*: symbol A⁺: the linker only occurs as the first word of the clause;

(b) *linker free position*: symbol Aᴸ: the linker occurs in several places in the clause.

Use the facts of the sentences above only, and refer to Fig. 6.1 if you like.

Notice that there are several examples of *FF* structures without linkers: just the two clauses in contact with each other. We will call this a *contact* relationship, and turn again to the linkers.

When two clauses are linked together, one of them may be without some element of structure that it seems to need. It is nearly always the *second* clause, and the necessary element of structure is found in the first clause. We will call this very close relationship *branching*.

Look at the following examples:

1. Mr Plumtree sat down carefully and his wife brought him his slippers.
2. Mr Plumtree sat down carefully and put on his slippers.
3. Mr Plumtree sat down carefully but didn't notice the cat on his chair.
4. Mr Plumtree might arrive soon or might 'phone from London.
5. Mr Plumtree will speak a few words and shake hands with all the parents.

In all the examples except no. 1, the second clause is **branched**. If no. 2 was not branched then *and put on his slippers* would have the meaning of a command. The same point is shown in no. 5, but here the branching-point is after *will*, i.e. in the middle of the predicator of the first clause. Here is an ambiguous example:

(1) They vote for the government and don't ask why.

This sentence (1) could be analysed as *FF* (branched), with both clauses in dec. mood. The sentence would be a statement. Such a meaning could be paraphrased as in (2).

(2) They don't ask why they vote for the government—they just do it.

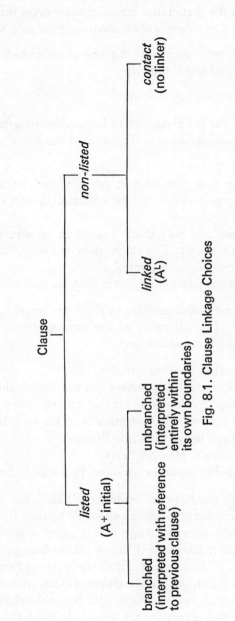

Fig. 8.1. Clause Linkage Choices

An alternative meaning comes from regarding the structure as *FF* (unbranched) with the first clause dec. and the second imp. Such a meaning would produce a *mixed-mood* sentence paraphrasable as in (3).

Unbranched (3) Don't ask me why they vote for the government—I don't understand why, I just know they do.

The ambiguity arises mainly because:

(*a*) *don't ask* can be the predicator of an imperative or a declarative clause.
(*b*) both interpretations have a fairly obvious sense; neither is very curious.

Such an ambiguity does not arise in no. 4 above, because *might* shows clearly that the second verb is not an imperative, and that the clause is branched.

The linkers that can introduce branched structures are specially distinguished from the rest. The name *lister* is useful, and the symbol is A^+. The other linkers have the symbol A^L.

There are two other features of listers that are quite important:

(*a*) They are in fixed initial position in their structure.
(*b*) Listers are found at all ranks of the grammar—particularly *and*, of course. Here are some examples:

1. Bill blushed scarlet. And no wonder.
2. We'll leave before the clock strikes but not before they've served tea.
3. Bill and his elder brother rode on the scooter.
4. You can have it now or in two months or on your fiftieth birthday.
5. The dress is made in red or white linen.
6. He can, but mustn't, play his harp.
7. Advances are being made in pre- and post-natal care.

Example 1 shows *and* between sentences. This is not very common in writing, perhaps because of a prescriptive rule against it, but perhaps also because the closeness of *and*-linkage is not often wanted between one sentence and another. Example 2 shows clause-listing; here with two B clauses, making an *FBB* structure. Example 3 shows two nominal groups combining to form the subject of the clause. Group structure is also shown in Example 4, where adverbial groups, with both adverbs and prepositions, are listed. In no. 5 two adjectives are linked; in no. 6 two auxiliary verbs; and in no. 7—also a rare case—two prefixes.

The non-listing linkers (A^L) are only loosely attached to a clause; since they commonly link sentences to each other, part of their grammar is

outside the scope of this book (see the beginning of Section 1). If we consider them *within* sentences only, we see them as optional elements of F
clauses, often initial but quite free in position; elements that specify the
relationship of F clauses to each other.

A summary of the choices in clause linkage appears in Fig. 8.1, page 53.
These are the main points, but a number of words have individual variations. Consider these examples:

1. Mr Plumtree was a small, yet bold man.
2. Mr Plumtree was rather small, so couldn't reach the apples.
3. Mr Plumtree didn't like fruit-picking, for he was rather small.

Linker	Fixed initial position in structure A	Links structures below clause rank B	Allows branching C
and, but, or			
yet			
for			
so			
however, unless, perhaps			

Fig. 8.2

Exercise 8.3

Fill in the matrix in Fig. 8.2 from the examples so far in this section. Tick
wherever a word can occur in the structure specified at the top of the
columns. If the type of linkage usually includes a *silent stress*, put a cross
rather than a tick.

Notes

1. Listing words (A+) will make up compounds with other linkers, for example:

(1) Bill was tired but nevertheless struggled on.
(2) He'll be sitting in his usual chair, or perhaps in the garden.
(3) Will we have a drink together and maybe go to a dance later?

The compounds occur in the same structures as simple listers.

2. Many linkers are ambiguous—they can also occur as adjuncts in clause structure. Consider (4) below, and three paraphrases in (5), (6) and (7).

(4) Then I'll stand up.
(5) At that time I'll stand up.
(6) After that I'll stand up.
(7) Because of that I'll stand up.

The meaning of (5) shows that *then* can be a timing adverbial group like *tomorrow*. (6) shows it as a lister with the same characteristics as *and*; and (7) shows it as a linker like *however*.

Exercise 8.4

Here are some more examples. Add from them to the two classes that you have in answer to Exercise 8.2, and study the particular features of each linker.

1. In fact, there was nothing we could do.
2. It was, in fact, the only time I'd ever seen him.
3. Bill said he would bring the books, but in fact forgot them.
4. It was big, in fact enormous.
5. But he promised to talk to us; he offered to indeed.
6. Indeed the only thing stopping us was money.
7. It was big, indeed bigger than I expected.
8. The mixture is finely strained; the sediment is thus separated from the liquid.
9. Thus, it is necessary for us to attend to the matter without delay.
10. We therefore resolved to write a strong letter to the *Guardian*.
11. Therefore the line AC lies outside the triangle BDE.
12. Mr Plumtree twisted his ankle and therefore couldn't play tennis last night.
13. He wrote to his M.P., organised a protest rally in Trafalgar Square, and finally tied himself to the lamp-post outside his house.

14. Finally, gentlemen, I have to report that the sales offices are to move to new premises on June 15th.
15. In effect he has a licence to print money in every country in Europe.
16. The Corporation is in effect acting as a banker for the Society for the first five years.
17. It is a rare and dangerous, in effect almost impossible feat.

Notice that the 'non-listing linkers' can be divided into sub-classes. One contains *yet, in fact, in effect, indeed, perhaps, maybe.* These linkers can occur in branched structures, and below clause rank (but normally when a silent stress separates them from the preceding structure). The other sub-class (*therefore, however, nevertheless,* etc.) does not have this power.

Example 13 shows another characteristic of listers. If there is a list of more than two items, the lister normally occurs only at the beginning of the last item.

The details of this will not be described—but there are several shades of meaning to be distinguished. See (8), (9) and (10).

(8) He wrote to his M.P. and then organised a rally and finally went on a hunger strike.
(9) He wrote to his M.P. and organised a rally—and then finally went on a hunger strike.
(10) He wrote to his M.P., he organised a rally, and he went on a hunger strike.

In (8) the *progress* of events is prominent; in (9) the first two events are grouped together and separated from the third; in (10) the three events might have been simultaneous, and in no particular order of importance.

That is an outline of *FF* and *BB* co-ordinations and the words that signal them. Last in this section we shall consider *BB* subordination, the feature called *depth.* Here are some examples:

1. Ring me up if you hear that Bill is still in London.
2. I wanted you to know that Bill, who is a really good chap, is getting a rise next month.
3. The bell will ring when everyone has finished; but not later than six p.m., when I have to leave.
4. I asked him how, if it was true that he had lost the car key, which I'd just lent him, we would get to the airport before the flight closed.

The examples show the sort of relationships that have been described in *FB* structures: *contingencies, additions* and *reports.* We now state that the distinction between F and B has to do only with the **sentence-actions** that we met in Section 1. *Any* clause may have another one subordinate to it. Example 4 shows several instances together. Let us split this sentence up according to the depth relationships.

  (i) I asked him = F
 (ii) how we would get to the airport = B (rep. by (i))
(iii) (*a*) if it was true = B (cont. on (ii))
      (*b*) before the flight closed = B (cont. on (ii))
 (iv) that he had lost the car key = B (rep. by (iii*a*))
  (v) which I'd just lent him = B (add. to (iv))

There is a depth of 5 here, all built up from simple structures which we have met many times. Compare the following FB sentences:

  (i/ii) I asked him how we would get to the airport.
 (ii/iii*a*) If that's true, how will we get to the airport?
(ii/iii*b*) We would get to the airport before the flight closed.
(iii*a*/iv) It was true that he had lost the car key.
 (iv/v) He had lost the car key, which I'd just lent him.

Of course, there are many details of very complex sentences that do not appear in this brief outline. What has been shown is summarised as follows:

1. *FF, BB* (and at ranks below clause) (*a*) **listing** by initial A+ (*and, but,* etc.)

 (*b*) **contact:** no marks of co-ordination

2. *FF* (and between sentences) (*c*) linking by initial, medial or final adjunct (*however, thus,* etc.)

3. *FB, BB* (*d*) subordination, by binder.

All these relationships are *recursive*; that is they can be repeated indefinitely in the same sentence. Example 4 above has the structure $F_1B_2[B_3B_4B_5]\,B_3$, and one could add *FS* and *BS* as often as desired, without making the sentence ungrammatical.

SECTION 9: REVISION OF SENTENCE STRUCTURE

Here is an exercise in which there are examples of most of the points made in this chapter. Analyse them as carefully as you can. The key presents the analysis as follows:

(a) the structure of the sentence in terms of F, B and [];
(b) the sentence-action represented;
(c) for each B clause (i) binding; P-bound, binder or P-binder, no marks
                 of binding
               (ii) type; cont., add., rep.
               (iii) depth number;
(d) split causes: places of split I, II or III according to Section 6;
(e) for each linkage: list or not, branched or not, linked or not.

Example

It was all right, in fact, for the first hour, but gradually, no matter what position you took, you got uncomfortable.

(a) *FF [B]*
(b) statement
(c)   (i) no matter what. A^{B}
   (ii) cont.
  (iii) 2
(d) II
(e) *FF* list

1. I saw in a flash that she was going to faint.
2. Everyone present, having been introduced to the bridal party, enjoyed a glass of champagne and a piece of wedding cake.
3. Although I hurried like mad, I found he had left ages before.
4. But in fact, once all the fuss has died down, don't you think that we'll get our own way?
5. The vicar, who will be retiring next year, visits everyone in the parish at least once a month.
6. It wasn't going to be too easy, he very soon found.
7. Two years later, just to see the development, Mr Plumtree called for a similar report.
8. He didn't know if he'd manage, so I went myself, and had a good time.
9. Start up the car once Bill has passed.
10. Then, in his garden, Mr Plumtree, trying not to show his excitement, pulled his new mouth-organ from his pocket.
11. Will you join us when you've finished?
12. If you see a parcel, don't open it unless your name is on it.
13. And again, if you do not consistently follow the strait path, great will be your fall.
14. Never before, he said, in the history of these islands, had such a profit been made.

15. Indeed, unless you do it now, I'll speak to your father.
16. Did you mention that Madge was coming back from Australia soon?
17. Bill concluded, after thinking a great deal, that he'd taken the best possible course.
18. In the late evening, when the pubs and cinemas are closed, give me a ring.
19. We wanted Bill to say that he would 'phone whenever he arrived in Amsterdam, where Hans was waiting.
20. You must visit Sutton Hoo, where they found Norse relics.
21. Do you think I'll do that just because you tell me?
22. I didn't ever imagine he'd jump.
23. Rarely would Bill, who was a kind-hearted chap, refuse anyone a loan.
24. In the end, when people had said what they wanted to say, he found the speaker had slipped out: however, no-one seemed very worried.
25. However, when the boat sailed, Bill wasn't on it.
26. After that Mr Plumtree arrived; peace descended on the company.
27. Inform the manager that I can't stand the noise any longer.
28. I wouldn't do that if I were you; it's too dangerous.

CHAPTER 2

Clause Structure

Introduction

This chapter describes structures inside clauses; the focus of the grammar drops down one rank. The ranks are not independent—choices made at one rank can affect choices at a higher or lower rank. Already several elements of clause structure are familiar, and the mood system—the title of the next section—has already been set out briefly in order to discuss contextual types (Section 1). Various linking and binding elements have also been set out so that the relations between clauses could be described.

Clauses are made up of *groups*. In many examples a group will consist of just one word, but when we are considering clause structure, we regard it as the equivalent of a group with several words. Groups form the elements of clause structure; the main elements are:

> (S)ubject
> (P)redicator
> (O)bject
> (C)omplement
> (A)djunct

The next few sections will show various elaborations of these elements of structure—more detailed classifications, elements which combine two functions, and extra elements like (Voc)ative, which is loosely attached to a clause. The organisation of the chapter is as follows:

Section 10 considers the elements that often start a clause—s and P: their behaviour is described by the Mood system. The next section (11) picks up another aspect of Mood—the way in which a mood can be added at the end of a clause. This section, on Tags and Responses, also considers several varieties of 'two-legged' clause structures.

If s or P is not at the beginning of the clause, then what is, and why? This question is answered in Section 12, on Theme, and the final details on position are tidied up in Section 13, as far as can be done in this size of book. Moving towards the end of the clause, there is the very important area of Transitivity—basically what can follow the verb; and two sections (14 and 15) are devoted to this subject. Then, finally, what if there is more than one P? The last section introduces Phase into the grammar.

SECTION 10: MOOD

The mood system of a clause concerns two elements of structure in particular: Subject (s) and Predicator (P). We need to know:

(*a*) if there is a P;
(*b*) if there is also an s;
(*c*) whereabouts s and P are in relation to each other.

The description in this section deals with *free clauses*, clauses which occur at F. There are a few notes on bound clauses at the end. Free clauses, it will be remembered, are clauses that determine the **contextual type** of the whole sentence; the mood system is one of the main ways in which they do it. (Bound clauses do not show a mood system; the arrangements of s and P in bound clauses have a different significance.)

In this section, we shall assume that the subject of a clause can only be found with reference to the predicator. So any clause without a P has no s either. This does not mean that we cannot interpret the grammar of a clause without P; just that we recognise two different types of structure (with P, and without P), and we keep the symbol s for structures with P.

First of all, consider clauses with no P. Although there are not many of these in paragraphs of written English prose, they are very familiar structures that carry a large amount of our daily communication. Here are some examples:

1. Yes.
2. At once, Sir.
3. Nice place, Falmouth.
4. What about me?
5. Horror scenes in death crash.
6. The Poetical Works of Thomas Chatterton.
7. Good evening.
8. Suffering goldfish!
9. A pleasure, my friend.
10. Why Mr Plumtree?

11. J. Squid, High-Class Fishmonger.
12. On my right, Bill Blood of Barnsley.
13. Dr Plumtree, Miss Wiggins.
14. Forward!
15. Him?
16. Merry Christmas, Mum.
17. Giant size Rinso 19p.
18. For Sale in Netton district, desirable modern Villa.
19. Not on your life!
20. lŏnganĭm/ ĭtў (-ngg-), n. (rare).
21. Nice evening.

Exercise 10.1

Guess the contextual type (statement, question, command, response) of
each of the sentences above. If none of the four types seems appropriate,
leave it blank.

Exercise 10.2

Write a paraphrase of or some notes on the meaning of each of the
sentences.

Examples

(a) *Certainly.* This is a response of agreement; agreement to do something,
    or agreement with something that has been said. It is quite strong;
    stronger than *yes.*
(b) *Many happy returns of the day.* A greeting, to wish someone a happy
    birthday.   *Some   unshod Someo. ——*
(c) *Gaumont Cinema.* This is a *title*, a name for something which is displayed
    on it. 'This is the Gaumont Cinema.'

The guide to the interpretation of these sentences is the sort of situation that we imagine for them, and not so much their grammatical structure. They can be any of the four contextual types. Because of the absence
of P they will be called **moodless clauses.**   *— really reduced (S)*

So much for clauses without P. We move on to clauses *with* P but *without* S.
The mood category is generally *imperative*, and the closest contextual
type is command, but not all clauses with P and no S are imperative.
Bound clauses are left till later, but we must also mention:

(a) branched structures;
(b) unstressed subjects in informal speech.

(*a*) (1) Bill went home *and had his dinner*.

The structure of the italicized clause is $A+PC$; but it is branched. One of the features of branched clauses is that the mood may be taken over from a previous clause (see Section 8, page 51). Examples (2)–(4) show how the same clause may have different moods when there is the possibility of branching.

    (2) Every evening Bill and his girl come to this bench *and sit down*.
    (3) Did they come here *and sit down*?
    (4) Come here *and sit down*.

Nos. (2) and (3) are branched; no. (4) is unbranched and imperative.

(*b*) (5) Could be, sometimes.
    (6) Sits there every night.

In informal utterances like (5) and (6), there is no subject, but the clause is not imperative. We interpret (6) in much the same way as a branched clause: the finite verb sends us looking for a suitable subject referent in the situation. It may be in the previous utterance ('What does he do?') or it may be in a gesture like pointing to someone. (6) often occurs with a tag, as (7) below. There is a section on tags (Section 11), which discusses the structure further.

    (7) Sits there every night, he does.

(5) is a little different. It is a response, and it would be easy to supply a subject like *it* or *there* or *that*. But the way it is used suggests that there is no subject referent at all, that *could be, should be, might be* are almost clichés, and are following *maybe* towards the status of linking adjuncts.

The examples show at least that it is possible for clauses with P and without s to occur, and yet not to be imperative. It is not very common, however, and it depends on the sound structure of the sentence. The following are impossible, or most unlikely, sentences in English (stress is marked by ').

    (8) *Could be cóming.
    (9) *Will sít there every night.

We recognize the imperative not only by the structure of the clause but also by the tone of voice (or an exclamation mark), and the verb form. Section 22 lists the various verb forms: and a rule of English is that the imperative is the base-form of the verb—when we talk of the verb *do* or the verb *come* or the verb *be* we write down the base-form, without any changes or endings. So Example (1) cannot be the imperative since *had* is not the base-form. *Sit* in (2), (3) and (4) is the base-form (and also a finite present tense form); but *sits* in (6) is not. *Could* and *will* are verbs that we shall see cannot occur as imperatives. (See Section 22, page 174.)

There is another small problem in the description of imperative clauses:

(10) You sit down!

The predicator, *sit*, is in the base-form, but there is what appears to be a subject—*you*, to go with it. However there are two important differences between *you* in (9), and the subject of a clause.

(*a*) *You* must be stressed if the clause is imperative. A pronoun which is the subject of a clause need not be stressed.
(*b*) The subject of a clause is normally a choice from a wide range of nominal groups. But *you* cannot be replaced by a range of nominal groups; only (rarely) by a proper name, for example:

(11) Bill sit down!

Bill and *you* in (10) and (11) are called *vocatives* and are discussed in the section on *tags* (Section 11). The clauses are imperative, with a structure *Voc. PA.*

All the other F clauses have both s and P present, and there are three common arrangements of s and P.

SP; s is in front of P.
P [S]; s is inside P (P must have at least two words).
PS; s follows P.

(*a*) *SP* clauses. These are called **declarative,** and they are usually statements. But note that they can occur as questions if they have a question intonation (Tone 2) in spoken English. *SP* is the commonest clause sequence in written English, both in free and bound clauses.

(*b*) *P [S]* clauses. Examples: (*S* italicized).

(12) Are *you* coming?
(13) Could *that fellow next door* have done it?
(14) What might *he* say?
(15) Does *Bill* like oysters?

The word that comes just in front of the subject is an *auxiliary verb*. Note these words carefully. We shall call clauses with *P [S]* structure **interrogative.**

There is one small point to make here. Compare sentences (14), (16) and (17).

(16) Who will light the candles?
(17) He will light the candles.

All three sentences are normally spoken with the same intonation (Tone 1). The sentences are compared in Fig. 10.1.

Example no.	Sequence of S and P	Mood	Sentence type	Interrogative pronoun	Subject
(14)	P[S]	Interrogative	question	*what*	*he*
(16)	SP	?	question	*who*	*who*
(17)	SP	declarative	statement	none present	*he*

Fig. 10.1. Interrogative Structures

A word like *who* or *what* goes at the front of the clause, and makes it a question. An interrogative clause usually takes *P [S]* sequence. But when *who* or *what* is the subject it cannot occur inside P. So the reason for *SP* sequence in (16) is quite different from (17). In (17) s comes before P because the clause makes an ordinary statement; in (16) s comes before P because it is a *wh-group*, and cannot occur anywhere else without changing the meaning a lot. So we recognise *SP*, with wh-group subject as a variety of interrogative mood. Fig. 10.2 summarises the choices here.

Exercise 10.3

Identify the mood of each of the following clauses.

1. Ought I to go to London?
2. Why can't you manage?
3. Be ready by six o'clock tonight.
4. The girl in the Post Office doesn't really know her job.
5. Who threw that stone?
6. Tomorrow morning pop round about coffee-time.
7. Been here for weeks.
8. How would Mr Plumtree make a living?
9. To the memory of E.K.
10. Lend me a cigarette.
11. I was watching her myself.

12. May I have a look?
13. Should be.
14. Get Bill an ice-cream, please.
15. Calm down everyone.

Exercise 10.4

Make a list of all the words that have come just before s in interrogative clauses so far in this section. Add to it from the examples below.

1. Am I walking with a limp?
2. Next week will you pay us a visit?
3. Has Mr Plumtree been bothering you?
4. When must you go?
5. Were Bill and Madge laughing all the time?
6. Should I send him a letter?
7. Why have you been so long?
8. Did Madge say that?
9. Are we bothering you?
10. How shall I tell him?
11. Had Mrs Plumtree lived there for long?
12. Isn't he speaking after all that fuss?
13. Which one was he looking at?

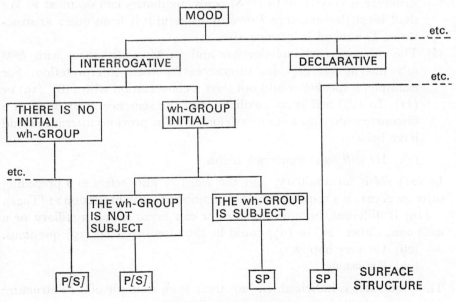

Fig. 10.2 Interrogative Structures

(c) PS clauses. The last type of clause that we shall consider is the one where s follows P. So far it is clear that each mood category roughly corresponds to a clause structure, and also to a contextual type.

If there is no P: moodless (response)
If there is P but no s: imperative (command)
If *SP*: declarative (question)
If *P [S]* (s inside P): interrogative (statement)

There is no mood category for *PS* structures. Instead, they must be related to one or other of the four categories that have already been described. Here are some examples of *PS* structures.

(18) Will he?
(19) Are you really?
(20) Is there anyone in?
(21) So did I.
(22) Here comes Bill.
(23) Near this spot lies the body of Mary Jane.
(24) 'Tomorrow?' asked Rupert.

Notice the following points:

(a) Some of them are questions (nos. (18), (19) and (20)). The words at P are *are, will, is*: all these words are auxiliaries. This kind of *PS* structure is very close to *P [S]*; only auxiliaries can occur at P. We shall label the structure $P^{aux} S$ to distinguish it from other PS structures. The mood is interrogative.
(b) The category P^{aux} includes *have* and *be*. Most structures with P^{aux} rely heavily on previous utterances for their interpretation. For example, a speaker would not start a conversation with (18), (19) or (21). In (18) *will* is an auxiliary, and the sentence must fit in to a discourse which has a main verb for *will*. The previous utterance could have been

(25) He *will finish* tomorrow night.

In (21) *did* is an auxiliary, and the word *so* also refers to a preceding utterance. (21) is a response which is mentioned again in Section 11 (Tags).

(19) is different, because the verb *be* can occur as an auxiliary or a *main verb*. Either (26) or (27) could be the utterance that (19) questions.

(26) I'*m* very happy.
(27) I'*m coming*.

The predicator is italicized. In (20) there is an example of a *PS* structure with *be* that is likely to start a conversation.

(*c*) Nos. (18) and (19) have pronoun subjects; (20) has the 'empty' subject *there*. The s of *P*aux s structures is very commonly such a word. In contrast, (21) makes an interest point out of the s, and (22), (23) and (24) cannot have a pronoun subject.

(*d*) Nos. (22) and (23) have an initial adjunct, usually telling of place or direction. The sentences are not grammatical without the adjunct, and the subject cannot be a pronoun. Section 12, on Theme, deals with initial adjuncts in more detail. Examples (28)–(31) show some of the variations that are possible with *SP* clause structure.

(28) Here he sits every day.
(29) She lies near this spot.
(30) Here Bill sits every day.
(31) Near this spot the body of Mary Jane lies.

A pronoun usually refers to something that has already been named in the discourse; something new is usually named by a noun. This is the basis of the distinction in the above structure: in (22) and (23) the subject is kept back till the end, and is the main point of interest in the clause; in (30) it seems to be *every day* that takes the main interest. (31) is an odd utterance because *lies* is hardly a point of great interest in the clause!

Because of these considerations we shall call (22) and (23) declarative clauses, but a special case of declarative structure.

(*e*) The clause in (24) is similar to (22) and (23) except that some *quoted speech* takes the place of the adjunct. The mood is declarative.

Exercise 10.5

None of the sentences below are acceptable in Modern English. Can you explain why, with reference to the notes on *PS* structures? Provide the nearest acceptable sentence.

1. *Came he?
2. *So threw Bill.
3. *Asked Mr Plumtree 'Why?'
4. *Here came they.
5. *Brightly shone the moon that night.
6. *Over there rises it.
7. *Stands a statue of Lord Nelson in Trafalgar Square.

There is a whole section on the front-placing of elements of structure, which is called *Theme* (Section 12, page 87). But we must anticipate it a little because of the effect of theme on mood. So far we have met two instances:

(32) Who will light the candles?

A **wh-group** normally comes at the front of its clause. But it takes a *P[S]* structure normally, and a problem arises when the wh-word is subject. The mood choice (interrogative) suggests *P[S]*, but the theme choice suggests *SP*. The theme choice wins.

(33) Here lies John Smith.

A thematic (that is, initial) adjunct of place allows the choice of *SP* or *PS* following, provided that s is not a pronoun. The mood is declarative in both cases.

Here is a third effect of theme on mood.

(34) Hardly had he sat down, when the phone rang.

The structure is *P [S]*, but the mood is declarative. Adjuncts like *hardly, seldom, never, scarcely* do not often come at the beginning of a clause, but if they do, the structure must be *P [S]*. Notice (35) and (36).

(35) He had hardly sat down, when the phone rang.

(36) *Hardly he had sat down, when the phone rang.

There are not *two* choices here, one of theme and one of mood; but a single choice of putting the adjunct to the front, which forces the *P [S]* arrangement.

These structures are rather old-fashioned in Modern English; even more so are (37) and (38), although they were once common in literary prose and verse.

(37) *Often would he sit at the water's edge.

(38) *A thousand times had he struck the great bell.

Fig. 10.3 summarises this discussion.

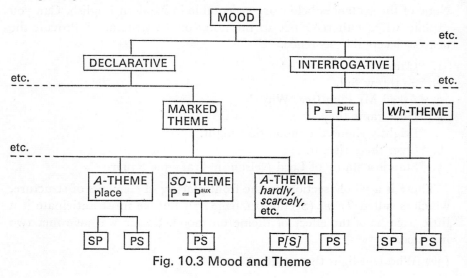

Fig. 10.3 Mood and Theme

Summary ✓

There are four mood choices for an F clause: interrogative, declarative, imperative and moodless. Interrogative is the most easy to define, because P^{aux} S is such a regular part of the structure. Any other structure with s and P is almost certainly declarative. Imperative mood is distinguished by the base-form of the verb and no s. Moodless clauses have neither s nor P.

The main influences which complicate the Mood System are:

(*a*) branched structures, which can confuse declarative and imperative;
(*b*) the tendency in conversational English not to pronounce initial un-stressed syllables—which also confuses declarative and imperative;
(*c*) the vocative, which can come just where a subject is expected, and again confuse declarative and imperative;
(*d*) wh-words, which regularly come first in the clause no matter what element of structure they are; confusing declarative and interrogative;
(*e*) auxiliary verbs as the only exponents of P, giving a *PS* structure for an interrogative mood;
(*f*) thematic place-adjuncts like *hardly*, which force a *P [S]* structure on declarative clauses.

The summary version of the free clause mood system is as follows:

Terms	Structures	Classes
Interrogative	(*a*) . . . P^{aux} S . . . (*b*) . . . S^{wh} P . . .	P^{aux}: a word which can be an auxiliary verb S^{wh}: wh-group
Declarative	(*a*) . . . S . . . P . . . (*b*) A^{place} P . . . S . . . (*c*) Q P^{rep} . . . S . . . (*d*) P . . . ⟨branched structure⟩	A^{place}: *here, there, near this spot, behind the shed, near by,* etc. Q: quoted speech P^{rep}: a reporting verb (see Section 4)
Imperative	. . . P° . . . ⟨no S⟩	P°: base-form of the verb
Moodless	⟨no P⟩ ⟨no S⟩	

Within the declarative mood we can see subsidiary systems: P is reduced in prominence.

Terms	Structures	Classes
Marked sequence	(a) A^{place} P . . . S . . . (b) Q P . . . S . . .	A^{place} Q } as previous diagram P^{rep} S : not a pronoun
Unmarked sequence	(a) . . . S . . . P . . . (b) P . . . ⟨branched structure⟩	As before

Exercise 10.6

For each clause in the following examples, note

(a) the sequence of s and P in clause structure (except for moodless clauses);
(b) the mood;
(c) the contextual type of the sentence.

1. Which car runs best?
2. Along the road ran three frightened boys.
3. Never again, my friend.
4. Ladies sit over there.
5. Was it cold in Anglesey?
6. The Balkan Sobranie smoking mixture.
7. Can you remember his name?
8. There goes a good man.
9. Been here for years.
10. 'Do you really love me?' whispered Greta.
11. Whose place has Bill taken?
12. Wait just a minute.
13. Hasn't there yet?
14. Mr Plumtree ate only two sardines, and left promptly at nine o'clock.
15. Seldom has mankind witnessed such depravity.

Subject and Predicator in bound clauses

It has already been pointed out that bound clauses do not choose a mood. There is one old-fashioned structure that has *P [S]* sequence, but it is not very common in modern spoken or written English.

(39) Had I but known his name . . .
(40) Should the track rod wear be excessive . . .

These are contingent clauses similar in meaning to (41) and (42).
(41) If I had but known his name . . .
(42) If the track rod wear is excessive . . .

Only *had* and *should* are used in this structure.

In all other bound clauses there is only one sequence of subject and predicator, namely *SP*, and only one choice—whether s is present or not. Some B clauses have no subject. We interpret many such clauses as referring to the subject of the F clauses to which they are bound.

A. *Without S*
1. In order to save the man's life, Bill jumped into the muddy canal.
2. The old man strolled down the road, smoking away at his pipe.
3. As if injured by his fall, Mr Plumtree lay quite still.

B. *With S*
1. In order for Bill to swim freely, he wriggled out of his jacket.
2. The old man strolled down the road, his horse nibbling at the verge.
3. Ribs bruised by his fall, Mr Plumtree could not get up for a few moments.

Note that the occurrence of a subject when the verb is non-finite is often affected by the choice of initial adjunct. Details have already been given in Section 7, page 46.

Very occasionally a finite verb can occur without s.

(43) As was pointed out in my Report, expansion is inevitable.

The binder must be *as*, the verb normally passive. Written office English is the main place where this structure is found. Unlike the clauses with non-finite verbs, the clause does not refer to the F clause for a subject. The sentence can be paraphrased in various ways, each showing a different subject:

(44) As my Report pointed out, expansion is inevitable.
(45) As I pointed out in my Report, expansion is inevitable.
(46) It was pointed out in my Report that expansion is inevitable.

The B clauses above are all contingent clauses. Sometimes a reported clause occurs without a subject.

(47) I don't know how to mend shoes.

(48) Have you decided which filling to put in the sandwiches?

(49) He said to sit quietly for an hour.

Again, the syntax of (47) and (48) gives no certain clue about who is to mend the shoes or fill the sandwiches. See (50)–(52).

(50) I don't know how I might mend the shoes.

(51) I don't know how shoes are mended.

(52) He said you/we/ I should sit quietly for an hour.

These points can be summarised in the following systems.

System at $B^{cont.}$: Binding type

Terms	Structures	Classes
A-bound	$A^B \ldots$	Ab : binding adjunct, e.g. *if, when*
P-bound	$\ldots P^x \ldots$	P^x : non-finite verb as *only* predicator
Sequence-bound	$P^{aux} S P^{lex}$	P^{aux} : *had, should* only P^{lex} : non-finite verbs according to the sequential rules (see Section 22)

System at $B^{cont.}$ P-bound : Subject reference

Terms	Structures	Classes
New subject	(A) S P . . .	See Section 7, for influence of A and P sub-class
Shared subject	(A) P . . .	

System at B^rep. : Subject specification

Terms	Structures	Classes
Subject specified	...S P...	
Subject unspecified	(Int) P^t...	Int: *who, whom, what, which, why, when, how, where* P^t: to-infinitive

SECTION 11: TAGS AND RESPONSES

In the spoken language in particular, there are structures that occur inside or after a clause, and appear to be separate from it, yet do not make up another clause. They are called *tags*, and in this section we examine some of the commonest of them. Consider the example:

(1) Madge is coming round tonight, *isn't she*?

Isn't she has all the marks of a P^{aux} S interrogative clause. But it is subject to a number of restrictions which suggest that the whole of (1) is a single clause, with the second part modelled upon the first part. We shall call a clause like (1) a **two-part** clause. The first part is the *proposition* (prop.), and the second part is the tag. This variety is the **checking tag**.

Note the following features of checking tags:

(*a*) the P^{aux} s sequence is necessary;
(*b*) the negative is necessary;
(*c*) the pronoun—referring to Madge—is necessary;
(*d*) the P^{aux} must be repeated;
(*e*) no other elements of structure can appear in the tag.

So none of Examples (2)–(6) is an acceptable checking tag. Example (2) does occur, but is an example of another tag—the *copy* tag (see later in this section).

(2) Madge is coming round tonight, is she?
(3) *Madge is coming round tonight, she isn't.
(4) *Madge is coming round tonight, isn't Bill?
(5) *Madge is coming round tonight, should she?
(6) *Madge is coming round tonight, isn't she tired?

(4), (5) and (6) can occur, of course, as two separate clauses, e.g.

(7) Madge is coming round tonight; isn't Bill?
(8) Madge is coming round tonight—should she?
(9) Madge is coming round tonight. Isn't she tired?

The main difference in speech between (4), (5), (6) and (7), (8), (9) is the need for a *silent stress* in (7), (8) and (9). This marks a syntactic break, which is not necessary between prop. and tag. The break frees the following clause from the five restrictions that are listed above.

So Example (1) is just one clause: Examples (7), (8) and (9) are each two clauses.

Now compare (1) with (10) and (11).

(1) Madge is coming round tonight isn't she?
(10) Is Madge coming round tonight?
(11) Isn't Madge coming round tonight?

Question	The speaker thinks I	Events suggest II	Expected response III
1. Is Madge coming round tonight?	—	—	—
2. Isn't Madge coming round tonight?	Yes	No	—
3. Madge is coming round tonight, isn't she	Yes	—	Yes
4. Madge is coming round tonight, isn't she	Yes	No	Yes

Column I depends on the verb *isn't*; column 2 on the rising intonation (no. 2 has rising intonation); column 3 on the negative tag. The negatives of 3 and 4 are:

5. Madge isn't coming round tonight, is she?	No	—	No
6. Madge isn't coming round tonight, is she?	No	Yes	No.

Fig. 11.1. Yes/No Questions

Nos. (10) and (11) are both interrogative in mood, and contextually they are questions.

All three examples ask very much the same question, but from different starting-points. In (10) the speaker shows no knowledge or assumptions about the question. In (11) he shows that he has assumed that Madge was coming, but something has happened to make it unlikely. In (1) also the speaker assumes that Madge is coming, and is merely checking.

There is actually a subtler distinction still, depending on whether the intonation of the tag is Tone 2—rising, or Tone 1—falling. A fuller picture is given in Fig. 11.1, showing how the different styles of Yes/No questioning reveal information about the speaker.

Exercise 11.1

Provide checking tags to each of the following props.

1. Mr Plumtree will buy a raffle ticket,
2. I should tell Mum,
3. That car has been parked there too long,
4. Bill and Madge must enjoy walking,
5. You're tired,

The main structural feature of the checking tag is the *polarity*: if the model is positive, the tag is negative, and vice versa.

There are a number of small points of concord between the tag and the prop.: they are summarised with examples in Fig. 11.2. From that figure it should be possible to construct a checking tag for any statement in English.

Exercise 11.2

Provide checking tags to each of the following props.:

1. He mightn't want it,
2. There's no-one here,
3. Your house in the country has a lovely garden,
4. Everyone thinks he's coming,
5. You'll come with us,
6. I used to like Brahms, . . . *didn't   pos - neg*
7. . . . but I don't now, *do I   neg - pos.*
8. You can do this,
9. Father should have made the speech,
10. It's not the rain we're worried about as a matter of fact,
11. That boy never came back,
12. All those people we met last night were Italian,

(contd. on page 79)

Prop.	Tag	Example
(a) any *negative*, e.g. *n't, never, nobody*, or even *hardly, seldom*	positive	He isn't coming, is he ?
(b) non-negative	P^{aux} n't S	He is coming, isn't he ?

Prop. Subject	Tag Subject	Example
(a) a personal pronoun (*I, you, he, she, it, we, they*)	same word	He's coming, isn't he ?
(b) non-personal *it*; *that, this*, etc.	*it*	It's raining, isn't it ?
(c) *there* (unstressed)	same word	There's coffee after, isn't there ?
(d) a rankshifted clause	*it*	Where we're going is nice isn't it ?
(e) an impersonal pronoun *no-one, nobody, someone, somebody, everyone, everybody*	*they*	Everyone's coming, aren't they ?
(f) no subject (imperative verb)	*you*	Don't touch, will you ?
(g) all other subjects	the appropriate personal pronoun	That man's coming, isn't he ? My hair looks nice, doesn't it ?

Prop. Predicator (first word)	Tag Predicator	Example
(a) *am*	*are*	I'm late, aren't I ?
(b) *used*	*did*	He used to come, didn't he ?
(c) any other P^{aux}	same word	He can come, can't he ?
(d) an imperative P	*will*	Sit down, won't you ?
(e) any other P	*do/did*, etc.	He sat down, didn't he ?

Fig. 11.2. Concord Rules in Checking Tags

13. I'm allowed to have oysters,
14. What he said oughtn't to matter,
15. Have an orange,

The Copy Tag

There is another tag which resembles the checking tag closely, except that the polarity of the tag is the same as that of the prop. See (12) below, and (2) earlier on.

(12) So he said that, did he? Wait till I get my hands on him!

The usual intonation is Tone 1 3: *that, did he?* This tag, called the **copy tag,** has a range of meaning. In an example like (12) it is a very aggressive, challenging remark; in (13*b*) it is little more than a response to (13*a*).

(13*a*) It's dark outside now.
(13*b*) Oh, it's dark, is it?

It is clear from (13) that the copy tag copies something that has just been said—it adds nothing except the reaction of the person who speaks it. It is often used to acknowledge statements that cause surprise, and it requests confirmation of the previous statement. It is one of the ways in English that we *repeat* information so that both parties can be sure that it has been passed correctly—like spelling out an address on the telephone, or repeating back complicated instructions.

Exercise 11.3

Provide a copy tag to each of the statements in Exercise 11.2. (No. 15 is a command, so miss it out.)

Responses

Fig. 11.2 is also useful for the description of some response structures which have P^{aux} in them, so we leave tags for a few pages.

(*a*) Response: *Restatement*

This is a response to a statement, meaning that the responder has fully understood—like 'Ah yes, I realise that.'

(14*a*) Madge is coming round tonight.
(14*b*) So she is.

The Predicator is always positive. Some speakers seem not to have a negative form of this response; others replace *so* by *neither* or *nor*. The subject is always a pronoun related to the subject of the previous statement (but note that with the change of speaker *we* becomes *you*, etc.).

Exercise 11.4

Provide restatement responses to each of the positive statements in Exercise 11.2.

(*b*) Response: *New Subject*

This is a response where the second speaker adds another subject to refer to the original clause.

(15*a*)   Madge is coming round tonight.
(15*b*)   So is Bill.
(16*a*)   That won't fit.
(16*b*)   Neither will what you've got.

Notice that the ᴾaux is always positive; concord is *so* to a positive verb in the model, and *neither* or *nor* to a negative verb. The sequence is *So P*aux *S*, whereas restatement tags have *So S P*aux. New subjects cannot be provided where the subject is an impersonal pronoun, e.g.

(17)   There's a hole in my bucket.
(18)   It's raining.
(19)   Nobody told me.

Exercise 11.5

Provide New Subject tags for the examples in Exercise 11.2, missing out nos. 2, 4, 10, 15.

(*c*)   Response: *Yes/No*

Very often in conversation, the minimum response to a question is simply *yes* or *no*, but the speaker adds a tag. The tag does little more than make the utterance a few syllables longer. Examples:

(20*a*)   Is Madge coming round tonight?
(20*b*)   Yes she is.
(21*a*)   Won't that fit?
(21*b*)   No, it won't.

The tag follows rules that should now be familiar. There is of course a choice of polarity in the answer; the sequence is sᴾ, subject is the appropriate pronoun and the ᴾaux is repeated.

Exercise 11.6

Provide yes/no responses to each of the following questions: (note that the negative of *I am* is *I'm not*).

1. Does he want it?
2. Isn't there anyone here?
3. Has your house got a garden?
4. Doesn't everyone look super?
5. Won't you come with us?
6. Did you used to like Brahms?
7. Can you do this?
8. Should father have made the speech?
9. Is it the rain that's bothering you?
10. Did that boy never come back?
11. Were all those people Italian?
12. Aren't you allowed to have oysters?

These P^{aux} tags and responses are worth reviewing in connection with the mood system of the previous section. Remember that the sequence P^{aux} *S* is ambiguous between affirmative marked sequence, and interrogative.

T_1: Checking tag (*he's coming*) *isn't he*? The model has *SP*, the tag P^{aux} *S*. The tag clearly is used to convert a statement into a question, so the whole clause is considered interrogative.

T_2: Copy tag (*he's coming*) *is he*? In mood this tag is the same as T_1.

R_1: Restatement *so she is SP* declarative mood.

R_2: New Subject *so is Madge PS* structure, like *there goes Madge*. Very occasionally, the verb can be other than P^{aux}; e.g. *says*. This structure is declarative marked sequence.

R_3: Yes/No. *SP* declarative mood.

Tags Continued

Another group of tags concerns the ways in which a speaker can amplify a clause as he utters it.

(*a*) The simplest tag of this type is the vocative; the name of the person spoken to (or written to). It usually occurs at the beginning or the end of the clause. It is just a name, what is called in Section 17 a *proper noun*. Occasionally it is the pronoun *you*; at times like the start of a letter, or during a formal speech it can be a special phrase (see the examples below with vocatives italicized).

(22) Have you seen it, *Bill*?

(23) *Ladies and gentlemen*, I am not going to speak for long.

(24) *Madge*, wait for me.

(25) Sit down, *you*.

(26) *Dear sirs*, I have your letter of the 16th.

(*b*) Another tag of this type is the *gloss*. This tag has various forms, as the examples show.

(27) Then he walked over, *this fellow*, and shook me by the hand.

(28) There they were in front of me, *two huge Shorthorn bulls*.

(29) I came out, *I did*, and no wonder.

(30) Bill spoke to him quietly, and he—*the man I was talking about*—started to sing.

(31) *My friend* she said it wasn't right to do that.

(32) So she made a cup of tea, *Madge did*, and we all drank it up.

These are all 'running repairs' to sentences. They are common in speech, and occasionally used in written prose (e.g. (28) and (30)). (27), (28), (30) and (32) are nominal groups amplifying the subject of the model. Traditional grammar would call them *appositional*. In (31) the gloss comes first; showing clearly the structural function of this tag. It separates a nominal group from the rest of clause structure, and allows the speaker to construct them separately.

Two examples—(29) and (32)—have a structure $S\ P^{aux}$ which simply emphasises the mood of the prop. In (29) especially there is no new information added in the tag.

Exercise 11.7

Identify the tags and responses in the following examples.

1. Good morning, Mr Plumtree; my name is Smith.

2. So he stayed out till three in the morning, did he? So did I.

3. He'll come tomorrow, Bill will, so don't worry, Madge, will you?

4. Then another man came up to me, an old man with a cap, and told me not to worry.

5. (*a*) This parcel, lady, it can be registered.
   (*b*) So it can.

Tags are an important feature of speech, but are not written down very often. They vary from time to time and from place to place and from person to person. Not long ago a novelist would use a vocative like *gentle reader*, but this is now out of fashion. In Scotland a checking tag with two negatives is common, e.g. *he's coming, isn't he not?*; in Wales checking tags are used very frequently, and *isn't it* can be used after any prop.; in the north of England a gloss tag can be *P*aux *S*, for example:

(33) Then he walked home, did Jack.

Some individuals use vocatives a lot, or checking tags, or gloss tags, as unconscious habits of speech.

Summary

Tags modify the structure of a clause by adding to it extra elements of structure. They allow a clause to be altered while it is being uttered. We divide tags into two types—those which affect the mood of the clause, and those which add further information or emphasis to some part of the prop.

1. *Mood tags.* The statement about interrogative mood in the summary to Section 10 has to be added to. (See Fig. 11.3.)

Terms	Structures	Classes
neutral	... Paux S ...	Paux = any positive auxiliary
query	... Paux, neg S ...	aux, neg : any negative auxiliary (ending in *n't*)
checking tag	(S)P...T1	T1 : see Fig. 11.2
copy tag	SP...T2	T2 : see Fig. 11.2 and notes

Sub-system of Free Clause mood
Fig. 11.3. Interrogative Type

2. *Further information tags.*

(*a*) Vocative: structure a nominal group, symbol *Voc*. Proper name or special form of address.
(*b*) Gloss: structure *S P*aux or just a nominal group. Symbol T3. Glosses are more common in impromptu speech than in writing.

On the basis of Fig. 11.2, a few common responses were described:

1. Restatement (*so it is*, etc.)

2. New Subject (*so is Bill*, etc.)
3. Yes/No (*yes it is, no it isn't*, etc.)

Tags and Theme

One effect of a gloss tag can be to present the vocabulary of a clause in a
different sequence from its non-tag equivalent. Look back to Examples
(27), (28) and (32) and compare with those below:

(34) Then this fellow walked over . . .
(35) There two huge Shorthorn bulls were, in front of me.
(36) . . . so Madge made a cup of tea . . .

Notice that the syntax of (34) is the same as the syntax of the prop. of
(27), and so with the other pairs. Now consider (37) and (31):

(31) My friend she said it wasn't right to do that.
(37) My friend said it wasn't right to do that.

Here the tag position affects the *theme* of the clause. Theme is fully
described in Section 12, page 87. Roughly speaking, the theme of a clause
is the first element in it, apart from binders and linkers.

There is another important type of two-place structure that is briefly
outlined here; it involves the word *it*. Just as the mood tags control the

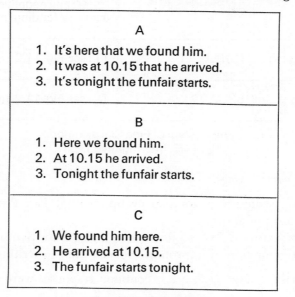

Fig. 11.4. *it*-theme

mood of the clause, these structures, beginning with *it*, control the theme of the clause. Fig. 11.4 gives contrasting examples.

Exercise 11.8 (refer to Fig. 11.4)

Work out a rule to derive B1 from A1, B2 from A2, B3 from A3 and another to derive C sentences from B ones.

In the example A1, *It's here* carries the theme of the clause, and the remainder, *that we found him*, is called the *rheme*. The theme portion consists of *it* as subject, *be* as Predicator, and the Adjunct *here*. The rheme portion starts with an optional *that* (see A3) and then a normal clause continues.

The B examples show Adjunct theme, and the C examples show the normal sequence of clause structure. Clearly the function of **'it-theme'** structures is to place great emphasis on the Adjunct. But other elements than the Adjunct can be singled out in it-theme. See Fig. 11.5, where subjects and objects are *thematised*.

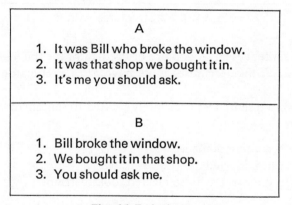

A
1. It was Bill who broke the window.
2. It was that shop we bought it in.
3. It's me you should ask.

B
1. Bill broke the window.
2. We bought it in that shop.
3. You should ask me.

Fig. 11.5. *it*-theme

Two-place structures within one clause must be carefully related to *FB* structures, to show the similarities and differences. Consider Fig. 11.6.

Group A sentences are *FB*rep. (see Section 4, page 30). Group C sentences have *it*-theme. In between are the sentences of Group B. Let us compare the three groups to see which category best suits Group B.

(*a*) *It*-theme clauses normally have *that* as the beginning of the rheme. Group B sentences can have a *wh*-group or *if*, *whether*; or a *to*-infinitive, just like a *B*rep. clause.

(38) It's doubtful whether he'll come.
(39) It's necessary to lock up every night.

A

1. He says that he's coming.
2. I know what he says.
3. We all believe Mr Plumtree will be elected.

B

1. It's nice that he's coming.
2. It's true what he says.
3. It looks certain that Mr Plumtree will be elected.

C

1. It's here that he's coming.
2. It's Bill that says these things.
3. It's Mr Plumtree that'll be elected.

Fig. 11.6. FB Structures with *it*

(*b*) Group B sentences have a choice of Predicator for the *it*—*be, look, seem, appear*, etc. *It*-theme clauses must have *be* as Predicator in the prop. portion.

(*c*) Most Group B sentences are closely related to sentences like (40), (41) and (42).

(40) That he's coming is nice.

(41) What he says is true.

(42) That Mr Plumtree will be elected looks certain.

In (40) the structure of the sentence is F; and within that clause the subject is *that he's coming*, which is therefore a rankshifted clause (see Section 18). Most of the examples of this structure are stilted and formal; the Group B structure is much more common. The only exception is (41), because *what* is frequently used in both (41) and B2 structures.

(*d*) There is no way of arranging *nice he is coming* to make a normal clause, in the way that Exercise 11.8 does for *it*-theme clauses.

The conclusion from this discussion is that Group B sentences should be considered a special variety of *FB*rep. structures. It was noted in Section 4, page 30, that the report structure showed much more interdependence of the clauses on each other than *FB*cont. and *FB*rep.. This new variety with *it* shows a closer dependence still.

Exercise 11.9

Analyse the following sentences in terms discussed in this section.

1. It was the pearl that your Mum lost.
2. No-one knows what to do.
3. Where we go for holidays is super.
4. It's next year the Festival is in Cardiff, isn't it?
5. Over there is the old churchyard.
6. It's lovely to see you.
7. Now Bill, he wanted beer.
8. It was the dog that laughed last.
9. It's unfortunate that Mr Plumtree has another engagement.

Note: Nos. 1 and 8 are ambiguous, because *it* can also be a personal pronoun referring to a dog or a pearl. In that structure, no. 8 would answer the question 'Which dog was it?'; but in the structures described in this section, no. 8 answers the question 'Who laughed last?'

In summary, we have done some description of the grammar of theme and rheme, as it is found in two-place structures. It has been related to other types of theme, anticipating Section 12, below, and also to *FB*rep. structures which often look like it.

The grammar of *it*-structures cannot be taken much farther in this book, but here are just a few examples of structures related to *it*-theme:

1. It took Bill twenty minutes to fix the bell.
2. Bill took twenty minutes to fix the bell.
3. To fix the bell took Bill twenty minutes.
4. It's almost as if he was here among us.
5. It's essential for him to walk.

SECTION 12: THEME

Theme is the way in which the elements at the front of a clause are organised. We have already seen how the mood system handles the organisation of s and p; how the tag systems deal with things added to a clause (usually at the end, but not always). Now we look at the beginning of a clause. What can occur there?

Let us start with the observation that the mood choice is usually made first in the clause. Since that is the regular situation, it will be called *neutral theme.* It gives no surprises. Now we consider what items can come in front of it.

A. Fixed position items

The italicized items in the following sentences must occur before mood choice.

1. (Bill walked) *and* Madge took the car.
2. (Bill must clear out) *or* I'll do something dreadful.
3. (I was going to buy one of these), *but* something happened at lunch *and* I clean forgot.
4. (He always plays with the children) *when* he comes home at nights.
5. *If* you won't do it (I'll have to, I suppose).
6. (I said) *that* I wasn't able to help the project.
7. (He didn't say) *whether* he thought (it was a good idea).
8. *Notwithstanding the fact that* the Commission may not interfere in civilian disputes (this matter falls outside their terms of reference).

Exercise 12.1

Nearly all these items have been met before. What are they? What happens if two are chosen in the same clause?

These words are not considered under theme, since they have no choice in their position. The theme of a clause is an element of structure which *could* occur somewhere else.

B. Very mobile items

The italicized items in the following sentences often occur in front of the mood choice, but they also can occur in several other places in clause structure (revise Section 8 for details). They don't have a *regular* place in the clause at all. So when they occur at the front, or in the middle, or at the end of a clause, they do not cause any surprise. We have seen how sometimes an element of structure is predicted by the rest of a clause (e.g. *Bill threw* . . . expects an object). These words are never predicted by the previous syntax.

1. *Furthermore,* we must be perpetually aware of the competitive nature of the enterprise.
2. *Also,* there's the question of money.
3. *Then* why did you bother phoning?

4. *After all,* that sounded good at one time.
5. *As a matter of fact,* Bill couldn't find the key.

Exercise 12.2

These items have been met before. What are they? Find at least three other positions for them in each sentence.

We reserve the name *minor theme* for these linkers when they occur at the beginning of the clause. They are not important in the development of a clause because their main function is to link clauses and sentences together.

C. Some adjuncts usually occur after the mood choice, but can also occur at the front of the clause. They are called lexical adjuncts, to distinguish them from linking and binding adjuncts. Linking and binding adjuncts have an important grammatical function to relate clauses to each other. On the other hand, lexical adjuncts mainly carry vocabulary words, or deal with the timing and placing of events. Section 13 gives more details of their patterns. Here we are just concerned with their front position.

1. *In the morning* we went home.
2. *At the end of the street* you'll find a pillar box and a 'phone box.
3. *In time,* he got to know us quite well.
4. *Carefully* he picked his way among the sharp stones.
5. When, *after ten,* we continued the debate (Mr Plumtree had a lot to say).
6. However, *between periods of pain,* he was able to tell his story.
7. *Seldom* have I listened to such poppycock.

(For the mood of no. 7 see Section 10, page 70.)

The effect of this word-order is to make the adjunct very prominent. It is called **Adjunct-theme** or *A-theme*. Notice in no. 5 that a binding adjunct *must* come in front; and in no. 6 that a mobile linker *can* come in front.

Exercise 12.3

Rewrite the seven examples above with the adjunct in another clause position. Try to find its regular position.

D. Occasionally the object occurs at the front, instead of in its usual place after the predicator. Here are some examples: notice how often the object is contrasted with a nearby nominal group (nos. 1, 4 and 6; implied in no. 3).

1. *Big nails* I need, not these little ones.
2. *As big a meal as that* I don't like, really.
3. On the other hand, *table linen* we can take easily.
4. I said there'd be mince for supper, and *mince* there is.
5. *Any aircraft you care to mention* he'll recognise first time.
6. *Chairs* put over here (tables down the corridor, please).

(The clause *you care to mention* in no. 5 is actually part of the object. Section 18 explains this sort of structure, called *rankshift*.)

An object at the front of the clause is very prominent, because objects have hardly any mobility in the clause. This pattern is called **Object-theme** or *O-theme*. The object is a special information point here, and it will have a tone group to itself.

Exercise 12.4
Rewrite the six examples above with the objects in their regular places.

Note that when a prepositional object comes to the front of a clause, that is A-theme.

(1) Money I can do without, but not love.
(2) These papers you're welcome to, but please leave those ones.

Example (1) is analysed *A [SP]* . . ., since *money* is part of the adjunct (see Section 25). This *split* structure is mostly due to the idioms *do without* . . . and *be welcome to* . . ., which would not give the same meaning in a different sequence.

(3) *Without money I can do, but not love.

E. There is a group-class which cuts across the theme choices that we have considered above. It is the class of *wh-groups*; they nearly always need separate notes on their grammar. What concerns us here is their strong tendency to occur at the beginning of a clause.

When they occur in B clauses, they have the status of binding elements, no matter what element of structure they are in. And binding elements must come first, as we noted in A above. Examples:

1. I spoke to Bill, *whose uncle* is Bishop of Bridgnorth.

2. *Whatever* he does, don't tell him the answer.
3. I don't know *which flight* he's on.
4. Madge asked her friend *why* the tickets cost so much.

Exercise 12.5

What elements of structure are the italicized groups? What kinds of clause do they introduce?

When they occur in F clauses, their normal place is at the front of the clause, again no matter what element of structure they expound.

1. *Whose dog* is this?
2. *What* do you want?
3. *Wherever* have you been?
4. *What job* interests you most?
5. *Why* can't I?
6. *However* did you manage?
7. *Who* did you get it from?
8. *When* did it happen?
9. *On whose authority* do you take this action?
10. *Who* told you to do that?

Exercise 12.6

What elements of structure are the italicized groups? What is different about clauses where the italicized group is subject?

Wh-theme, then, is different from neutral theme, A-theme and O-theme, because it can be chosen with any element of structure except P. It applies only to F clauses, because there is no choice in B clauses.

The choice in F clauses is interesting. Consider the following dialogue:

A (i). Who do you want for President?   (structure *O P [S] A*)
B.   I want Hubert Plumtree.   (structure *S P O*)
A (ii). You want *who*?   (structure *S P O*)

The clause in A (ii) shows the alternative place for a wh-group—in this case in the normal place for objects in clause structure. Clause B has the same structure as A (ii), and A (ii) is used as a surprised reaction to hearing something. Its intonation is a very sharp rise (tone 2) on the wh-word, with a high *pretonic*. Here are some more examples:

1. He shouted *why*?
2. He said *what*?
3. She did it *how*?

    4. They came *when*?
    5. The dog is *whose*?
    6. You got it from *whom*?
    7. I'm going *where* on Sunday?

Notice that *wh*-words that end in -*ever* (like *wherever, whatever*) only occur initially.

Exercise 12.7

Note the themes of the following clauses. Where there is more than one theme, note the sequence in which they occur.

    1. Nevertheless, can you supply us in time?
    2. Thus five weeks hence, when in England you are sitting under your umbrellas, I'll be enjoying myself in Madeira.
    3. I told him all about it.
    4. Therefore, early this morning I slipped out of bed quietly.
    5. All of a sudden jumping to his feet, Bill asked a penetrating question.
    6. Come round tomorrow at ten.
    7. Who told you that next Tuesday is the date?
    8. His last chance he let slip like all the others.
    9. If after all this you still want to go, in Africa how will you contact us?
   10. Will you manage an early lunch?
   11. What is the man running for?
   12. Tomorrow, what'll we do?
   13. Your latest consignment, however, I found quite satisfactory.
   14. Mr Plumtree, who is my landlord, wakes me up every morning at seven with his singing.
   15. When, the very next day, he returned, we drove to London and there we had a marvellous time.
   16. Madge I like a lot.
   17. It came via *where*?
   18. Whatever is she saying?
   19. Calmly and skilfully, Bill edged the yacht round the buoy.
   20. How did you clear it up so quietly, when you were so busy otherwise?

Note the following points about the sequence of themes:

(*a*) minor theme can occur before or after any of the others (Examples 1, 2 and 4);

(*b*) A-theme comes in front of *wh*-theme (Examples 9 and 12).

This is a suitable point to summarise the choices of theme that have been described so far.

Terms	Structures	Classes
minor theme	...A^L...MOOD...	A^L = mobile linker MOOD = SP, P[S], P : the mood choice
non-theme	any other structure	

System of the clause : Minor Theme

Terms	Structures	Classes
major theme	(i)...A...MOOD... (ii)...O...MOOD...	A = Lexical adjunct MOOD = SP, P(S), P... O = object of clause
neutral theme	any other structure	

System of the clause : Major Theme

Terms	Structures	Classes
A-theme	...A...MOOD...	See above
O-theme	...O...MOOD...	See above

System of Major Theme : Theme Element

Terms	Structures	Classes
Theme *wh-*	(A) *wh*...	A : see above *Wh-* : element of structure containing *wh*-group
Contrast *wh-*	any other structure containing *wh*-group	

System of the *F* clause : *Wh*-theme

Fig. 12.1. Theme Systems

The theme of a clause is the first element of its structure that appears by a choice of position. There can be three themes in a clause:

(i) minor theme;
(ii) neutral, o-theme or A-theme;
(iii) wh-theme on an element different from the choice at (ii).

Wh-groups have an unusual position in F clauses as well as their thematic place at the front. This is the position they would most likely occupy in the clause if they were not *wh*-words. It will be mentioned again below this summary. The systems are set out in Fig. 12.1.

A final note about *wh*-words. All the examples below have neutral major theme.

(4) Who came today?

This clause chooses *wh*-theme on the subject (which explains the sequence *SP*).

(5) What did you say?

This clause chooses *wh*-theme on the object.

(6) You said *what*?

This clause chooses contrastive *wh* on the object.

(7) *Who* came today?

This clause chooses contrastive *wh* on the subject. Since the regular place for the subject is in front, it does not move its position from Example (1); it can only be recognised by the intonation, and by italics in print.

Two-place structures and theme

At the end of Section 11, page 84, there was some discussion of this subject and it is continued here.

Most of the tags occur late in the clause, and so do not affect theme. The two that can occur early are the gloss tag on the subject, and the vocative tag.

(8) Then this sailor he walked off in a fury.
(9) Madge, did *she* like it?

(Assume that *Madge* in (9) is the person *she* refers to, and is not a vocative.) In these examples the subject is made prominent by the tag structure, in contrast with its usual neutral effect. So we shall call (8) and (9) examples of *S-tag theme*, a marked theme.

(10) Bill, are you coming tonight?
(11) Are you coming tonight, Bill?
(12) Are you coming, Bill, tonight?

The vocatives are very mobile, and they have no regular structural position. In this they resemble the mobile linkers (A^L); for their function is to link a sentence with the situation in which it is uttered, by mentioning the name of the person being spoken to. When they start a clause they are a variety of *minor theme*.

The theme-and-rheme structures show *it*-theme choices with A, S, O and prepositional objects.

(13) It was last year that he died.
(14) It's Bill who's doing that.
(15) It'll be me that he'll charge.
(16) It was this cat you sat on.

Exercise 12.8

What is the theme of sentences (13) to (16)?
Finally, here is a sketch of the theme choices available in a clause.

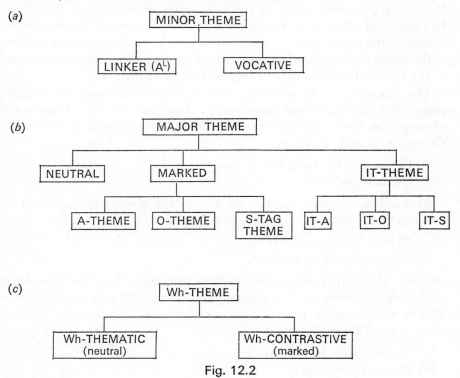

Fig. 12.2

Exercise 12.9

Identify the themes in the following clauses:

1. Last Friday he had a meeting, hadn't he?
2. Are you ready yet?
3. Now Mr Plumtree, he got out quickly.
4. Madge looks like *whom*?
5. Doris, it was Bill who told you.
6. It's *whose* party you're going to?
7. The dog, it disappeared.
8. It was around here that the battle took place.
9. Sir John, last night at what time did you hear the noise?
10. I like school.

SECTION 13: ADJUNCT POSITION

In this section some more of the patterning of adjuncts is described. Grammatical adjuncts have been dealt with briefly, and the theme systems described the rather unusual cases where a lexical adjunct comes in front of the mood choice. Now it is time to look at the position of adjuncts later in the clause. Lexical adjuncts only will be described.

The first point is to establish what positions there are. An English clause with one predicator has no more than one subject and one complement, no more than two objects. But it doesn't need to have any. Compare (1) and (2) below:

(1) I gave him the book later.
(2) He managed later.

The adjunct is final in the clause, but the clauses are different in construction.

(3) *I gave him later the book.
(4) *I gave later him the book.

Neither (3) nor (4) is acceptable, so there are no positions like 'between P and o' or 'between the two objects'—unless in very rare circumstances that do not concern us here. So we can call (1) and (2) 'after P' or 'final'—there is no difference.

(5) I nearly gave him the book.
(6) He nearly managed.

(7) I had nearly given him the book.

(8) He'll nearly manage.

In (5) and (6) the adjunct is 'between s and p'; in (7) and (8) it is 'inside p'. But there is no important difference between these positions; the adjunct will occur between s and p when p is just one word, and inside p when p is more than one word. Compare (9)–(12).

(9) Did you nearly give him the book?

(10) Had you nearly given him the book?

(11) Did he nearly manage?

(12) Will he nearly manage?

When the interrogative P [S] sequence is chosen; the adjunct occurs in exactly the same place in all four clauses, namely P [SA] 'after s, inside p'.

(13) You nearly had given him the book.

(14) He nearly will manage.

(13) and (14) show SAP sequence, even when p has more than one word in it. This is an unusual sequence which makes either the adjunct or the first word of p very prominent. Note, however, the following examples:

(15) Bill just used to sit here.

(16) Bill used just to sit here.

(17) You always ought to be kind to animals.

(18) You ought always to be kind to animals.

(19) Later I gave him the book.

(20) Later he arrived.

In (19) and (20), *Later* is thematic and quite prominent: see Section 12, page 88.

When the verbs *used* and *ought* are at P^{aux} it is common for the adjunct to come before them; especially in informal speech. The *SAP* structure of (15) and (17) does not force emphasis on the adjunct or the verb, as it does with the other auxiliary verbs.

Since theme has been described, there are only two other adjunct positions that concern us:

(a) *In*-p—including 'between s and p' when p is one word.

(b) *Post*-p—anywhere in the clause after p.

Exercise 13.1

Note the position of the italicized adjuncts in the following examples. Classify them as

(*a*) thematic;
(*b*) *SAP*: unusual emphasis;
(*c*) In-P (i.e. *P[A]* or *AP* without unusual emphasis);
(*d*) Post-P.

1. He'll *never* manage to finish it.
2. I *usually* like strawberries.
3. I *only* mentioned it.
4. We hadn't *ever* done it *before*.
5. He's coming *tonight*.
6. You *just* can't keep quiet, can you?
7. He'll *quite* understand your position.
8. The man next door *always* takes his dog *for a walk* at night.
9. *Usually* I like strawberries.
10. The car started *noisily*.
11. I *rather* do like steak.
12. Madge *nearly* died.
13. We could *hardly* speak for laughing.
14. The ship will *only* have been at sea a week by then.
15. Madge *quite* terrified me.
16. I *merely* wanted to stop arguments at this point.
17. They go to school *now*.
18. Mr Plumtree may *just* want to collect his things.
19. You *nearly* fell then.
20. *Last week* I wrote four letters.

Exercise 13.2

From the examples so far, make a list of adjuncts which occur in-P and post-P.

Some adjuncts are restricted to one of the two positions, and some occur readily in both. Consider the following sentences:

A1	A2
1. Bill even washed up.	1. Bill always makes breakfast.
2. *Bill washed up even.	2. Bill makes breakfast always.
3. Bill washed up, even.	

The comma in A13 shows that *even* in post-P position, must have a tone group of its own. *Always* does not need this, but can carry the tonic syllable of the clause.

For reference we shall call adjuncts based on the in-P position, Class A adjuncts; Class A1 adjuncts are those restricted to in-P positions. If one occurs post-P it will have a separate tone group. Class A2 adjuncts can occur post-P but are more frequently found in-P.

B1	B2
1. Bill quietly made breakfast.	1. *Bill at home made breakfast.
2. Bill made breakfast quietly.	2. Bill made breakfast at home.

Both *quietly* and *at home* are what we shall call class B adjuncts—occurring regularly post-P; but *at home* does not occur in-P.
Class B adjuncts are based on the post-P position.
Class B1 adjuncts can occur in-P but are more frequently found post-P.
Class B2 adjuncts do not occur in-P.
As well as this positioning, of course, some adjuncts can be theme in their clause.

Exercise 13.3

Here are a large number of examples of adjuncts in different positions. Find them, and state their position in-P, post-P or theme. Then add in the answers to Exercise 13.2 and make a table of classes of adjunct according to position. First of all, discover whether the adjunct occurs both in-P and post-P without having a new tone group. If it does, it will belong to either Class A2 or Class B1. Decide which seems to be its most natural position.

If the adjunct does not go into Classes A2 or B1, the choice between A1, and B2 is easy. Note if the adjunct can be thematic, but do not classify on this basis yet.

1. Never have I seen such a mess.
2. We've scarcely painted the window frames . . .
3. Scarcely had they started, when the roof fell.
4. Hardly had we begun, when two men shouted slogans.
5. He didn't drink, hardly.
6. He wants a drink, merely.
7. Bill and I would rather like to try those biscuits.
8. I'd join the army, rather.
9. He dropped his cup, nearly.
10. Bill was almost finished.
11. It was a palace, almost.
12. The shops will still be open.
13. He's there still.
14. Still the waves beat the sandy shore.
15. He sits here always.
16. Always he gave me twenty-five pence.

17. You must get depressed often.
18. Mrs Plumtree doesn't often cry.
19. Often, the traffic annoys me.
20. He may already have left.
21. I've told you already.
22. Already, it seems more dangerous.
23. Tonight we'll have a party.
24. Madge quickly stitched her dress.
25. He recovered quickly.
26. Quickly, Mr Plumtree started the car.
27. The dog was quietly removed.
28. Everyone spoke quietly.
29. Quietly, things were being changed.
30. Mr Plumtree willingly moved his seat.
31. He agreed willingly.
32. Willingly, they gave their valuable time.
33. We're having our holidays at home.
34. At home there was a visitor.
35. It will happen on Tuesday.
36. On Tuesday the Plumtrees came.
37. Put it in the kitchen.
38. In the kitchen Madge had a new fridge.
39. I live here.
40. Here lies Mary Jane.
41. Here the corn is ripening.
42. Nothing grows there.
43. There goes a happy man.
44. There I used to sit.
45. I couldn't see him, scarcely.
46. He lost his temper, almost.
47. You'll be meeting them on Tuesday.
48. In the kitchen there's a lot to eat.
49. Did you enjoy the match last week?
50. Noisily they washed the dishes.
51. Mr Plumtree washed the dishes.
52. Have you seen him ever?
53. Before, he was tall and strong.
54. We were later released.

Note that Class A1 can be divided according to theme. The class of *never*, *hardly* and *scarcely* is the class sometimes called 'seminegatives' (remember their influence on checking tags in Section 11). The clause sequence is *P [S]* when they are thematic. The other A1 adjuncts are only rarely found in theme position.

Class A2 adjuncts mainly concern time, but not particular points of time in the past or in the future.

All the Class A adjuncts focus on the whole clause, and not just the verb. Class B adjuncts focus on the verb more directly. The syntactic distinction between B1 and B2 follows closely the type of group—whether **adverb-head** (B1—*quietly*) or **preposition-head** (B2—*at home*). Class B1 includes all the many 'quality' adverbs ending in *-ly*.

The classification is just an outline. A word like *just*, or *now*, has more than one meaning, and the position may depend on the appropriate meaning.

(21) Now I want you all to look at this.
(22) I want you all now to look at this.
(23) I want you all to look at this now.

Now, at the front of (21) is probably unstressed, and links the sentence with what goes before. It has a similar function to *well*, *so*, etc. and we would classify it as A^L. In (22) *now* is at in-P position and is stressed. It shows that the sentence is part of an orderly presentation. proceeding step by step. Such words—like *then*, *therefore*, are also A^L items. In Example (23) it means 'at this moment', and would be classed as a B2 adjunct, along with *tonight*.

Exercise 13.4

Look for ambiguities in the following examples, and try to classify the adjuncts.

1. Sir Jasper leaped easily astride his horse.
2. I can easily manage that!
3. The chairman spoke definitely.
4. The chairman definitely spoke.

Place, manner and time

It quite often happens that two or even three adjuncts occur post-P in the same clause. The main classes are **place**, **manner** and **time**. These terms refer to the meaning of the adjuncts, but as well as the meaning there are some positional rules that help in the classification.

(*a*) Adjuncts of the same class occur in any sequence without showing prominence, e.g.

(24) Bill arrived at half past two yesterday.
(25) Bill arrived yesterday at half past two.

(*b*) Adjuncts of different classes usually follow the sequence *place, manner, time*.

(26) Bill arrived unexpectedly yesterday.
(27) Bill arrived at the office unexpectedly.
(28) Bill arrived at the office yesterday.
(29) Bill arrived at the office unexpectedly yesterday.

Exercise 13.5

(*a*) Classify the adjuncts in Examples (24)–(29) as place, manner or time.
(*b*) Make a set of clauses like (26)–(29). Start with *Mr Plumtree lived* and add the adjuncts *here, happily* and *before the war*.
(*c*) If x, y and z are adjuncts, and the clauses below are all in normal sequence, which classes do x, y and z belong to?

1. Madge sang z x
2. Madge sang z y
3. Madge sang y x

Exercise 13.6

Add to your classification the adjuncts in the following examples.

1. Put it on the table by yourself.
2. Bill threw it across the room to me.
3. He's going by train tomorrow.
4. We're off to Scotland tomorrow.
5. The baby was born last night at 23.27.
6. Bill threw it to me across the room.
7. He walked across the room with a smile.
8. The baby was born at 23.27 last night.
9. He did it by himself with a smile.
10. Put it on the table tomorrow.
11. He greeted us with a smile yesterday.
12. He did it with a smile by himself.

Exercise 13.7

Go back to Exercise 13.3, and list the adjuncts of class B which do not occur in-P. Add them to the classification of 13.4 and 13.5, but don't just do it on their meaning. Try them out positionally. For example, if you think *quickly* is a manner adjunct, then it should occur naturally after *here* and before *yesterday*, e.g.

> *He ran here quickly yesterday.*

SECTION 14: TRANSITIVITY I

Objects, Complements and Adjuncts

Most grammars make the predicator the main element of clause structure. In traditional grammar a clause was recognised by its 'finite verb'; in this grammar the mood system shows how the position of P indicates the mood. In the rest of the clause, too, the choice of verb is closely related to the presence of objects, complements and adjuncts. This section begins the description of such relationships.

Individual verbs can be classified according to the clause structures in which they occur; there are many different classes and much recent grammatical research is in this area. This book is too small to say much about the detailed classification of verbs, though the Introduction sets out a fragment of this sort of grammar.

Object, complement and *adjunct* are the names given to the three elements of clause structure that remain to be described. Here are some examples, with comments:

A. Objects

(1) Mr Plumtree drank *the milk*.
(2) Can you collect *them*?
(3) *The bones*, you throw away.
(4) Bill hurt *himself* badly.
(5) I've baked *a cake* for tea.
(6) You should visit *Wales* next summer.

Notice some grammatical features of objects.

(*a*) They are nominal groups, with noun *headwords* (*milk, bones, cake, Wales*) or pronouns (*them, himself*).

(*b*) A pronoun that does not end in *-self* can always replace the object:

(7) Mr Plumtree drank *it*.
(8) *These* you throw away.

(9) Bill hurt *him* badly.
(10) I've baked *it* for tea.
(11) You should visit *it* next summer.

(c) Any group that can be the object of a clause can also be the object of a preposition:

(12) I saw a fly in *the milk* | under *them* | among *the bones* | near *myself* | on *a cake* | in *Wales*.

(d) Objects are highly predictable in the syntax of the clause. In the examples none of the objects is absolutely essential, but the environment usually has to be carefully contrived to allow the verb to occur without an object.

(13) The milk was in the tumbler, and Mr Plumtree drank.
(14) They're here—can you collect?
(15) The bones? *You* throw away.
(16) Bill hurt badly whenever he fell.
(17) I've baked for tea.
(18) We're here all the time; you should visit next summer.

(e) Usually, the object of a clause can occur as subject of the same verb in the *passive* voice. Thus:

(19) *The milk* was drunk.
(20) Can *they* be collected?
(21) *The bones* are thrown away.
(22) *Bill* was hurt badly.
(23) *A cake* has been baked for tea.
(24) *Wales* should be visited next summer.

Notice in (22) compared with (4) that *himself* cannot be the subject of a clause. There are further remarks about the relationships between objects and subjects later on in this section.

Notice also that the object of a clause names something different from the subject. Compare sentences (4) and (9): in sentence (9) we assume that the object refers to someone other than Bill. The only time the object refers to the same person as the subject is when it is a *reflexive* pronoun, as in (4). In the following examples we must assume that two people are involved.

(25) William Pitt hurt the Prime Minister.
(26) *Bill hit Bill.

B. Complements

(1) Madge felt *fine*.
(2) It seemed *a good party*.
(3) That soup tastes *really delicious*.
(4) Mr Plumtree doesn't look *himself* today.
(5) Everyone grows *old* eventually.
(6) They were *machines*.

Notice some grammatical features of complements.

(*a*) They are usually *adjectival groups*. Less often they are nominal groups, which can be replaced by adjectives, e.g. (7)–(9) compared with (2), (4) and (6).

(7) It seemed *suitable*.
(8) Mr Plumtree doesn't look *fit* today.
(9) They were *mechanical*.

The nominal groups are never pronouns except in the case of reflexives like (4) *himself*.

(*b*) Complements are hardly ever *thematic* (placed to the front of the clause —see Section 12). Sentence (A3) shows a thematic object, but the sentences of group B do not all have an exact equivalent. Consider the following:

(10) A good party, that.
(11) Really delicious, that soup.
(12) Machines they were.

In these changes to sentences (2), (3) and (6), the Predicator is omitted unless it is the verb *be*, and sentences (10) and (11) are now moodless.

(*c*) The complement of a clause is highly predictable, like the object.
(*d*) The complement of a clause cannot usually be the subject of similar constructions with the verb in the passive voice.
(*e*) The complement of a clause does not name anything distinct from the subject, but describes the subject. Consider the two meanings of:

(13) Bill and Henry parted bitter enemies.

(i) *SPC*: Bill and Henry were not the enemies: but they interrupted a fight between some other people.
(ii) *SPC*: Bill and Henry had become enemies of each other when they went their separate ways.

C. Adjuncts

(1) He left *eventually*.
(2) We have three teachers *in our Chemistry Department*.
(3) Bill has eaten his dinner *rather greedily*.
(4) A parcel arrived *the next morning*.
(5) Madge smashed the clock *in a fury*.

Notice some grammatical features of adjuncts.

(*a*) They are usually adverbial or prepositional groups, occasionally nominal, like (4). Here is an ambiguous sentence, depending on whether the italicized nominal group is read as object or adjunct.

(6) He booked *the next weekend* for his holiday.

If *the next weekend* is object, then he reserved those days as a holiday period; if adjunct, he booked at that time for some later holiday.

(*b*) Their position in the clause is very mobile. Some regularly occur between s and p—see (7).

(7) He eventually left.
(8) In the Chemistry Department we have three teachers.
(9) Bill has rather greedily eaten his dinner.
(10) The next morning a parcel arrived.
(11) In a fury Madge smashed the clock.

(There is more detail on this point in Section 13, page 96.)

(*c*) Adjuncts are much less predictable in the clause syntax than complements and objects. All the sentences (c1)–(c11) are acceptable without adjuncts. A few verbs predict an adjunct, for example, in sentence (12) *under the table* cannot be left out.

(12) Bill put the book *under the table*.

Also, the constructions known as **phrasal verbs** are combinations of predicator and adjunct which develop a new meaning. They are further described in Section 25, page 211.

Adjuncts in a clause do not usually relate or refer to any one element of the clause. They develop the meaning of the clause as a whole by descriptive detail including timing and placing.

Exercise 14.1

Mark the italicized group in each of the following examples as object, complement or adjunct.

1. Mr Plumtree became *an important person*.
2. He gets *rather too friendly* often.
3. The boy dropped *his new toy*.
4. I do my exercises *every morning*.
5. We got a letter *from Dad* yesterday.
6. Mother ordered *five tins of beans*.
7. Haven't you seen *a haggis* before?
8. It smells *horrible*.
9. The trapped insect wriggled free *gradually*.
10. *Philip* I've already met, but not Sonia.
11. The children amused *themselves* for hours.
12. She was going to be *a very unhappy woman*.
13. Bill found his jacket *this afternoon*.
14. I noticed *two vases* on the table.
15. At the hairdressers, tipping appeared *the custom*.

Exercise 14.2

(a) Change each object to a pronoun that is not reflexive.
(b) Change each complement that is a nominal group into an adjectival
    group.
(c) Change each adjunct that is not an adverbial group into one.

In the rest of this section, there are some notes on the occurrence of
objects, complements and adjuncts in addition to the distinctions that are
set out above.

Clauses which contain a complement are not often in the imperative mood.
Consider (B1)–(B6) above, and compare with (1)–(6) here.

(1) *Feel fine!
(2) *Seem a good party!
(3) *Taste really delicious!
(4) *Look yourself today!
(5) *Grow old eventually!
(6) *Be machines!

None of them seems acceptable as a command. The clauses refer to
matters that are not normally in our control, making it unlikely that we
should issue commands about them. When these structures do occur, we
interpret them as if the situations *could* be controlled.

(7) Look nice tonight!
(8) Be a good boy!
(9) Well, *seem* happy then!

(7) is not telling someone to alter their physical appearance, but just the matters of dress, tidiness, make-up, etc. which can be controlled. (8) assumes that children decide whether to be good or bad, and (9) tells someone that, if he can't *be* happy, he should appear outwardly as if he was happy.

Another point to note about complements is that they are not often found in the same clause as a class of adjuncts that we shall call, informally, 'manner adjuncts'. (See Fig. 14.1.)

A	B
1. Madge felt fine *in the water.*	1. *Madge felt fine *sweetly.*
2. It seemed a good party *for a while.*	2. *It seemed a good party *thoroughly.*
3. That soup tastes delicious *initially.*	3. *That soup tastes delicious *carefully.*
4. Mr Plumtree doesn't look himself *today.*	4. *Mr Plumtree doesn't look himself *easily.*
5. Everyone grows old *eventually.*	5. Everyone grows old *gracefully.*
6. They were machines *at one time.*	6. *They were machines *strongly.*

Fig. 14.1. Adjuncts and Complements

Nos. A1–6 have *time adjuncts* or *place adjuncts* which fit the clauses: Nos. B1–6 have *manner adjuncts* that do not fit grammatically, except B5 because it includes a cliché. The exact rules are very complicated: for example *quickly* would fit in nos. 1, 5 and perhaps 2, of column B where it could be interpreted as a time adjunct, but not in the others.

This point leads to two other points. First, a number of verbs occur with a complement only as clichés. Here are some examples to show the tendency. *Turn* can be used with quite a number of adjectival groups, whereas *rest* and *wax* have only one or two.

(10) The big man *turned nasty.*
(11) That fish *has gone funny.*
(12) They all *fell sick.*
(13) *I rest content.*
(14) Mr Plumtree *waxed eloquent.*

Secondly, the –*PC* structure is related to the passive voice. This arises because past participles of verbs (*n-forms*) share a lot of syntactic patterning with adjectives. The following sentences are ambiguous:

(15) The cloth was torn.
(16) The job was finished.
(17) The wallpaper was marked.

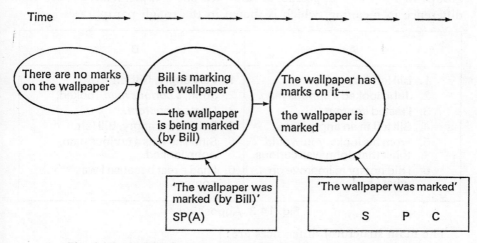

Fig. 14.2. Ambiguity of n-forms. 'The wallpaper was marked'

Fig. 14.2 shows the difference between the meanings of these sentences. For example if (17) is roughly similar to (18) below, its structure is *SPC*; if (19), it is *SP*.

(18) There were marks on the wallpaper.
(19) (Bill) marked the wallpaper.

Exercise 14.3
Make grammatical notes on the following clauses, particularly on any italicized words.

1. The older boys drove *them* home.
2. They stayed *a happy family*.
3. My cousins *visit every week*.
4. Be *reasonable*, Dad.
5. Good chap, Bill.
6. Madge seemed cheerful *normally*.
7. The search *proved* hopeless.
8. Bill *was tired*.
9. He's *sitting pretty*.

This is the place to start a discussion of **apposition**, which is the name given to a number of different grammatical relationships. Section

11 deals with some points about apposition. Here the main concern is to distinguish the complement relationship from an appositional one. Study the examples in Fig. 14.3. Nos. 1–3 have the structure *SPC*; the italicized groups in B1–3 are 'appositional' and are not complements. Notice the difference in meaning, which is shown in the rough paraphrases 4–6.

A	B
1. Bill left *very angry.*	1. *Very angry,* Bill left.
2. John looked *a curious man.*	2. John, *a curious man,* looked.
3. I rested *content.*	3. I rested, *content.*
4. Bill left in an angry state.	4. Being very angry, Bill left.
5. From his looks, you would think that John was curious.	5. Since he was a curious man, John looked.
6. I did not try to improve on what I had.	6. I had a rest because I was content.

Fig. 14.3. Apposition

The main structural differences are:

(a) Appositional groups can occur in several different places in the clause. On the other hand, we have already noted that complements are not often thematic, and do not occur between s and P.

(b) The appositional groups are separated by commas from the clause. In spoken English, they cannot contain the only *tonic syllable* of the clause.

In the analysis proposed here, appositional groups of this type are not part of the clause at all, but are separate B clauses. The clues are given in the paraphrases in Fig. 14.3: they can all be regarded as a type of B clause similar to P-bound clauses but without a verb at all: it is easy to insert the word *being* in front of each of the 'appositional groups' in the examples in Fig. 14.3; this is shown in box B of Fig. 14.4.

All the examples of initial apposition are Bcont. clauses. Medial apposition is more tricky, and Fig. 14.5 contrasts two types. The examples in box A have been chosen so that there is very little meaningful connection between the 'appositional' clause and the surrounding clause. Note the following points:

(a) When an adjectival group is appositional, it must have some clear meaningful connection with the surrounding clause. Thus in (20) below we are forced to assume that people over a certain height were singled out, asked to leave, or that the venue was very low-roofed, or in some way relevant to height.

finite B clause	A.	1. Since he had become very angry, Bill left.
		2. Because he was a curious man, John looked.
		3. Now that I was content, I rested.
non-finite B clause	B.	1. Being very angry, Bill left.
		2. Being a curious man, John looked.
		3. Being content, I rested.
initial apposition	C.	1. Very angry, Bill left.
		2. A curious man, John looked.
		3. Content, I rested.

Fig. 14.4. Apposition and B Clauses

	A.	1. Bill, very angry, left.
		2. John, a curious man, looked.
		3. I, content, rested.
	B.	1. Bill, very tired, left.
		2. John, my cousin, looked.
		3. Madge, a hairdresser, rested.

Fig. 14.5. Medial Apposition

(20) Bill, very tall, left.

(*b*) When a nominal group is between s and P, as in B2 and B3, there is no need to make such an assumption. B2 and B3 could be paraphrased as:

(21) John, who was my cousin, looked.
(22) Madge, who was a hairdresser, rested.

Notice that here the paraphrase uses an add. clause rather than a cont. clause.

(*c*) Now return to Examples c1–3 of Fig. 14.4. Again there is the compulsory connection in meaning between appositional clause and the following clause. Look how odd are (23), (24) and (25) below.

(23) Very tall, Bill left.
(24) My cousin, John looked.
(25) A hairdresser, Madge rested.

It is implied by the *B*cont. structure that Bill left because of his height, John looked since he was my cousin, and Madge, being a hairdresser, needed to rest.

We conclude from these points that an appositional element occurring before the F clause is *B*cont.. (Remember that add. clauses cannot come in front of their F clause.) An appositional element occurring between s and P is either *B*cont. or *B*add., and usually it will be interpreted as *B*cont. if it is adjectival, *B*add. if nominal.

Exercise 14.4

Mark the italicized parts of each of the following clauses as object, complement, adjunct or appositional element, and if appositional whether *B*cont. or *B*add..

1. He wrote, *full of promises*.
2. He grows *radishes*.
3. . . . but *the licence* they sent later.
4. It seemed *a forgotten part of England*.
5. Madge went home *a happier girl*.
6. *A sailor*, Bill took a drink readily.
7. I wasn't feeling *very depressed* last night.
8. Madge blushed, *a young girl in such a crowd*.
9. I'm *fine*, thanks.
10. We all got *ready*.
11. They arrived, *ready for anything*.
12. Madge blushed *bright red*.
13. He talks *a great deal*.
14. I obtained *a permit*.
15. *Furious*, he walked out.
16. *The next morning*, Mr Plumtree left for France.
17. He might have become *a great artist*.
18. Mrs Plumtree cabled at once, *unhappy at the news*.
19. The next person, *a fruit salesman*, told his story.
20. The mixture turned *bright yellow*.

The last point about complements concerns the general classification of verbs. Many of the verbs that have been used in examples can also occur with objects—and with slight differences in meaning.

(26) Madge felt *his hand* in the darkness.
(27) Mrs Plumtree tasted *the soup*.
(28) Everyone grows *potatoes*.
(29) I smelled *something*.
(30) He got *a new job*.
(31) You should rest *your legs* a little.
(32) Bill left *his watch* at the cinema.

With some of these verbs, there is a systematic relationship between the object of the *SPO* structure and the subject of the *SPC* structure. Compare (26)–(29) with (33)–(36)

(33) His hand felt warm and sticky.
(34) The soup tasted delicious.
(35) Potatoes grow big around here.
(36) It smelled horrible.

Summary

In this section we have begun to deal with transitivity—one of the main grammatical relationships in the clause. First, three elements of clause structure are distinguished—o, c and a. Objects can always be replaced by pronominal groups. Complements can always be replaced by adjectival groups, and adjuncts can always be adverbial or prepositional groups. The object names something distinct from the subject, the complement refers back to the subject, and the adjunct times, places or otherwise describes the rest of the clause.

Complements rarely occur in imperative clauses; and they rarely occur with qualitative adjuncts. They have to be distinguished from the n-forms of passive verbs, and from 'appositional groups'. Verbs can be classified according to the structures (*SPO*, *SPC*, *SP*, etc.) in which they occur.

SECTION 15: TRANSITIVITY II

Double Transitivity

The structure of some clauses includes more than one object, or an object
and a complement. In this section the main patterns of **double transitivity** will be examined. As with single transitivity, the choice of the particular verb is important, and there are many classes of verb which can be
identified. Some of the classes are very small, numbering only one or two
verbs, and there is no space in this book for a detailed treatment of the
individual verbs.

First of all, clauses which have two objects.

(1) I made Mr Plumtree a piperack.
(2) Bill lent his father some books.
(3) Tell me the answer.
(4) I'll pick you some apples.
(5) Madge read her mother the notice.
(6) He made me the lampshade.

The traditional names for the two objects are *indirect* for the first one,
(*Mr Plumtree, his father, me, you*) and *direct* for the second one (*a piperack,
some books, the answer, some apples*). The indirect object usually refers to a
person, but not always, e.g.

(7) I got the car a new set of tyres.
(8) I gave the library some old manuscripts.

Nearly always the two objects occur in the sequence indirect-direct.
The only freedom occurs when both objects are pronouns, and in these
cases the pronoun which refers to a person is assumed to be the indirect
object. There is a slight chance of ambiguity in examples like (9) and (10),
but it is very rare.

(9) I fed it him.
(10) I gave her them.

(9) is more likely to be understood like 'I fed the food (it) to the animal
(him)' rather than 'I fed my friend (him) to the lion (it)'. (10), where both
pronouns can refer to people, will be understood by the sequence rule, as
'I gave them to her', not 'I gave her to them'.

There is a close relationship in meaning between the indirect object of a
clause, and prepositional groups with *to* and *for*. Notice the possible and

A.	Prepositional group with *to*
1.	Bill lent some books *to his father.*
2.	Tell the answer *to me.*
3.	I gave some old manuscripts *to the library.*
4.	I fitted a new set of tyres *to the car.*
5.	Madge read the notice *to her mother.*

B.	Prepositional group with *for*
1.	I made a piperack *for Mr Plumtree.*
2.	Pick some apples *for me.*
3.	I got a new set of tyres *for the car.*
4.	We bought new curtains *for the bedroom.*
5.	Bill lent his father some books *for me.*
6.	I want a biscuit *for them.*
7.	Madge read the notice *for her mother.*

C.	Impossible, or very doubtful clauses
1.	*Bill lent some books for his father.
2.	*I made a piperack to Mr Plumtree.
3.	*I fitted the car a new set of tyres.
4.	*We bought the bedroom new curtains.
5.	*Bill lent me some books to his father.
6.	*He mended me the lampshade for Bill.
7.	*I want them a biscuit.
8.	*He mended the man across the road the lampshade.

Fig. 15.1. Indirect Objects and Prepositional Groups

impossible clauses in Fig. 15.1. From these examples we notice particularly:

(a) the normal position for a prepositional phrase;

(b) the *to* and *for* prepositions cannot be interchanged (see Examples c1 and c2);

(c) clauses with indirect objects cannot normally also have prepositional groups that name someone or something in addition to the subject and the two objects (c5, c6);

(d) although indirect objects can usually be replaced by *to-* or *for*-groups, this rule does not always work in reverse (compare A4 and C3, B4 and C4, B6 and C7);

(e) the indirect object that can be replaced by a *for*-group is easily added to many verbs (though not all—see C7). But the other one—replaced by a *to*-group—is restricted to a small class of verbs;

(f) where there is ambiguity, the *to*-group type is the first to come to mind. Look at clause (5) on the original list: it could be replaced by A5 or B7, but we naturally think of A5 first of all.

In many clauses with two objects, the direct object cannot be omitted. In some, the indirect object cannot be omitted either. It depends again on the verb chosen, and on the situation surrounding an utterance. The pattern of the verbs that have been used so far in examples is shown in Fig. 15.2. *want* and *fit* are not double-object verbs.

Verb	Without indirect object	Without direct object
1. lend	I lent some books. *	
2. give	I gave some old manuscripts. *	
3. make	I made a piperack.	
4. pick	I'll pick some apples.	
5. read	Madge read the notice.	
6. mend	He mended the lampshade.	
7. get	I got a new set of tyres.	
8. buy	I bought new curtains.	
9. tell	Tell the answer. *	tell me
10. feed		I fed him

*Not common

Fig. 15.2. Double-transitive Verbs

The classes of verb shown here are:

(a) *give* and *lend*. They normally occur with both objects. It is possible for them to occur with only one—or even none, when the environment allows it, e.g.

(11) There was a collection for Mrs Plumtree and I gave willingly.

(b) *make, pick, read, mend, get* and *buy*. They regularly occur without the indirect object. Traditional grammar often uses the term *ethic dative* for the indirect object with verbs of this class. It is a very large class.

Almost any action can be done on behalf of someone else, so most transitive verbs allow an indirect object, usually a *for*-type rather than a *to*-type.

(c) *tell*, which can occur without the direct object, and occasionally without the indirect. Some other reporting verbs are in this class.

(d) *feed*, which can occur without the direct object, but not without the indirect. This verb is included to emphasise the variety of patterns shown by different verbs. Perhaps *him* in *I fed him* should not be analysed as indirect object at all. There are many problems of detail like this one.

*Exercise 15.1**

Classify the italicized verbs in the examples below. Use the four categories that have been identified:

(a) regular double-object verbs, e.g. *give*, which normally occur with both objects;

(b) single or double-object verbs, e.g. *make, read*: the indirect object is optional;

(c) reporting verbs which have an indirect object, e.g. *tell*. They can occur with both objects, or just with one; but the construction with direct object only is uncommon;

(d) minor types.

1. Bill *has asked* him hundreds of questions this morning.
2. I *paid* them a deposit.
3. But you *promised* me!
4. I *granted* his request.
5. Mrs Plumtree *finished* her soup carefully.
6. Who *will ask* his name?
7. *Did* you *bring* Madge a souvenir?
8. I *promised* £5.
9. *Finish* me this dress by tomorrow morning.
10. *Ask* me, then.
11. Bill *allowed* him ten minutes only.
12. Mr Plumtree *promised* his wife a long holiday.
13. We *wish* you a long and happy retirement.
14. *Have* you *paid* the guide?
15. My employers *granted* me some sick-leave.
16. I'll *bring* some milk.
17. I'm afraid you *must pay* £2.50 for that.

After double-object clauses, we turn to clauses which have one object and one complement. In the first examples the complement is an adjectival group.

(12) The acid turned the litmus paper red.
(13) That flask will keep the coffee piping hot.
(14) Can you make her happier?
(15) People consider Bill very successful.
(16) The jury find the defendant guilty.

Note the following grammatical points:

(*a*) In many cases the complement can be a nominal group (but not a pronoun). The same point was noted about single complements.

(17) The acid turned the mixture a funny colour.
(18) People consider Bill a very successful lawyer.

There is a small class of verbs which have a nominal group only as complement. Here are some examples.

(19) The people elected him *President* by a narrow majority.
(20) The company appointed Mr Plumtree *secretary*.

The italicized nominal group in (19) and (20) must refer to an official position. Therefore it cannot be an adjectival group. We include these clauses as *SPOC* structure mainly because of the similarity in meaning between, say (14) and (19) or nos. (21)–(25) below.

(21) They made Bill captain.
(22) They made Bill their leader.
(23) They made Bill important.
(24) They made Bill happy.

(*b*) There is another reason for including *President, secretary, captain* as complements. It is a general point distinguishing objects and complements, just as in the previous section. Consider first some passive clauses (all with double-object verbs), shown in Fig. 15.3.

These examples are not intended to be another classification of verbs that take two objects; so they are not complete. Group A shows the indirect object in the *SPOO* clause as subject of an *SPO* clause. Group B shows the direct object of an *SPOO* clause as subject of an *SPO* clause. Group C shows the direct object of an *SPOO* clause as subject of an *SP(A)* clause.

The main point to be made here is that either object of a double-object clause can be subject of the same verb in the passive. Of the verbs above, the only doubtful case is the following:

(25) *I was finished the dress.

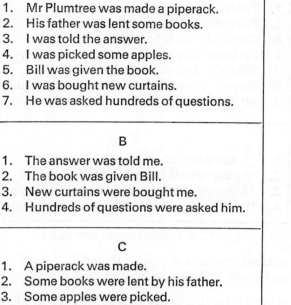

A

1. Mr Plumtree was made a piperack.
2. His father was lent some books.
3. I was told the answer.
4. I was picked some apples.
5. Bill was given the book.
6. I was bought new curtains.
7. He was asked hundreds of questions.

B

1. The answer was told me.
2. The book was given Bill.
3. New curtains were bought me.
4. Hundreds of questions were asked him.

C

1. A piperack was made.
2. Some books were lent by his father.
3. Some apples were picked.
4. New curtains were bought.
5. Hundreds of questions were asked.
6. The dress was finished.

Fig. 15.3. Double Transitivity and Voice

Finish is a verb of class (*b*) which does not often take an indirect object, and that accounts for the rarity of a clause like (25). Examples A1 and A4 are also fairly unusual. Indeed the *for* type of indirect object is less common as subject than the *to* type. But they are all potentially subjects of a passive clause with the same verb.

In contrast, there are some examples formed from *SPOC* structures in Fig. 15.4. Compare them with (12)–(16).

As before, the complement can never be subject to the same verb (Example B3 is grammatical, but is understood as the passive of *People consider a very successful lawyer*).

Notice also:

(*a*) The clauses with the verbs *elect* and *appoint* fall in with *SPOC* clauses in this test.

(*b*) The verbs *turn* and *keep* remain active in box A. They could be forced into the passive in the following rather clumsy structures.

A

1. The mixture turned a funny colour.
2. The coffee will keep piping hot.
3. Can she be made happier?
4. Bill is considered a very successful lawyer.
5. The defendant was found guilty.
6. He was elected President by a narrow majority.
7. Mr Plumtree was appointed secretary.

B

1. *A funny colour was turned by the acid.
2. *Piping hot will be kept by the flask.
3. *A very successful lawyer is considered by people.
4. *President was elected him by a narrow majority.

Fig. 15.4. Complements and Voice

(26) The mixture was turned red by the acid.
(27) The coffee will be kept hot by that flask.

This class of verb is similar to the class mentioned in the previous section, of verbs such as *grow*, which can have the same nominal group as o in *SPO*, and s in *SP* (with P active in both cases).

In the outline so far of *SPOC* structure, the complements have been important in the interpretation of the verb. Compare the original examples (12)–(16) with the following:

(28) The acid turned the litmus paper.
(29) This flask will keep the coffee.
(30) Can you make her?
(31) People consider Bill.
(32) *The jury find the defendant.

(32) in particular is most unlikely; but in all of them the verb has a different meaning from its meaning in an *SPOC* structure. For example *keep* in (29) means roughly 'store', while *keep . . . hot* means 'insulate'.

We now turn to *SPOC* structures where the complement is much more of an 'extra' in the clause. The meaning of the verb is not affected. Here are some examples:

(33) We'll eat the lamb *cold*.
(34) Bill cut the pieces *very large*.
(35) He certainly built this *solid*.

(36) I like my weekends *quiet*.

(37) He entered the room *cold*.

A complement refers to another element of clause structure. In *SPC* structures it refers to s; in *SPOC* structures it usually refers to o, and only rarely—e.g. in (37) above—to s.

Notice one final point about *SPOC* structures. Later in this chapter (Section 16, page 124) there is a description of the structure known as *phase* in English grammar, which has a lot of similarity to *SPOC* structures. Here are some examples of phase to compare with the clauses in this section:

(38) People consider Bill to be very successful.

(39) The jury find the defendant to be guilty.

(40) We'll have the lamb fried in butter.

(41) He certainly made this last a long time.

(42) I like my weekends to be quiet.

The main difference in phase structures is the occurrence of a second verbal group (*to be, fried, last*). It could be held that *SPOC* structures are a reduced variety of phase. But it is difficult to see how a clause like

(43) That flask will keep the coffee hot.

can be related to a phase structure, since no other verbal group can be inserted. The same is true for many *SPOC* clauses. So in this book a distinction is kept between the two types of structure.

Exercise 15.2

There are several verbs which can occur in *SPOO* and *SPOC* structures. *Make* has been used in the examples

I made her a piperack *SPOO*

You make her happier *SPOC* (c refers to o)

Below are some more examples. Mark them *SPOO* or *SPOC*, and state the most likely reference of c (either to o or to s, according to the way you understand the sentence).

1. Bill left the office content.
2. He got his neighbour a new garden shed.
3. We found him irresponsible.
4. Bill left the office a fortune.
5. We found him a dejected man.
6. I'd call him a good salesman.
7. Bill left the office a mess.

8. We found him some antiques.
9. I'll call you a porter.
10. He got his neighbour furious.

Summary

A clause can have one object or two.
A clause can have a complement.

If there are two objects, the indirect object occurs first. The indirect object usually refers to a person, is often a pronoun, and usually does not occur without the direct object. Indirect objects are related to prepositional groups with *to* and *for*.

A complement comes after an object. In *SPOC* structures the complement normally refers to the object, but it can sometimes refer to the subject. Individual verbs can be classified as follows, with reference to transitivity

(a) which structures can follow them;
(b) which objects can be subject of the same verb;
(c) what effect on (a) and (b) is made by changing the verb to the passive voice;
(d) what changes in the meaning of the verb occur with different structures.

Summary of systemic choices

Object and complement in the clause.
Notes: (i) The structural notation assumes neutral theme, affirmative mood and normal adjunct positions.
(ii) There is a great deal of overlap in the verb classes, and the examples are for illustration only.

Note

A clause which is both double transitive and complemented will be for example:

(44) He gave her the book dirty (SPO^I O^D C; $C = O^D$)

Revision Exercise: Transitivity and Complementation

Exercise 15.3

What place in clause structure is occupied by the italicized groups in the sentences below?

1. TRANSITIVITY

Terms	Structures	Classes
Transitive	...$P^t O^D$...	O^D: a nominal group P^t: a class of verb, e.g. *throw, eat, watch*
Double transitive	...$P^{tt} O^I O^D$...	O^I: a nominal group; very often a personal name or pronoun P^{tt}: a class of verb, e.g. *give, lend, buy*
Intransitive	...P^i...⟨no object⟩	P^i: a class of verb, e.g. *fly, speak, rest*

2. COMPLEMENTATION

Terms	Structures	Classes
Complemented	...P^c...C...	P^c: almost any verb C: (*a*) an adjectival group (*b*) a nominal group which can be replaced by an adjectival group
Uncomplemented	⟨no complement⟩	

Fig. 15.5. Transitivity and Complementation

1. J. Rubble will build *you* a house for £2250.
2. I taught him *arithmetic*.
3. The committee considered *the matter*.
4. He soon came *clean*.
5. Madge fell *last night*.
6. Did *anyone* call?
7. Bill cabled *an urgent message*.
8. Nothing makes me *upset* these days.
9. The Corporation sent *Mr Plumtree* a rude letter.

10. She bought *frozen peas* for supper.
11. That ticket saves *you* sixpence.
12. That should make *it* safe.
13. They voted him £*200*.
14. They made *him* chairman.
15. The judge refused *him* bail.
16. He died *a hero*.
17. Boil *me* an egg, please.
18. Bill returned the towels *clean*.

SECTION 16: PHASE

In this section there is a discussion of clauses that have more than one predicator. It introduces a major complication of clause structure, since with more than one predicator there can be more than one subject, more than one complement, more objects and adjuncts, and these duplicated elements may have a variety of relationships with the two (or more) predicators. Most of the examples in this section have only two predicators in them, but the structure is recursive, and one predicator (of the right type) can lead to another indefinitely.

We begin with the simplest case, where the phase is *PP*.

(1)   I want to go.

The second P is always non-finite. In the first batch of examples the *to*-form of the verb is the only one used; other non-finite forms are discussed later. Also all the clauses at present are *active* in *voice*. Notice that the subject of *go* is *I*, and that the sequence of elements is fixed.

Here are some more examples:

1. We all agreed to work very hard.
2. Did you remember to bring the sandwiches?
3. I can't bear to touch it.
4. I absolutely refused to see him.
5. You deserve to be awarded a medal for this work.
6. I meant to come earlier.
7. I didn't expect to be caught in the act.
8. All five chose to take the bus.
9. We all pretended to be asleep.
10. The great aircraft began to climb steeply away from the runway.

Exercise 16.1

(a) Make a list of the finite verbs in the examples above.
(b) Which of them can be transitive?

The next phase type has a nominal group between the two predicators. Examples:

(2) I wanted Bill to wash the dishes.
(3) I ordered Bill to wash the dishes.

Although superficially similar, these structures are not identical. The notable differences are:

(a) The nominal group *Bill* can be left out of (2). The whole clause changes its meaning, of course, but note that *Bill* cannot be left out of (3).
(b) One has a feeling that 'I ordered Bill' is a constituent of (3), while 'I wanted Bill' is not a constituent of (2).

The similarities between the two examples include:

(c) *Bill* appears to be the subject of the second predicator in both examples.
(d) If *Bill* is replaced by a pronoun, it is *him* and not *he*, suggesting that *Bill* is grammatically the object of the first predicator.

There are many more points in the argument than these, and this one is of the most complex areas of English grammar. For the moment we shall regard *Bill* in the two examples as having the same basic grammatical function, namely object to the left and subject to the right. This is a new element of structure that can be symbolised O/s to emphasise the 'two-faced' relationship. So the phase type is P O/s P in both cases, despite the fact that O/s is optional in (2).

Here are some more examples, some with an optional O/s and some like (3).

1. I can't bear him to touch it.
2. I meant your friends to come earlier.
3. No-one expected Bill to be caught in the act.
4. All five chose me to take the bus.
5. The Commission found Mr Perks to have carried out his duties quite satisfactorily.
6. Ask Madge to write a bit more often, will you?
7. His early life taught him to save money.
8. The porter told us to wait on this platform.
9. We thought him to be tall.
10. I command you to divulge the contents of that communication.

Exercise 16.2

(a) Make a list of the finite verbs in these $P\,^{\text{o}}/_{\text{s}}\,P$ structures.
(b) Which of them also occur in *PP* structures – see key to Exercise 16.1.

Exercise 16.3

Identify the phase type *PP* or $P\,^{\text{o}}/_{\text{s}}\,P$ in the following examples. Add the verbs to the lists from Exercises 16.1 and 16.2.

1. I managed to get it out with a chisel.
2. Please continue to read.
3. Madge would like you to sing some folk-songs.
4. The cat is forever trying to catch butterflies.
5. I'd like to thank you for your kindness.

Until this point examples of phase have concerned the *to*-form of the second predicator. The other type has the *ing*-form. This is an area of English grammar where several structures overlap, producing a complexity that cannot be fully described here. But the main lines are as follows:

1. Mr Plumtree finished ironing his suit at ten o'clock.
2. The others can't bear swimming in the lake.
3. I didn't fancy eating hamburgers at breakfast.
4. Bill managed walking a few steps.
5. Just continue talking.
6. Don't you remember dancing all night?
7. I rather like calling on people as a surprise.
8. The accused denied ever being there.
9. Have you tried asking your dad?
10. That cat keeps mewing outside my window.

Exercise 16.4

Which of the finite verbs that have exemplified *ing*-form phase can also occur in phase with *to*-forms?

These are examples of *PP* phase. There is also $P\,^{\text{o}}/_{\text{s}}\,P$ phase, as the second set of examples shows:

1. A passing motorist saw him lying in the road.
2. He remembers Queen Victoria laying the foundation stone.
3. Several of my friends have fancied him doing the catering.
4. I felt little insects crawling up my arm.
5. Just keep him waiting a bit longer.
6. Some people can smell rain approaching.

7. They like him singing.
8. Music-lovers couldn't bear him singing anything at all.

Exercise 16.5

Which of these verbs also occur in *PP* phase?

This structure must now be compared with two other similar structures:

(4) I prefer him setting the table.
(5) I prefer his setting the table.
(6) I prefer his setting of the table.

Only the first of these sentences is an example of *P* o/s *P* phase. In (5) *his setting the table* is a rankshifted clause which is the object of the outer clause. It can also be subject, while (4) cannot. (See also Section 18, page 142.)

(7) His setting the table is preferable.
(8) *Him setting the table is preferable.

Him and *setting* are separate elements of clause structure in (4); but in (5) *his* and *setting* are elements in the rankshifted clause only, forming one element only in the outer clause. Fig. 16.1 shows the structural difference.

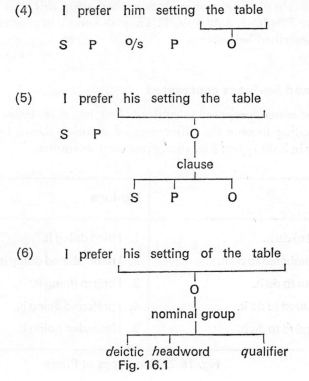

Fig. 16.1

The clause in (6) has as its object the nominal group *his setting of the table*, where *setting* is not in subject-verb or verb-object relationships, but is fully 'nominalised', as (9) and (10) show.

(9) His side of the table is preferable.
(10) His elegant setting of the table is preferable.

A diagram of the analysis of (6) is also shown in Fig. 16.1, bringing in some symbols of nominal group structure (see Chapter 3 for details). In particular note that *his* in (6) is a member of the word-class *deictic*, and can be replaced by *the, a,* etc.; but in (4) and (5) *his* is a complete nominal group – compare the different meanings of (11) and (12).

(11) I prefer another setting the table.
(12) I prefer another setting of the table.

In (11) we read *another* as equivalent to 'someone else', but in (12) we take *another* as a modifier of *setting*.

Many of the verbs that occur in *ing*-form phase have related meanings. *Like, prefer,* and all kinds of hating and loving are of this class; also *remember, recollect, fancy, imagine* and other verbs of 'secondary perception'. Ordinary verbs of perception such as *see, hear* are of this class too, but they do not take *PP* phase, only *P* ^{o}/$_s$ *P*. They also occur in another phase type, which is described below.

to-form and *ing*-form contrasted

There is no system proposed to contrast these two main types of phase, but it is interesting to note the differences in meaning shown by some verbs that occur in both types: Fig. 16.2. gives some examples.

to-form	*ing*-form
1. I tried to do it.	1. I tried doing it.
2. I remembered to do it.	2. I remembered doing it.
3. I began to do it.	3. I began doing it.
4. I preferred to do it.	4. I preferred doing it.
5. I intended to do it.	5. I intended doing it.

Fig. 16.2. Two Types of Phase

Compare (13) and (14).

(13) That boy needs washing.
(14) That boy needs to wash.

Although similar as printed above, there is a big difference between these structures. In (14) we expect the boy to wash himself; in (13) we expect someone else to do it. Contrast the following:

(15) Those clothes need washing.
(16) *Those clothes need to wash.
(17) *That boy needs washing the dishes.
(18) That boy needs to wash the dishes.

It seems that a few verbs, *need, want* and *deserve* among them, select only transitive verbs for *ing*-form phase, and use them intransitively; while for *to*-form phase they fall in with the general pattern. Recall the contrast at the end of Section 14.

(19) She washes the clothes well.
(20) The clothes wash well.

This section has outlined the two important types of phase, using the *to*-form and the *ing*-form of the second predicator. There is also a less common type using the *base*-form (ø) of the second predicator. Most of the structures are $P \, {}^o/_s \, P$, as the examples show.

  1. She felt the stone whistle past her ear.
  2. Don't make me go tonight.
  3. Have you ever seen him perform well?
  4. Madge helped wash the dishes.
  5. I noticed a motor-cyclist overtake on a bend.
  6. The stranger helped Bill to push his car to the garage.
  7. No-one has heard Madge sing for three years.
  8. Will you help me shift this wardrobe, Bill?

Exercise 16.6

(a) Analyse the clauses above as fully as you can, into $S, P, O, {}^o/_s, A$, voc.
(b) What structures can the verb *help* occur in?
(c) Make a list of the other verbs that occur in $P \, {}^o/_s \, P$ phase with P base.
(d) Which of them occur with *ing*-form phase? Look back to Exercise 16.5 for a clue.

Phase with adjectives

A structure *PC* with certain adjectives can initiate *to*-form phase.

1. I am happy to introduce the speaker for this afternoon.
2. He seemed sorry to leave.
3. Bill was lucky to escape with his life.
4. The stranger appeared most anxious to communicate.
5. Are you content to settle for half its value?
6. Mr Plumtree was quite ready for me to begin.

Notice that these adjectives can be modified in the usual ways, and also that in some cases a second subject can be introduced after *for*, e.g. no. 6.

Exercise 16.7

Check that these adjectives can all be modified, and find out which allow the second subject.

The notation for this phase is *PCP* (without new subject) and *PCASP* when a second subject is introduced with *for*.

There is a risk of confusion in structures involving the *to*-form of the verb. Fig. 16.3 gives contrasting examples.

A	B
1. I wanted to let him in.	1. I moved over to let him in.
2. I told him to while away the time.	2. I told him, to while away the time.
3. Bill helped to avert an accident.	3. Bill braked to avert an accident.
4. They were happy for him to go abroad.	4. They saved for him to go abroad.

Fig. 16.3. Contrasting Examples Involving *to*-form Verbs

Phase and Voice

The examples in column A are true phase, of various types. Those in column B are all *FB* sentences, with P-bound B clauses. In all of them the B clause has the meaning of 'in order to . . .' . In fact, wherever *in order* can be added in front of *to* without changing the meaning much, the structure is *FB* and not phase. Notice also that in most cases Column B structures can be reversed to *BF*. This is regular for *FB*cont. structures but not in phase. All the examples in this section have been in the active voice, so that the different phase types could be shown as clearly as possible. But the selection of passive voice normally removes one object, so that *P* o/s *P* phase should become *PP*:

(21) I ordered Bill to go.
(22) Bill was ordered to go.

Here are some notes on the verbs used in this section.

(23) *Bill was wanted to go.
(24) *Bill can't be borne to do it.
(25) *Madge was liked to sing folk-songs.

Find and *think* (Exercise 16.2) are not much used in *to*-form phase in the passive.

Ing-form phase presents some difficulty. In the examples for Exercise 16.5, the only natural passives are:

(26) He was seen lying in the road.
(27) He was kept waiting a bit longer.

The other examples resist a passive structure for one of two reasons. Some verbs (see (28)) are only rarely found in the passive; others (see (29)) make a clumsy structure that is most likely to be interpreted as a two-clause sentence *FB*.

(28) *He was liked singing.
(29) Queen Victoria was remembered, laying the foundation stone.

Summary

Phase is the name for the system which introduces a second predicator into the clause. There are three main structural types, corresponding to the main choices in transitivity.

(a) *PP*
(b) *P* o/s *P*
(c) *PCP*

The second predicator is non-finite; usually either the *to*-form or the *ing*-form of the verb. As with transitivity, the classification of individual verbs is very complex, and only a few examples are given.

CHAPTER 3

Nominal Group Structure

Introduction

We now leave clause structure and consider the next type of structure below it. The rank diagram shows that *group* structure is immediately below clause structure.

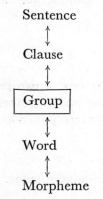

Sentence

Clause

Group

Word

Morpheme

According to the diagram, we should find (*a*) that groups are made up of words and (*b*) that groups are constituents of clauses. The term *group* is used rather than 'phrase' since 'phrase' is already used to mean many different parts of a clause, and of a sentence.

Here are two clauses, divided into groups:

(1) all my lovely green cushions / can't have been pushed / so far under the sofa
(2) he / came / then

The first thing to notice is that the groups are not all constructed in the same way. There are three main kinds; in this book we shall deal separately with each kind. The names are already familiar.

(*a*) nominal group: *all my lovely green cushions; he*
(*b*) verbal group: *can't have been pushed; came*
(*c*) adverbial group: *so far under the sofa; then*

The other important thing to notice in (2) is that a group often has only a single word as its exponent. This should not be surprising, since we have already met one-word clauses, and one-word sentences.

In general, the different groups correspond to the different elements of clause structure.

Predicators	are always **verbal groups**	*John is* COMING
Adjuncts	are usually **adverbial groups**	*John came* VERY QUICKLY
		/ IN FIVE MINUTES
	but occasionally nominal groups	*John stayed* FIVE MINUTES
Subjects		*The man* CAME
Objects	are usually **nominal groups**	*I liked* THE MAN
o/s elements		*I asked* THE MAN *to go*
Complements	are sometimes **adjectival groups**	*He went away*
		VERY HAPPY
	and sometimes nominal groups	*He went away*
		A HAPPY MAN

SECTION 17: NOMINAL GROUPS

This account of group structure starts with nominal groups.

First of all, a few more examples of nominal groups at various places in clause structure:

(1) *The little dog* ran away (subject)
(2) Call *that old man* (object)
(3) They elected him *the new chairman* (complement)
(4) He asked *me* to leave (o/s)
(5) Come *next week* (adjunct)

In addition to these are a few common uses of nominal groups which do not fit directly into clause structure.

(*a*) Prepositional groups

(6) down the steps
(7) in the garden
(8) to John

These are **prepositional groups.** The prepositional group is a combination of a preposition and a nominal group which together make up one single adjunct in the clause. The term used for the nominal group in a prep-group structure is object, and a small o symbol is used to distinguish prepositional objects from clause objects (*O*). Prepositional groups are a variety of adverbial group (see Section 25, page 205).

Clause	A = Nominal group	A = Prepositional group
1*a*. He stayed three weeks. *b*. He stayed for three weeks.	three weeks	for three weeks
2*a*. He ran many miles. *b*. He ran for many miles.	many miles	for many miles
3*a*. Do it this way. *b*. Do it in this way.	this way	in this way
4*a*. He arrived this morning. *b*. He arrived during this morning.	this morning	during this morning
5. He jumped off the wall.		off the wall

Fig. 17.1

Fig. 17.1 shows some relationships between nominal and prepositional groups as adjuncts. Examples 1*a* and 1*b* are very similar in meaning; and at the other extreme there is no nominal group to contrast with 5. In between are various shades of similar meanings. Sometimes the lack of a preposition marks a specialised variety of English, for example (9) as against (10)

(9) You touch down Athens 0200 sir.
(10) You land at Athens at 2 a.m. sir.

(*b*) Rankshift

(11) *The boy's* book was on the table.
(12) A hat *this size* will be fine.

These are cases where one nominal group plays a part in the structure of another nominal group (*the boy's* in *the boy's book*). *The boy's* comes at the beginning of the group and is called a **modifier**; *this size* comes at the end and is called a **qualifier**. The structure of one group inside another one is called rankshift; see Section 18, page 142.

Exercise 17.1

Some of the nominal groups in the examples below are underlined. Mark each of them with one of the symbols, *S, C, O, O/s A* (clause structure) or *m, q, o* (group structure).

1. A piece that shape won't do.
2. He sat in front of the statue for hours.
3. A boy your age should know how to tie his own tie.
4. Send the groceries round to the house at once, please.
5. I told the boy to be quick.
6. Next week we'll give you what John has made.
7. I persuaded Madge's uncle to come last night.
8. My best friend's mother is coming this way soon.
9. He came early.
10. We went to the station.

Headwords

The most important word in the nominal group is the *headword* (*h*). Every nominal group has one, and the structure of the group depends on the headword, which is usually some kind of *noun*. Here are the nominal groups in some of our recent examples with the headwords italicized.

(1) The little *dog*.
(2) That old *man*.
(3) the new *chairman*.
(4) *me*.
(5) next *week*.
(6) the *steps*.
(11) The boy's *book*.
(11) The *boy's*.
(12) A *hat* this size.

Exercise 17.2

Pick out the headwords of all the underlined groups in Exercise 17.1.

As well as the headwords, we have seen that there can be modifiers and qualifiers, but not in every case. Modifiers are the words that precede the headwords, and qualifiers are the words that follow the headwords. Modifiers are not often rankshifted, but qualifiers usually are.

Exercise 17.3

Pick out the modifiers of the underlined nominal groups in Exercise 17.1. Here are our earlier examples, with the modifiers italicized:

(1) *the little* dog.
(2) *that old* man.
(3) *the new* chairman.
(4) me.
(5) *next* week.
(6) *the* steps.
(11) *the boy's* book.
(11) *the* boy's.
(12) *A* hat this size.

The first statement of the structure of the English nominal group, then, is: (m) h (q)

that is, a headword, with or without a modifier in front, with or without a qualifier afterwards.

Here are some sentences with examples of different headwords:

1. Cows like milk, don't they?
2. Are we all ready?
3. He left satisfied.
4. That's how you should do it!
5. Anyone for tennis?
6. Bill looks anxious.
7. We've had several.
8. Beer is grand when you're thirsty.
9. Walking makes me tired.
10. I don't go to meetings.

Exercise 17.4

Pick out all the headwords of nominal groups in the sentences above.

Now here are the same headwords, and other ones like them, in more complex nominal groups:

(*a*) 1. *Those cows* are *fine animals*.
       2. *Pianos out of tune* sound like *tortured cats*.

3. *The three boys we danced with last night* were *American sailors,* weren't they?

4. I'm very fond of *the cheese from France.*

5. *My friends* don't like meat.

6. *Walking when you're tired* is *a bad thing.*

7. *The going* was rough.

8. *Fast running* tends to overstrain *the heart.*

9. We'll finish your portrait in *another three sittings,* your ladyship.

(b) 1. *We all* like *her.*

2. *They both* like dancing.

3. *You there* stand up properly!

4. *I myself* don't swim.

5. *Those who don't want to go,* put up your hands!

6. *Everyone in Italy* takes a siesta.

7. *All these* are for you.

8. *No-one else* is coming.

9. *Somebody I met last summer* worked there.

(c) 1. *Mr Plumtree* called me.

2. There are extensive moors in *Devon, Yorkshire* and *Scotland.*

3. Don't tell me you're called *Tabitha* too!

The headwords of the groups in Section (*a*) are *common nouns,* or just nouns. They occur with or without the whole range of modifiers and qualifiers. In particular they occur with modifiers like *the, this, my,* words which are called *deictics* (and sometimes 'determiners').

The headwords of Section (*b*) are *pronouns* of various kinds. They cannot be modified by adjectives (except in a few phrases, e.g. *Poor you!*), nor by *the, this, my,* etc. (deictics). Fig. 17.2 gives some examples of the very small range of modifiers and qualifiers that can be used, and of course the clause qualifiers, shown in (13), (14) and (15).

(13) Anyone who's left behind will have to walk home.

(14) We who are left must work harder. (very formal English nowadays.)

(15) Those who don't pay don't get a lift.

(As in *Poor you,* the vocative structure allows some exceptions, e.g. *You with the red hat.*)

The headwords of Section (*c*) are *proper nouns,* which are not normally modified or qualified at all. Their job is to name something or someone uniquely, so they are unlikely to need deictics, numerals, adjectives or qualifiers. In written English they usually start with capital letters.

There is a sort of grammar of proper nouns that we do not describe here – *Mr Plumtree, John Smith, Clacton-on-Sea, Mount Everest, The River*

Pronoun class	Examples	Modifier/Qualifier
indefinite pronouns	anyone, anything, anybody, no-one, nothing, nobody, someone, something, somebody	*else* qualifier *himself*, etc. qualifier
personal pronouns	I you he she it we they, etc.	*myself*, etc. qualifier *both, all* qualifier
demonstrative pronouns	this that these those	*all, both,* modifier

Fig. 17.2. Pronoun Modification

Thames, Lyme Regis, The Dog and Duck, Sheffield Wednesday. In English syntax, each of these phrases is one proper noun, because it uniquely names something, and we don't bother about how it is put together unless we are doing a special study. (So *Mr Plumtree* is regarded as just one word in this grammar.)

The word *father* (*Father*) is ambiguous: when it is used as a name, it has no modifiers or qualifiers and it is spelt with a capital letter; when it is used as a common noun it nearly always has a deictic (e.g. *the*) and it is spelt with a small letter.

(16) Father says you're to wash your hands
(17) Who is the father of this child?

Proper and common nouns overlap like this quite a bit: what is important is the syntactic function, rather than what word it is or whether it is spelt with a capital letter. Consider these examples:

1. *Nurse* wants you to stay in bed.
2. This isn't *the Walsall I used to know.*
3. There is *the happy Shakespeare,* and there is *the sad Shakespeare.*
4. *Captain's* coming!
5. Sit on *Uncle's* knee, there's a dear.
6. There are *six John Smiths* in the Telephone Directory.

Exercise 17.5

(a) Pick the headword in each group italicized.

(*b*) If it is a common noun, in the sentence above, make one up using it as a proper noun – and vice versa, so you end up with pairs like (16) and (17).

In nos, 2, 3 and 6 the headwords are most commonly found as proper nouns, but in these examples it is suggested (or stated, in no. 6) that there are several towns or people of the same name. Although Walsall and Shakespeare are unique names, we can think of them as changing over a period of time, or in different moods, and then speak as if there were two or more Walsalls and Shakespeares.

There are, then, three classes of nominal group headwords:

(*a*) (common) nouns
(*b*) pronouns
(*c*) proper nouns

and the criteria used to define them are syntactic. Note the following small points.

(*a*) Words that we expect to find as adjectives can occasionally function as headwords of nominal groups, but the structure is a bit stilted nowadays.

(18) *The wicked* shall be thrown into the Pit.
(19) Please help *the needy*.
(20) *The poor* of our country are getting organised.

(*b*) The word *one* deserves a paragraph on its own. It is a member of three different word-classes.

(21) There's just one important point I want to make.
(22) One is rarely faced with a problem like this.
(23) This is a good one.

  (i) In (21) it is a cardinal numeral in the series *one–two–three–four* . . .
 (ii) In (22) it is a pronoun like *he, you, everybody*. Because it has no referent, it introduces an impersonal structure in English, of a kind that is no longer common in speech (where *you* has taken over the job).
(iii) In (23) it looks just like a common noun, and can go in the place of a noun almost anywhere. (24) and (25) show exceptions.

(24) *I haven't got a one.
(25) *Ones are ready now.

In a nominal group structure *h* or with the article *a* in front, *one/ones* does not occur.

One in this last usage is perhaps the only true 'pronoun' in English — because the words that we call pronouns, like *he, she, anybody*, are substitutes for nominal groups, not nouns.

Exercise 17.6

Label each occurrence of *one* below (i), (ii), (iii) or (iv), referring to the three paragraphs above and reserving (iv) for occurrences which do not fit any of the other three categories.

1. One or two people voted for him, but he didn't stand a chance against the other one.
2. Today's programme is better than those ones we suffered last week.
3. I've lots of short-sleeved coats, but I haven't a blue one.
4. There's only one thing one can do.
5. More mechanical trouble, I'm afraid; your one's back axle went in the third lap.
6. One must fight for one's life in this business.
7. One fellow would say one thing, and the other something else.

Exercise 17.7

Supply *one* or *ones* as *h* in the gaps below:

1. Her red dress was nice but her blue——worries me.
2. Talking of paintings, did you fancy Tom's ——?
3. Do you like lettuce? I've a lot of big —— in the garden.
4. My car is a Ford, but the man across the road's —— is a Bentley.
5. Our noodles come in all shapes and sizes; big ——, little ——, square ——, round ——, thin ——, diamond-shaped ——, etc.

Exercise 17.8

Go back to the twenty-one sentences of the headword examples (*a*), (*b*), (*c*) on pages 136–7. In each case write out the structure of all the nominal groups in italics, using the following symbols:

deictic: **d** ⎫
numeral: **o** ⎬ modifiers
adjective: **e** ⎭
headword: **h**
qualifier: **q**

write **x** if you are not sure of a word.
Here are some examples from Exercise 17.1.

a piece that shape	**dhq**
the statue	**dh**
hours	**h**
a boy your age	**dhq**
his own tie	**dxh**
the groceries	**dh**
next week	**xh**
we	**h**
Madge's uncle	**xh**

Exercise 17.9

Do the same sort of analysis for the groups in italics below. But here also state the class of headword (noun, pronoun, proper noun). If you think a headword is an unusual exponent of its class, mark it so.

1. It was *the smell of it* I first noticed.
2. He lived in *Little Chipping Sodbury*.
3. We went fishing and I caught *two huge trout*.
4. *Five people* left early.
5. *The sorting of the mail* is done very quickly.
6. *Sir William Nocknee of Glumm* carried the standard.
7. Mummy, *Cook* wants you.
8. *Ten dogs this shape* would be too much!
9. *A party of tourists* climbed *Ben Lomond this morning*.
10. *Both those* came this morning.
11. Blessed are *the meek*.
12. *The journey* took *a long time*.
13. Give him *a big hand*!
14. *We ourselves* are in favour.
15. *Nothing Bill could do* saved her.
16. I don't like *meetings*, do you?
17. *A man standing in the doorway* waved at me.
18. *Someone else* told me your name.
19. *The Madge Smith I used to know* was much plumper.
20. *All hers* are for you.

Summary

Nominal groups are structured round headwords. Words occurring in front of the headword are modifiers, and words occurring after the head-word are qualifiers. The type of modification and qualification depends on the selection of the headword, of which there are three classes:

(*a*) common nouns – what we usually call just 'nouns'
(*b*) pronouns
(*c*) proper nouns

There is overlap among the numbers of classes (*a*) and (*b*), for some words may be used either to name an individual (proper nouns) or refer to a type (common nouns). Adjectives are rarely headwords.

SECTION 18: RANKSHIFT

So far in our description of English grammar, it has been assumed that the grammatical patterns divided neatly into units of various sizes. Then we started with the largest unit, the sentence, and continued through the clause to our present concern with the group. A sentence, we have assumed is made up of one or more clauses, with nothing left over. A clause is made up of one or more groups, and as we have seen in the case of headwords and modifiers in the nominal group, a group is made up of one or more words. Also each element of sentence structure will be one clause, each element of clause structure will be one group, etc.

The structure of a language is not as simple as this, however. There are quite a number of places where the pattern is broken. Some of these are fairly trivial, e.g. when *John Smith*, obviously written as two words is called a single headword. For cases like that we just have to consider a word, not as a sequence of letters between spaces, but as a sequence of letters and/or spaces with a particular job to do.

Sometimes a fairly simple and obvious rule explains many cases. If *my brother* is a nominal group and *the man next door* is another one, do we say that this clause has two subjects?

(1) My brother and the man next door went off together.

Not usually. The linking by *and* is so general in English that we almost take it for granted. So two groups (or more) joined in certain ways make up just one element of a clause. There is more about this kind of structure in Section 8, page 51.

In a few cases, there are more complicated structures still, and we use what is called *rankshift* to explain them. This section deals with rankshift.

Consider the following sentence:

(2) *The car I had last winter* started much quicker than this.

The italicized portion is undoubtedly the subject of the clause. Now according to the rank scale the subject of a clause should be a group, but it seems likely that the subject italicized above is not one group but several. Not only that, the organisation of most of these groups is exactly the same as we have been meeting in our work on clause structure. *I had last winter* is very close to a conventional clause; it has a subject, predicator and adjunct.

Why should we not argue thus: because *I had last winter* has the shape of a clause, it should be an element of sentence structure like other clauses? The reason comes from the meaning that is present in the nominal group structure. *I had last winter* allows the speaker to point out which car he is talking about. The word *the* means 'some particular car is being referred to: details follow after the headword.' If the qualifying clause is not present, i.e.

(3)   *The car* started much quicker than this.

there is a clear change of meaning: *the* now refers to 'my car', 'the family car we have'; or it may follow some previous description of the car. Also the thing referred to by *this* in (3) cannot be a car — it must be a van or a motor-cycle or something of the kind. So (3) is really quite different from (2) — in a way that was not shown anywhere in Chapter 1, where we looked at the way clauses joined together. The second clause of (2), *I had last winter* is part of the identification of the car, and it cannot be safely missed out. That is the reason why we label it *q* for qualifier in the nominal group, and not a separate clause in sentence structure. It is a stretch of language which *looks* like a clause, but *behaves* like a word; internally it is a clause, externally it is a word. Such a structure is called a rankshifted structure, in this case a *rankshifted clause*.

For a fuller display of rankshifted clause-qualifiers, in the nominal group, compare the two sets of examples in Fig. 18.1. Column A contains examples of rankshifted clause-qualifiers, while column B contains examples of *B*add. clauses (see Section 3, page 28).

Exercise 18.1

Make a list of the headwords of all the nominal groups in Fig. 18.1.
    Look at the list you have in Exercise 18.1. Compare:

1. place — Lake Lebro
3. man — Sir William Plumtree
6. season — April

Here clearly the clause in A1, A3 and A6 is used to identify the place, person

A	B
1. The place *we're going to this year for a holiday* is a village high up in the mountains.	1. Lake Lebro, *which is our holiday spot this year*, is high up in the mountains.
2. Anyone *who calls himself a doctor* will do.	2. I called my brother-in-law, *who is a doctor,* immediately.
3. A man *whom I've heard speak very often* has a voice like yours.	3. Sir William Plumtree, *whom I've heard speak very often,* talks like that.
4. I don't like spinach *that's been boiled into a mush.*	4. I don't like hot-pot, *which is just boiled mutton and potatoes.*
5. The remarks *made by the first speaker* were very well received.	5. I must apologise for that remark, *which I made in the heat of the moment.*
6. I love the season *when all the flowers begin to bloom.*	6. I love April, *when all the flowers begin to bloom.*

Fig. 18.1. Rankshift

and season respectively. The person required in A2 is not just anyone, but one of a particular group of people – those who call themselves doctors. In A4 the speaker may like spinach very much indeed – except in one case, namely, when it has been boiled into a mush. But in B4 the speaker does not like hot-pot at all any time. In A5 we do not know how the remarks were received except in the case of the first speaker. So it is clear that the headwords in Column B have to identify their referents *without* the aid of a following clause, whereas the headwords in Column A need the qualifying clause to help in the identification.

In many grammar books the q-clauses of Column A would be called 'defining relative clauses' or 'restricting relative clauses', as against the bound clauses of Column B which would be called 'non-defining/non-restricting relative clauses'.

Note the commas that isolate the adding clauses of Column B, and remember from Section 3 that there are clear differences in intonation in the spoken language.

There are two other types of rankshift related to nominal groups that must be mentioned here, now that the principle has been explained. Rankshift does not occur throughout the grammar – it is typical of only a few places in the structure of a language.

(*a*) At the place *d* in structure – at the beginning of the nominal group, there is the structure with '*s*, where any nominal group can be a modifier in the structure of another:

(4) *her best friend's mother* called
(5) *the man's curious behaviour* was noticed
(6) *the girl next door's cat* comes into our house

Here the three groups *her best friend's*, *the man's*, *the girl next door's* are complete nominal groups. But they occupy the place of a single deictic (e.g. *his*, *this*, *a*) in the structure of the larger groups. Consider the first example of a nominal group in this chapter: *all my lovely green cushions* and note that the three *possessive* groups of (4), (5) and (6) can all replace *my* above; e.g.

(7) *all the girl next door's lovely green cushions*

There is an interesting point to be made briefly in support of this argument. There are paraphrases of the three sentences above, where the *'s* structure changes to a prepositional qualifier with *of*.

(8) The mother of her best friend called.
(9) The curious behaviour of the man was noticed.
(10) The cat of the girl next door comes into our house.

Sometimes they sound a bit clumsy and pompous, because the *'s* structure is common in conversation. But notice that in each case there is an extra *the* at the beginning of the sentence. It has to be added to fill the place *d* in structure, vacated by the possessive group. An extreme example will show how this always happens, and it is set out in Fig. 18.2.

(*b*) A clause can be subject of another clause. Examples:

(11) *Running a big house* keeps me pretty busy.
(12) *To rush off like that* was bad manners, really.
(13) *Filling in all these forms* is a full-time job nowadays.
(14) *To finish off the edge like this* takes a lot of practice.

This type of rankshift is only loosely connected with nominal group structure – the clauses occupy a place where we would expect, in the simple rank-scale, a nominal group. They look very like the p-bound cont. clauses of Section 7 but with more restrictions on their structure. There are others which look like rep. clauses:

(15) *What he does* is none of your business.
(16) *That you even thought of it* was dreadful.

These clauses are called, simply, *subject-clauses*. They should be distinguished carefully from *FB* rep. structures with initial *it*. Note the examples below and the discussion in Section 11, page 84, particularly Fig. 11.6.

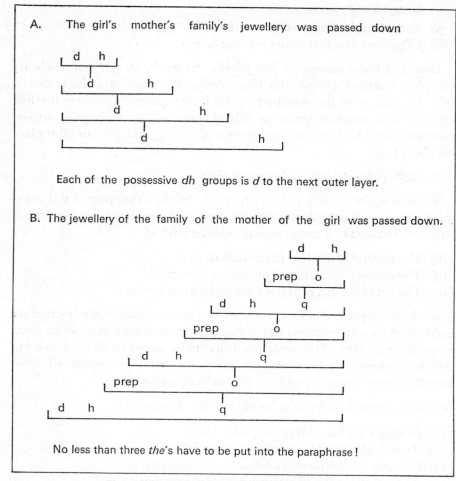

Fig. 18.2. Rankshift of Possessive Structures

(17) It keeps me pretty busy, running a big house.
(18) It was bad manners, really, to rush off like that.
(19) It's a full-time job nowadays filling in all these forms.
(20) It takes a lot of practice to finish off the edge like this.
(21) It's none of your business what he does.
(22) It was dreadful that you even thought of it.

Exercise 18.2

Consider the italicized portions of each of the following sentences. Say whether you think they are clauses or groups, whether they are rankshifted or not, and what place they occupy in the structure of a higher unit.

1. *Catching trains* is always a hectic rush.
2. The cinema *that used to show continental films* is closed now.
3. Among the foods *which must be avoided* are starches and sugars.
4. Mr Plumtree, *who was an expert in these matters*, advised caution.
5. *My best friend's* hat blew off!
6. Hydrofluoric acid is a substance *which must always be handled with great care*.
7. *Why he drinks so much* beats me.
8. I suppose an island in the South Seas is *everyone's* ideal.
9. Everyone *I meet* tells me to have a holiday.
10. I'm afraid a matter *that I couldn't leave till tomorrow* cropped up.
11. He agreed to come at once, *which was very good of him*.
12. A man *you used to know* called to see you this morning.

Finally in this section on rankshift, there is a ragbag of nominal group qualifiers that must be listed. A fuller analysis would relate each one by its internal structure to various clauses and groups, but here the concern is mainly with their occurrence at *q*, and we shall notice only the surface structure of them; all are common varieties in spoken English.

(23) A hat *this size* won't fit anyone.
(24) The meeting *next week* terrifies me.   } nominal
(25) The passage *quoted* caused a lot of interest.
(26) The best man *to see* is Mr Plumtree.   } verbal groups
(27) The bit *showing* can't be helped.
(28) A cottage *in the country* is my dream.
(29) An appointment *right away* would help.   } adverbial groups

In English, the greatest amount of rankshift is found in the nominal group. In fact, almost everything that occurs at *q* is rankshifted.

Exercise 18.3

Pick out any rankshifted material in the following examples and note:

(a) what structure it is rankshifted into;
(b) what structure it has in itself.

1. I teach two nights a week.
2. A screw the same length should do.
3. I spoke to the vicar, whom I hadn't met before.
4. Whatever he said, I can't do it.
5. To discuss the matter, a meeting the next day was agreed on.
6. Tripe occasionally is my limit.

7. The car approaching veered sharply left.
8. What he thinks doesn't matter.
9. The person you saw was just a clerk.
10. Have you any books to read?
11. Yesterday, Bill's cousin got married.
12. All he said was 'bother'.
13. The books recommended were unobtainable.
14. We met a man in a green suit.
15. People's complaints are the limit.

Note on Prepositional groups

Rankshift could be used to describe the structure of prepositional groups, and frequently is. It is argued that any nominal group can occur within a prepositional group, so it must be 'group-within-group' rankshift. An alternative, which is accepted here, is that a prepositional group is a compounding of an adverbial and a nominal group without either of them being rankshifted. There are several important differences between the prepositional group and the cases of rankshift that have just been described; in particular:

(a) the nominal group is essential to the structure of a prepositional group, whereas the rankshifted elements in the other cases are optional;
(b) there are no special restrictions on the nominal group in a prepositional group structure. In all the cases of rankshift, there is some restriction, as this section has shown.

Another alternative is to regard prepositional groups as a set of *cases* for nominal groups. Many languages have a choice of several cases for nominal groups – we can see the remains of the English one in the personal pronouns, e.g. *they, them, their, theirs*, chosen according to the syntactic function of the pronoun. Some modern approaches to English grammar describe prepositional groups in this way.

This book is not the place to follow the arguments for and against different analysis; but in Section 25, page 209, there is some more detailed analysis of the structure of prepositional groups.

Summary

In general, the structure of grammatical units of a language can be stated in terms of the occurrence of structures of the unit next below. The only important cases where this is not so are cases of *rankshift*, where units are found in the structure of a unit of the same rank or a higher one. In each language there are a few cases of rankshift; in English the typical ones are:

(*a*) where a clause is subject of another clause (one type of traditional noun clause);

(*b*) where a possessive nominal group is deictic to another nominal group;

(*c*) where a group or a clause is qualifier to a nominal group.

Prepositional groups are analysed in several different ways in current grammars. In this one they are described as a compounding of an adverbial group and a nominal group.

SECTION 19: DEICTICS

In studying headwords, nominal group structure was left as

$$(m) \ h \ (q)$$

The next stage is to make an important distinction in m between words which give a meaning of selection, and those which describe or classify. The distinction can be clearly seen in extreme examples, such as A1 and B1 in Fig. 19.1.

A	B
1. these cows	1. Jersey cows
2. five cows	2. fat cows
3. a cow	3. brown cows
4. I bought five cows	4. I bought brown cows
5. I like five cows	5. I like brown cows

Fig. 19.1. Deictics

These cows means an act of selection – by pointing or some other reference, a particular group of cows are identified. *Jersey cows* classifies cows into two types – Jersey and non-Jersey – but does so without referring to any actual cows.

The distinction is present, but not so clear, in A2, A3 and B2, B3. The

contrast in meaning is shown with reference to A4, A5, and B4, B5. A4 and
B5 are quite normal sentences; but in A5 the selection of *five* is odd in
relation to the verb *like*: we would probably interpret this sentence as
similar to 'there are five cows that I like', and not 'five cows are what I
like'. But A4 and B5 are similar in meaning to 'five cows are what I bought'
and 'brown cows are what I like', respectively.

The other odd sentence is B4, and an English speaker would normally
put a tonic syllable on *brown* in reading it out. It is likely that the object
of *buy* will be *selective*, since the action of buying involves a fairly precise
selection of what one buys: the reader is thus surprised to find a nominal
group without deictic or numeral.

The distinction is important. Selective nominal groups are more frequent than the others, and have a much wider range of use. The others –
we shall call them *global*, can only be used for the most general statements
– 'birds fly', 'man is mortal', etc. Global groups occur very commonly
with the so-called simple present tense of the verb – the neutral form, used
for statements which are true irrespective of time (see Section 23, page 183).

These examples are plural because there are other restrictions on singular nouns that are described later. At the moment it can be shown with an
example that singular nouns can occur in global meaning.

(1) Trouble is good business.

The distinction between global and selective groups is in the choice of
the first word: if it is a deictic such as *these*, *a* or a numeral such as *five*, the
group is selective; if not, it has a general, global reference.

Term	Structures	Classes
Selective	d...h... ...o...h...	d: deictic o: numeral h: common noun
Global	⟨no *d* or *o*⟩...h...	

System at *m:* Selectivity

Number

The numerals (*one*, *two*, *three* . . . etc.) show the normal English system
of *number* at its clearest.

(2) one cow
(3) five cows

The headword of a nominal group containing a numeral normally *agrees* with the numeral, and we call the agreement in (2) *singular* number, and agreement with any other number *plural* number. A noun that occurs in *o . . . h* structures is a *countable* noun – see (4) and (5) for examples of nouns that do not occur with numerals.

(4) *one furniture
(5) *five honesties

There are three brief notes to be made here.

(*a*) There are occasional special forms of counting in some varieties of English, and where numerals are used in measurement (e.g. *six foot*) the noun often remains singular.

(*b*) A few nouns (particularly *sheep*, *deer* and *fish*) do not show any distinction between singular and plural, although used with numerals. A few others have special plural forms retained from an earlier state of the language (e.g. *mouse–mice, child–children*).

(*c*) There are several varieties of noun which have special characteristics, for example *trousers, scissors* which are not normally singular, *measles, shingles*, never singular.

This book does not study the structure of individual words in much detail, and so the notes above are just an introduction to a great amount of information that is fully set out in standard reference grammars and dictionaries of English.

Examples (4) and (5) above show that there are in English some nouns that cannot occur in *o . . . h* structures, and they are called *uncountable* nouns (sometimes *mass* nouns). There are also many nouns which can occur as countable or uncountable with a difference in meaning. Fig. 19.2 gives some examples. The relationship between the countable meaning and the uncountable meaning is not the same in each example.

Some deictics show agreement (concord) in countability and number with the headword.

Exercise 19.1

Note the deictics in Fig. 19.2, page 152 and the examples below. Put them into the following classes:

Uncountable	Singular	Plural
1. He's looking for some trouble.	You are a great trouble to me.	Everyone has their troubles.
2. The wood for that wheel came from Sweden.	There's another wood down by the lake.	The woods are full of insects.
3. Have you had enough cabbage?	I'd like a large cabbage, please.	These cabbages are poor.
4. I was impressed by his obvious virtue.	Veracity is a virtue.	There are many virtues in that suggestion.
5. The coffee here is super.	There's one lump of sugar in each coffee.	I spilled both coffees.

Fig. 19.2. Uncountable and Countable Nouns

(*a*) singular: occurs only with singular countable nouns;

(*b*) non-plural: occurs with singular countable nouns, and uncountable nouns;

(*c*) non-singular: occurs with plural countable nouns and uncountable nouns;

(*d*) plural: occurs only with plural countable nouns;

(*e*) neutral: occurs with any common noun.

1. His books and his bicycle are his greatest treasures.
2. Their equipment was loaded on to their lorry.
3. Get rid of that rubbish!
4. This money will buy enough chocolates for everyone.
5. Those soldiers sang some songs last night.

(N.B. the word *some* in these examples is unstressed.

The key to Exercise 19.1, page 239, gives the basic choices of number within the English nominal group. Where nouns occur other than as headword, they do not have a number choice. See Section 21, page 168, for details.

The English verb also shows number in the third person of the present tense, e.g.

(6) The boy has seen you.
(7) The boys have seen you.

There are two main points to note here:

(*a*) uncountable nouns take the singular verb form (although this is perhaps better called *non-plural*).

(8) The furniture has arrived.

(*b*) A class of nouns — sometimes called *collective* nouns — occur regularly as countables, but can also occur in singular form with a plural verb, and neutral deictic, as in (9).

(9) The team are without a leader.

Fig. 19.3 shows a range of possibilities with the noun *government*, including usage as an uncountable noun.

Reference

The most important system in the deictic position relates to the type of reference made by the deictic. Extreme cases are the familiar *articles*

(10) I saw a cow.
(11) I saw the cow.

The indefinite article tells us that the cow referred to is not being identified. It has not been mentioned before, and there is no need to say just which cow it is. In (11) the definite article tells us that the cow must be identified — perhaps someone has just mentioned a particular cow. It is commonly used to refer forward to a qualifier, like (12).

(12) I saw the cow that was making the noise.

---

1. Government is the art of good management.   (global)

2. They just need some proper government.   (uncountable)

3. A new government seems inevitable.   (countable singular: verb non-plural)

4. Three separate governments have been   (countable plural: verb plural)
   dismissed.

5. The government have a lot to answer.   (collective: singular noun, plural verb)

Fig. 19.3. Number Choices with the Noun *Government*

We call *a* a word of **general** reference, and *the* a word of **specific** reference. All the deictics can be put into one of these two classes. For a syntactic test, we must anticipate a little and say that any specific deictic can be preceded by *all*, but general ones may not.

(13) I saw all the city from the viewpoint.
(14) *I saw all a city from the viewpoint.

Exercise 19.2

Look again at the sentences of the previous exercise, and try out the syntactic test on the deictics; check with the distinction in meaning that is set out above, and classify the deictics as *specific* or *general*. Then see how this system of *reference* fits the system of number (in the key to Exercise 19.1, page 239).

Exercise 19.3

Add the deictics in the following examples to the lists in the key to Exercise 19.2.

1. All employees should sign.
2. Bill's friends stood by him.

3. I'll take any maps you have.
4. He wants every penny you possess.
5. My leg is hurting.
6. No person must move.

Note that *any* and *no* are neutral in the number system.

The specific deictics include:

(*a*) the definite article *the*;
(*b*) the demonstrative pronouns *this, that, these, those*;
(*c*) the possessive pronouns *my, his, their, your*, etc.;
(*d*) rankshifted possessive nominal groups *Bill's, my friend's*, etc.

The general deictics can be subclassified by several distinctions in meaning; only an outline is given here.

(*a*) whether the coverage of their reference is total or partial. When total, their meaning is close to the meaning of a global nominal group without any deictic at all. *Each* is a typical deictic of total coverage, and *some* is partial.

Exercise 19.4

Go through the list of general deictics, and decide whether their coverage is total or partial.

(15) Jersey cows give milk.
(16) Every Jersey cow gives milk.

(15) has a global nominal group, which says that it is normal for Jersey cows to give milk. (16) is a general deictic of total coverage which says that there cannot be an animal called a Jersey cow that does not give milk.

(*b*) whether or not they agree with a singular noun; this is already covered in the number system, but it helps to distinguish *all* and *every*, for example.
(*c*) negative (*no, neither*) and positive. A full account would discuss here the occurrence of *any* in negative clauses, where it alternates with positive *some*.
(*d*) dual number. There are strong reminders of a special class of words used to refer to two noun referents: *both* is a clear example. *Either* and *neither* are less common.

Exercise 19.5

Complete the classification of general deictics as well as you can.

Partitives

It was stated earlier in this section that the deictic is the first element of nominal group structure. But there are constructions with *of* and with a specific deictic that need to be examined to see if they are best considered as one nominal group or two.

(17) Take another of the books.

According to the description so far, the analysis of *another of the books* would be *hq*; *another* is headword and *of the books* is a prepositional group qualifying. But there are good reasons for suggesting *another of* as a *pre-deictic* which gives a *partitive* meaning; *the books* specifies a selection of books, and *another* selects within that. Some of the reasons are:

(a) *books* must be countable if *another* is the partitive – this is not a normal head/qualifier relationship, but more like a deictic/head concord.

(b) *hq* constructions are recursive; partitive constructions are not, because in their usual form the pre-deictic is a general one, and the deictic is specific.

(18) the house in the street with the green lamp-posts
(19) *another of some of the books

(c) It seems too superficial to analyse (20) as if *deal* was headword, and *of coffee* qualifier

(20) a great deal of the coffee.

The position is similar to the rankshifted possessives, which function as specific deictics. The pre-deictic has the status of a group, so is rankshifted; notice that *a* does not occur in the partitive construction, because it cannot be headword of a group; while *none* does occur although it is not a deictic – it is the form of *no* used as headword.

(21) *a of the books.
(22) none of the books

The class of pre-deictic includes:

(a) general deictics, but not *a*
(b) numerals, *one, two, three*, etc.
(c) nominal groups of measurement, *a lot, a great deal*, etc.

Specific deictics cannot occur as pre-deictics. There is one similar-seeming construction with *those* and *these*.

(23) Those of my friends who were in town came.

Here the qualifying clause is essential, and it qualifies *those* and not *friends*; so it is more natural to see *those* as headword in an *hqq* structure here.

There is more about deictics in the next section, when we study their influence on the rest of the modifier. This section has mainly considered the significance of the occurrence of a deictic at all (global — selective), the concord with the headword (number) and some of the main features of classification of deictics, particularly the distinction between specific and general.

SECTION 20: ADJECTIVES

This section continues the description of modifiers in the nominal group. As before, most of the examples have a common noun as headword. Fig. 20.1 gives examples of typical modifier-head structures.

dh	oh	eh	nh
1. the man	1. two men	1. good food	1. copper kettles
2. this chap	2. five cars	2. fine wine	2. Morris cars
3. every single book	3. many people	3. red houses	3. fish soup
4. his own car		4. old men	4. jute warehouse
5. all those people		5. fine old buildings	5. cotton frock
6. a car		6. medieval tortures	6. noun modifier

Fig. 20.1. **mh** Structures

All except the class at **n** should be familiar; deictics and numerals were introduced in the previous sections, and the class at **e**, of adjectives or epithets, holds no surprises. **nh** structures show one noun modifying another — notice that we distinguish between the word-class *adjective* and the larger word-class *modifier*, which includes nouns, deictics, numerals and, as we shall see, participles too. The most striking feature of the nominal group is the way in which words of many classes can occur within it; the other types of group are normally composed of closely related word-classes; e.g. the verbal group is almost entirely composed of verbs.

The different structures of the modifier are shown mainly by sequence: **d** comes before **o**, which comes before **e**, which comes before **n**. Here are some examples:

1. the fine houses
2. every five cars
3. an old cotton warehouse
4. the many medieval orators
5. that copper warehouse
6. the few noun modifiers
7. my two good copper kettles

Exercise 20.1

Use the symbols *d, e, h, n, o* to label each of the examples above, and check that their sequence is correct.

Exercise 20.2

Now try the following italicized groups. Most of the words have already been used in this chapter.

1. I'd like *three animal books* for *my boy*, please.
2. Mr Plumtree visited *those five huge book warehouses*.
3. *Two copper ones*, please.
4. *Two American boys* bought *a piano*.
5. He'd prefer *a morning appointment*, I think.
6. She wore *an attractive cotton thing*.
7. We need *a long screw* for *the car*.
8. These are *bigger cows* than ours, surely.
9. *Another ten men* told me about *these exciting meetings*.
10. I'm going to meet *my sailor boy*.

Submodifiers

Some of the deictic examples in Fig. 20.1, page 157, need further explanation. No. 5 is a reminder of Section 19, but *single* in no. 3 and *own* in no. 4, show a new structure which is called *submodification*. The modifiers are themselves modified.

The symbol for submodifier is **s**. Notice how the deictic submodifiers emphasise the meaning of the deictic: *every* occurs with a singular head, and refers individually, 'singles out' without identifying, and *single* brings up that aspect of the meaning; *his* implies possession, which is the normal meaning of *own*; *very* (in this sense) emphasises the specific nature of the reference.

	I	II	III	IV
1.	a beautiful view	a very beautiful view	a more beautiful view	the most beautiful view in the world
2.	good paintings	moderately good paintings	better paintings	my best paintings
3.	her nice shoes	her rather nice shoes	some nicer shoes	the nicest shoes

Fig. 20.2. Adjective Submodifiers

Adjectives can be submodified also. Fig. 20.2 gives a set of examples to begin the discussion. In the first row, the submodifiers *very*, *more* and *most* add the notion of *degree* to the description of adjectives. *More* indicates what is called the *comparative* degree (s^c), and *most* indicates the *superlative*. *Very*, *moderately* and *rather* in Column II are *tempering* submodifiers (s^t). If we imagine a scale of beauty, then *a beautiful view* simply places the view on the scale; *very*, *fairly*, *awfully*, etc. shift it up and down the scale. *More* places the view relative to other views, as does *less*; and *most* puts it at the top of the scale of beautiful views, *least* at the bottom.

Beautiful is chosen in the first row because there is no word **beautifuller*; but *nicer* and *nicest* draw attention to the fact that many common English adjectives retain an *inflection* for the comparative and superlative. Roughly speaking, adjectives of one syllable inflect; two-syllable adjectives follow a set of rules depending on the sound of the second syllable and the derivation of the word (*cleverer*, *easier*, *simpler*, *more active*, *more dreadful*, *more pleasant*). Adjectives of more than two syllables take submodifiers regularly.

In comparative structures, like Column III, a specific deictic is rare. When it occurs (e.g. in *the more beautiful view*) it means that only two views are being compared; but special forms for a *dual* number are not regularly used in modern English.

When there is no specific deictic, it is very common for a clause or prepositional group introduced by *than* to occur in a comparative structure. Its normal position is after the headword, as in (1).

(1) It was a more beautiful view than I had ever seen before.

Compare this example with (2)

(2) It was more beautiful than I had ever seen before.

The structure of adjectival groups is not set out until Section 25, and the types of adjective submodification really belong there. At present, we simply label the *than*-clause of (1) a *subqualifier* (q^s), and note that when it is present, and especially when it is lengthy, it can occasionally allow a structure where the adjective comes after the headword, as in (3)

(3) It was a view more beautiful than I had ever seen before.

A superlative structure nearly always has a specific deictic in front of the adjective. In fast colloquial speech it is sometimes omitted, but only at the beginning of an utterance. The demonstrative deictics (*this* and *that*) pick out a referent precisely and so do not occur with a superlative; the definite article commonly occurs with a qualifier after the headword to limit the reference.

(4) It was a most beautiful view.

In this example *most* is not being used to place the view relative to a scale of beauty; it is just an emphatic substitute for *very* and has a tempering meaning, as the indefinite article indicates.

A few words form subqualifiers of superlatives, e.g. (5).

(5) It was the most beautiful chair *possible*.

Possible, imaginable, conceivable occur occasionally as subqualifiers.

Not all adjectives have degrees; it is uncommon to find *reddest* or *more physical*. In a moment we shall turn to such adjectives, but first we must summarise the choice among the *qualitative* adjectives, like *beautiful, good, nasty*. Qualitative adjectives come before the others, and we shall label them structurally as e^a (the others, according to position, will be e^b and e^c).

Terms	Structures	Classes
simple	...e^a...h ⟨no s⟩	e^a: qualitative adjective, *good, beautiful*, etc.
tempering	...$s^t e^a$...h	s^t: *very, moderately, really, quite, awfully*, etc.
comparative	...$s^c e^a$...h (q^s) ⟨or inflected adjective⟩	s^c: *more, less* q^s: *than*-group or *than*-clause
superlative	...$d^s s^s e^a$...h (q) ⟨or inflected adjective⟩	s^s: *most, least* d^s: *the* (allows q) *my, his*, etc. (no q)

System at e^a: Scaling

e^a is the structural position of qualitative adjectives; e^b is where we find the 'colour' adjectives. They have a few general submodifiers like *deep* and *light*, but in addition each colour has some submodifiers that occur with it:

(6) dark grey   cobalt blue   funereal grey
     bright red   flame red   royal blue
     deep purple   shocking pink   lemon yellow

All these pairs have the structure se^b. Submodifiers of colour adjectives are used a lot in advertising English, and the English of fashions in clothes, cars, etc. So every year sees some new ones, and some dropping out.

Examples (7), (8) and (9) show colour adjectives with the sort of sub-modification that is associated with e^a position.

(7) She had very blue eyes.
(8) The sky was bluer than I'd ever seen it before.
(9) SPLASH for the whitest woollies.

In these examples is another instance of the mobility of exponents in the nominal group classes – compare it with the account of proper nouns and adjectives as headwords in Section 19. The main points are:

(a) in a neutral group like (10), blue suggests just the colour. In (7) and (8) it suggests that blueness is a quality rather than a wave-band of light.

(10) She had blue eyes.

(b) If a qualitative adjective is added to (7), it will normally follow *blue*, and will be separated by a comma from it (and if spoken, be on a separate tone group). This is the regular indication of a double selection from the same class; if *interesting* is added in (10) it will precede *blue* without commas, showing the normal $e^a e^b$ sequence. (11) and (12) show the difference, and (13) shows a double selection at e^a.

(11) She had very blue, interesting eyes. ($s^t e^a e^a h$)
(12) She had interesting blue eyes. ($e^a e^b h$)
(13) She had interesting, charming eyes. ($e^a e^a h$)

The conclusion here is that *very blue* has the structure se^a: both the meaning and the structures indicate this. We have to allow that *blue* is normally a colour adjective at e^b, but it can be 'converted' into a qualitative adjective at e^a if that aspect of its meaning is to be brought out.

There is a third adjective class and a structural place $\mathbf{e^c}$. But before moving to it, a word about the numerals and their submodification.

Fig. 20.3 shows the familiar contrast between *cardinal* (column A) and *ordinal* (column B) numerals. The ordinals occur in similar circumstances to superlative adjectives – virtually always with *the* or a possessive deictic: they number a particular referent, and they do not need to agree in number with the headword. Cardinals, on the other hand, are used in numbering, but not in picking out individuals. The system can be summarised:

Terms	Structures	Classes
Cardinal	...oᶜ...h	oᶜ: *one, two, three,* etc. h : common noun in number agreement with oᶜ
Ordinal	dˢo°...h	dˢ: *the, my,* etc., *Bill's* etc. o°: *first, second, third,* etc.

System at o : Numeral Identification

Exercise 20.3

Note the structure of each italicized nominal group, as in Exercise 20.2, but adding the details of the two systems given in this section – numeral identification and adjective scaling.

Example:

He wore *a rather smart grey coat.*

Structure: *d sᵗ eᵃ eᵇ h*

1. Mr Plumtree is *very pleasant company.*
2. I don't think I've ever seen *a better black paint than this.*
3. There were *three fine yellow tulips* in *an earthenware vase.*
4. *Bill's favourite navy blue tie* was ruined.
5. Bill has *a really gorgeous house.*
6. *Those two brown clay bowls* represent *a more valuable find than anything we had last year.*
7. We're spending *the summer months* in *a country cottage.*
8. He wore *a dark grey suit* and *a nylon shirt* with *a red silk tie.*

(contd. on next page)

A		B	
1.	one boy	1.	the first boy the first boys
2.	the three boys three boys	2.	the third boys the third boy

Fig. 20.3. Numerals

9. She has *very black hair* and *a little nose*.
10. *The nicest part of it* is *the prize money*.

Notes

(*a*) Consider the nominal group *a light grey suit*. It could mean two different things

(i) a suit whose colour is light grey. This meaning is the most likely one, and the group structure is $d\ s\ e^b\ h$.

(ii) a suit which is light in weight and grey in colour. The word *lightweight* would probably be used instead of *light*, and the structure is $d\ e^a\ e^b\ h$.

This ambiguity comes because *light* can occur at e^a or as a submodifier to e^b. The same ambiguity arises with *deep*, *shocking* and *royal*, of the submodifiers at e^b.

(*b*) *dark*, which submodifies *grey* in example (8) above, is an adjective which can be *scaled* as a submodifier, in the same way as when it is at e^a.

(14) *a very dark suit*
(15) *an awfully dark red mark*

The group structure of (15) is thus $d\ s^t\ s\ e^b\ h$, if the darkness applies to *red*; and $d\ s^t\ e^a\ e^b\ h$ if the darkness applies to *mark*.

Several of the colour submodifiers can themselves be submodified according to the system of adjective scaling (e.g. *light*, *deep*, *shocking*, *bright*—all those which also appear at e^a).

It has already been pointed out that a specific deictic at the beginning of a nominal group can allow a choice of ordinal numeral and superlative adjective. Its influence is also found in a more general way in any structure *dnh*. Compare the italicized groups in (16), (17) and (18).

(16) he gave *an excellent address*.
(17) *his excellent address* was followed by stimulating questions.
(18) *the only excellent address* was given by Professor Plumtree.

Excellent in (18) picks out one address as against others: its excellence distinguished it. In (16) and (17) the address is merely described as excellent; but (17) is actually ambiguous. It could have a similar meaning to (18), that is, it could be used to identify the address if *his* is not sufficient, that is, if the person gave several addresses, one of which was excellent.

Classifiers

Fig. 20.4 introduces a third class of adjective, coming after qualitative and colour adjectives in position. The structural place is e^c, and the meaning is classifying rather than descriptive. In the first row of examples in the figure, the difference between *unusual* and *plural* is clear; a verb is either plural or it is not, and *plural verb* is a technical term. On the other hand, *unusual* is a word that can be scaled; it is a subjective impression about the verb; there is no established classification of verbs according to their oddity.

The figure also shows that classifying adjectives come before noun modifiers; the sequence is $e^c n$.

Most classifying adjectives have a distinctive word-structure, because they have been formed, at one time or another, from other words, usually nouns. Some of the suffixes are shown in (19)

(19) -al: classical
   -en: golden
   -ic: metric
   -ish: Danish
   -ern: eastern
   -ar: tubular
   -an: urban

(d)e^{c}h		
1. a plural verb	an unusual verb (de^{a}h)	an unusual plural verb (de^{a}e^{c}h)
2. the decimal system	the currency system (dnh)	the decimal currency system (de^{c}nh)
3. an eastern county	a powerful county (de^{a}h)	a powerful eastern county (de^{a}e^{c}h)
4. classical sculpture	marble sculpture (nh)	classical marble sculpture (e^{c}nh)
5. Danish pastries	luscious pastries (e^{a}h)	luscious Danish pastries (e^{a}e^{c}h)
6. an angular pattern	a red pattern (de^{b}h)	a red angular pattern (de^{b}e^{c}h)

Fig. 20.4. Classifying Adjectives at e^c

The relationship with nouns emphasises the classifying meaning of e^c adjectives; but, as with colour adjectives, it must be pointed out that there is great mobility in the nominal group, giving a variety of shades of meaning.

(20) he showed me lots of brown medieval pottery
(21) it was rather medieval brown pottery
(22) it was medieval pottery

There is a quality of 'medievalness', whether genuine or bogus, and (21) can use the word at e^a. (22) shows that when it occurs as the only modifier, it is a classifying adjective at e^c.

There is a chance of ambiguity from the mobility of exponents between e^a and e^c; note example (23).

(23) a dramatic performance

(23) could mean an exciting performance (de^ah) or the performance of a play (de^ch).

There are several more points of detail that could be made about adjective classification; notice briefly some combinations of e^a selections.

(24) a sweet little house
(25) a lovely old tapestry
(26) a fine new plan
(27) a nice hot drink
(28) a great big bung

It was said above that a structure e^ae^ah would require a comma between the e^a exponents. But two common classes of qualitative adjective relax these rules.

(a) *old* can occur after almost any e^a adjective without separation; *little* in many people's speech has the same feature; *new* and *big* less commonly.

(b) *nice* is so general in meaning that it can submodify other e^a adjectives, like *great* does in (28). The meaning of (27) is a compound of nice and hot – the drink was nice because it was hot; and (29) shows that *nice* is not used as a direct modifier of *drink*.

(29) She made me a nice hot cup of tea, but I couldn't take it because there was no sugar in it.

A few other common qualitative adjectives (e.g. *lovely*, *grand*) are occasionally found instead of *nice* in this structure.

Exercise 20.4

Given the words *a, house, red, small, suburban, very*; make up the following nominal groups:

  1. three groups with the structure *deh*
  2. *de^ae^ch*
  3. group with *red* at e^a

4. group with *suburban* at e^a
5. $d\ s^t\ e^a\ e^b\ e^c\ h$

Exercise 20.5

Give the structure of the nominal groups in italics in the following examples.

1. Mr Plumtree lived in *a very pleasant suburban bungalow.*
2. I found the examination *a physical strain.*
3. *Three Australian nuclear specialists* visited London for the conference.
4. Bill quickly made *a wooden door-stopper* for *the bedroom door.*
5. *Some rare botanical specimens* were lost in transit.
6. I just don't understand *oriental music.*
7. He suffers from *an unfortunate muscular complaint.*
8. *The dark grey Norman castle* was outlined in the moonlight.
9. *Vehicular traffic* prohibited.
10. You'll find it in *a small yellow plastic food-container* in the fridge.

Summary

Modifiers in the nominal group can themselves be submodified. A special list of deictic submodifiers give an intensifying meaning; numerals have a choice of cardinal or ordinal, qualitative adjectives choose from four possibilities of scaling, colour adjectives have special submodifiers.

There are three classes of adjective corresponding to the structural positions $e^a\ e^b\ e^c$ and the meaning: quality, colour, classification. There is great mobility among the exponents.

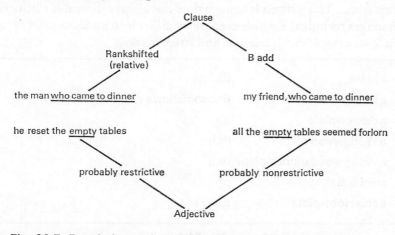

Fig. 20.5 Restrictive and unrestrictive meaning in Adjectives

The influence of the deictics, particularly the specific deictics is considerable. Ordinal numerals and superlative adjectives depend on a prior selection of a certain deictic, and there is a systematic ambiguity on *deh* structures, corresponding roughly to the distinction between rankshifted relative clauses, and bound adding clauses, as Fig. 20.5 shows.

SECTION 21 : NOUN MODIFIERS

Nouns can modify nouns. If you knock a small hole in a wall you can call it *a vent* (*dh*); if you fit a *control* on it for opening and shutting it you can call that *a vent control* (*dnh*). If the control has a *knob* so that it can be operated, that can be *the vent control knob* (*dnnh*). If it is a knob that unscrews with a special *key* that can be *your vent control knob key* (*dnnnh*) – and, to become slightly absurd, you could require a special *lubricant* for the key, supplied in a *can* (*a vent control knob key lubricant can* (*dnnnnh*) and then the can could have a control, with knob, key, etc. There is no limit to the power of compounding nouns in modern English.

Much technical jargon is of this kind, and it is difficult to understand because the precise meaning relationship between each noun and the next is not clear from the syntax; also each pair of nouns can make up a special compound which then operates as a single word, and eventually gets written with a hyphen between the two words, or a single compound word. When you invent a vent control, you speak of it with the stresses on *vént* and *contról*; if you manufacture it, it will soon be called *a vént-control*, with only one stress. The written language does not always show this distinction, which makes technical English even more difficult to understand. Fig. 21.1 gives a few examples with analysis and stress marks.

1.	a pláte	dh
2.	a fóot-plate	dh : sometimes written *footplate*
3.	a dińner-plate	dh
4.	a Wédgwood pláte	dnh
5.	a Wédgwood dínner-plate	dnh
6.	stéel pláte	nh
7.	a stéel fóot-plate	dnh

Fig. 21.1

a film	dh
a colour-film	dsh
a colour-film advertisement	dsnh
a technicolor film	dnh
a horror-film	dsh
a technicolor horror-film	dnsh
a technicolor film epic	dnnh
a vistavision technicolor horror-film epic	dnnsnh
a vistavision technicolor horror-film epic star	dnnsnnh

Fig. 21.2

In speech, then, we can recognise the headword because it contains the last stressed syllable (unless there is some special emphasis or contrast). So *plate* cannot be the whole headword in Examples 2, 3, 5 and 7 of the figure. In writing we take what clues there are in hyphens, etc. This section adopts a special convention to make the examples clear: hyphens will be used in all cases of compounding. The symbol **s**, as used for submodification, will be retained in the structural shorthand. Fig. 21.2 lists a variety of noun modification structures; Fig. 21.3 contrasts different structures of three nouns each.

A	B	C
snh	**nnh**	**nsh**
1. instruction-manual holder	chrome kitchen fittings	army trials driver
2. coal-merchants foundation	Latin grammar texts	Latin word count
3. buffet-car service	Worthing cantilever bridge	transistor radio-set
4. radio-control facilities	factory lightning strike	police patrol car
5. car-battery filler	ebony desk calendar	pocket address book

Fig. 21.3

Exercise 21.1

Mark with a т all tonic syllables in the example of Fig. 21.3 and use (т)
for any that are optional. Then mark with an s all the remaining syllables
that are stressed, or (s) if there is a choice. Terms:

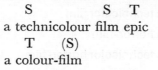

Now let us examine the meanings closer by altering one of the
examples of Fig. 21.2.

(1) ebony desk calendar
(2) ebony desk-calendar
(3) ebony-desk calendar.

(1) – structure *nnh* – refers to a calendar which is made of ebony and is
suitable for a desk. But (2) – structure *nsh* – refers to a particular, established type of calendar, as against a wall-calendar, say, which happens to
be made of ebony. And (3) – structure *snh* – denotes a special type of
calendar for use on ebony desks. There probably is no such object as (3),
but the structure can refer to it none the less.

Exercise 21.2

Most of the following examples fit into one of the types A, B and C in Fig.
21.3. Mark which type. Those that do not fit mark D, and suggest an
analysis.

1. Textiles price-control	10. executive-committee member
2. test-ban treaty	11. Bradford school-leavers
3. town-centre traffic-jam	12. college extension-programme
4. state-school pupils	13. express-train speeds
5. X-ray-diffraction studies	14. Hull Council Library-Committee
6. *Guardian* book-reviews	15. Hull Council-Library Committee
7. London crash inquiry	16. pest-control laboratory
8. Savings-Movement report	17. Champion kitchen scissors
9. Government defence crisis	18. two-inch steel screw

Lastly in the description of modifiers, a word must be said about the
participles, which are common at *e* and *n*. It was noted in Section 19
that words ending in *-ing* behave like common nouns when they are headwords. As modifiers they have several roles: Consider the examples in Fig.
21.4. Groups A, B and C are all fairly familiar. Group A contains examples

A. 1. She really is a very exciting person.
   2. It was a thrilling moment.
   3. This seems an exceptionally soothing ointment.
   4. The boring spectacle continued for hours.
   5. That was most interesting.

B. 1. The sinking ship radioed for help.
   2. The galloping horse pounded through deserted streets.
   3. Growing boys need lots of milk.
   4. I saw his smiling face at the window.
   5. He was surrounded by whining dogs.

C. 1. The meeting-place is fixed.
   2. Have you got a bathing-costume?
   3. It's a fishing-tackle shop.
   4. Let me see your driving-licence.
   5. Put it in the roasting-tin.

Fig. 21.4

of -*ing* words at e^a — they can be submodified by *very, more*, etc. just like qualitative adjectives. Those in Group B cannot; they are roughly similar to adjectives at e^c. The hyphens in Group C show that the -*ing* words are *sub-classifiers* of nouns at *n* and *h*.

Notice also that the words in Group A are transitive when they expound P, and their object can always be *me*. On the other hand, the words in Group B are commonly intransitive at P. See (4) to (7).

(4) The ointment soothed my ache.
(5) The spectacle bored me.
(6) The ship sank.
(7) He smiled from the window.

Exercise 21.3

Test the participles italicized below to see which of them can be submodified by *very, rather, more, most*, etc. If so, label them e^a, if not, e^c.

1. a *sliding* scale
2. the *moving* components
3. the *amazing* conjuror
4. a *puzzling* problem
5. a *convincing* demonstration
6. the *rising* sun

7. a *worrying* moment
8. the *gathering* clouds
9. an *enthralling* picture
10. a *fitting* remark
11. a *moving* story

12. my *aching* limbs
13. a *surprising* story
14. a *promising* performance
15. an *ageing* style

Notes

(*a*) Some interesting ambiguities can arise with *-ing* words. Examples 2 and 11 above show that the verb *move* can be transitive or intransitive, so that *moving pictures* can mean 'pictures which move me' — $e^a h$, or 'pictures which move' — $e^c h$. Also, the combination of an *-ing* word and a following noun can suggest a verb-object structure, e.g.

(8) Moving pictures can annoy people.
(*moving pictures* can also be a rankshifted clause at *S*, meaning 'if pictures moved').
(9) I love enthralling children.
(*enthralling children*, as well as $e^a h$ meaning 'children who enthrall me' can be a predicator and object in phase with *love*, meaning 'I love to enthrall children').

(*b*) There are very few cases of *-ing* words at *n* in the modifier — only a few idioms like *a knowing look, his saving grace*.

The patterning of past participles, or *-en* words, is similar to *-ing* words; in positions e^a and e^c. Examples:

(10) a determined man
(11) very restrained comments
(12) the tired runner
(13) a faded portrait
(14) the beaten egg
(15) corrugated iron

The first three examples, nos. (10), (11) and (12) have an *-en* form as e^a; (13), (14) and (15) show it as e^c.

There is one more point to complete the description of the participles. They are difficult words to describe, because some (like *exciting, amazing, determined*) are probably most familiar to us as modifiers or complements than as exponents of P. So the following examples are rare and rather stilted.

(16) This action has determined me. (*SPO*)
(17) The conjuror was amazing his audience. (*SPO*)

Participles can themselves be *submodified* by adverbs or *sub-classified* by nouns:

(18) a well-fed calf
(19) a milk-fed calf

Adverbs as submodifiers indicate the e^a position; nouns indicate e^c.

(20) a well-fed brown calf (*de^a e^b h*)
(21) a strong milk-fed calf (*de^a e^c h*)
(22) a well-fed bottle-fed calf (*de^a e^c h*)
(23) an ill-fitting grey suit (*de^a e^b h*)
(24) a magnificent record-breaking jump (*de^a e^c h*)

Exercise 21.4

Assign each italicized item either to the class at e^a or the class at e^c.

  1. a *cable-laying* device
  2. *gently-falling* snow
  3. a *pipe-smoking* parson
  4. a *carefully-painted* sign
  5. a *well-built* house
  6. a *weight-lifting* competition
  7. *hard-drinking* companions
  8. *care-laden* housewives
  9. the *colour-printed* brochure
 10. *long-lasting* polish
 11. a *badly-stained* suit
 12. a *stone-built* house

Summary

There are two main kinds of noun modification

(*a*) *nh* structures, where *n* classifies the headword.
(*b*) *sn*, *sh* structures, where the subclassifier classifies its own headword.

The written language is not very good at making distinctions of this kind, and a convention of hyphens is used as a guide to the stress-patterns for the reader.

Verbal participles operate at *h*, *e* and *n*, and they fit in easily with the categories already set up; according to the transitivity of the verbs in clause structure. When submodified they are clearly either e^a or e^c.

CHAPTER 4

Verbal and Adverbial Group Structure

SECTION 22: VERBAL GROUP STRUCTURE

The structure of verbal groups in English is rather simple. There are two main kinds of verb, auxiliary verbs and main verbs, and verbal groups very often consist of one each of these verbs, like *will eat, is eating, has eaten*.

Longer verbal groups are made up of more than one auxiliary verb, and still just one main verb. The main verb of a group always occurs at the *end* of the group. There are many thousands of main verbs, but only a few auxiliary verbs.

Exercise 22.1

Pick out (*a*) the verbal groups (*b*) the main verbs in the following clauses.

1. He has gone home.
2. Bill works all day.
3. You might have fallen over it.
4. Little boys can't be spoken to like that.
5. Do you want me?
6. That great big dog is very cowardly.
7. He should be being questioned for another hour or so.
8. See those birds all in a row on the clothes line.
9. Mrs Smith is needed in the front lounge.
10. I used to be praised for my croquet.

Each main verb has several principal parts, known by such names as *infinitive*, *participle*. They are usually inflections of the verb, like *walk*, *walking*, *walks*, *walked*, but the infinitive is formed by placing *to* in front of the base or uninflected form. Also a few English verbs are irregular in their inflection. There are not many such verbs, but some of them are very common.

For this chapter we need to have a name for each of the parts of a verb, and a symbol for each name to make the structural statement easier. Table 22.1 gives some examples.

Notes on Table 22.1

1. *n-form*: often called 'past participle', this form is the same as the d-form in most verbs in English. The 'regular' verbs have forms like *walk* in the table.
2. *d-form*: the 'simple past' or 'inflected past' tense.
3. *base*: sometimes called 'to-less infinitive', 'unmarked form'. The minimum form of the verb, also used as the imperative.
4. *to-form*: the infinitive form of the verb. This chapter avoids calling it the 'infinitive' because several other forms can be non-finite, and the reader might get confused.
5. *ing-form*: the 'present participle', formed by regular rules from the base.
6. *s-form*: the '3rd person singular present indicative active' to give it its traditional name.
7. The most important irregularity in English verbs is *be* which has some extra forms.

to-form	ing-form	base	n-form	d-forms	s-form	extra forms	
to be	being	be	been	was were	is	am	are

The extra forms *am* and *are* take on some of the functions of the base – the *finite* functions, as we shall see. *Am* is restricted to occurrence with *I.* the distinction between *was* and *were* is roughly singular/plural. There is still, however, a trace in English of the old subjunctive mood, whose form is also *were*. The trace is so slight that it should be considered idiomatic rather than grammatical. The idiom is:

'*if* + pronoun were – –'

(1) *If I were you, I'd leave quietly.*
(2) *If he were to come early, what would we do?*

Substituting *was* for *were* in these examples would sound stilted to many speakers, particularly in the case of (1).

name :	to-form	ing-form	base	n-form	d-form	s-form
symbol	t	ŋ	ø	n	d	s
	to break	breaking	break	broken	broke	breaks
	to come	coming	←——— come ———→		came	comes
	to hit	hitting	←——— hit ———→			hits
	to walk	walking	walk	←——— walked ———→		walks

Table 22.1. Principal Parts of Verbs

Concord

The first word in the verbal group has quite a different role from all the others. It is the only place where the d-form and s-form can appear, and it is the only word that has an independent choice of form. All the other words in a verbal group depend for their endings on the word in front.

Examples
ought takes the to-form of the next word.
must takes the base of the next word.
have often takes the n-form of the next word.
be often takes the ing-form of the next word.

Exercise 22.2
Fill out the examples above by looking at the sentences of Exercise 22.1. What other form follows the verb *be*?

The verbs *have* and *be* offer alternative endings on the next word, along with systematic distinctions in meaning. Let us take them in turn.

(a) *have*. Table 22.2 contrasts *have* with the n-form and the to-form. The first is a verb form commonly called the *perfect* tense, and it has the symbol *h* in verbal group structure. Compare the to-form with the examples below.

(*a*) with n-form

    1. They have gone now.

    2. It's lovely to have travelled so much.

    3. We all had shown our passports.

(*b*) with to-form

    1. They have to go now.

    2. It's lovely to have to travel so much.

    3. We all had to show our passports.

Table 22.2. Have

(3) They want to go now.

(4) We wanted to show our passports.

Examples (3) and (4) are phase structures (see Section 16, page 124); the *have* + to-form seems to fit there, in which case *have* is a main verb and not an auxiliary when it is followed by the *to*-form. Its meaning, however, remains different from *have* as a main verb without the to-form.

(a) main verb	1. I am your leader. 2. There's a hole in my bucket.
(b) be + ing-form	1. Bill is waiting for you. 2. He was coming a minute ago.
(c) be + n-form	1. The pianist was cheered for several minutes. 2. You're not allowed to smoke.
(d) be + going + to-form	1. I'm going to leave this minute. 2. He was going to stay, but he changed his mind.
(e) be + to-form	1. Officers are to assemble at 0600 hours. 2. He was to have paid, I thought.

Table 22.3. Be

(5) I have three cars.

(6) He has a large red nose.

(*b*) *be*. With this verb, there is its common use as a main verb, and no less than four auxiliary uses. Table 22.3 gives examples. The ing-form after *be* signals the *continuous* tense, as it is often called. The n-form is of course the mark of the passive voice. The complex form *be going to* is a future tense in English, where the verb *go* becomes an auxiliary and, like *ought* and *used*, takes the to-form after it.

The meaning of these three forms is discussed in Section 24.

be + to-form is less common than the others; it is a *modal* verb (see below) which has the meaning of a very strict order.

Exercise 22.3

In the sentences below, the italicized verbs are given in their base-form. Change them (if they need changing) into grammatically correct groups that fit into the rest of the sentence. If there are alternatives, list them all and note whether or not they fit into the sentence.

Example: Mr Plumtree *be play* golf yesterday.

Answer: 1 *was to play* (*was*-tense goes with *yesterday*)

2 *was playing*

3 *was going to play*

(*was played* does not fit since *play* does not have an object in the passive)

1. Bill *could have go* earlier.
2. I *must wash* my hands.
3. They *have* all *sleep* since one o'clock.
4. Bill *be drive* to work every morning.
5. *Sit* too long in the sun *be* dangerous.
6. *Do* Madge *like* cherries?

Exercise 22.4

The same instructions as 22.3. After doing the exercise, refer to your answers to 22.2, and bring your list up to date by adding the auxiliaries of the last exercises.

1. We *needn't run*.
2. Mr Plumtree *ought have arrive* by now.
3. They*'ll be come* soon.
4. It *may be announce* by the headmaster.

5. We always *used fish* in this stream.
6. I *shall speak* for twenty minutes or so.

Auxiliary and modal verbs

An auxiliary verb is one which can precede a main verb in a verbal group. We have seen that *have* and *be* often occur as auxiliaries, although, in other meanings, they can be main verbs too. The contrasts can be seen clearly in (7) and (8), where the verbs occur as both auxiliary and main in the same sentence.

(7) He is being silly this afternoon.
(8) Has the dog had his walk today?

The other auxiliary verbs cannot occur as main verbs (we discount the rare verbs *to will, to can*) – in fact they must come first in the verbal group. These are called modal verbs. Unlike *have* and *be*, they do not show a full range of forms. They do not have any **non-finite** forms (see Section 23). Only one of them (*be* + to-form) has an s-form. They do not have a separate d-form.

Historically, *would* is the d-form of *will*, and *should* of *shall*, *might* of *may* and *could* of *can*; *ought* is an old d-form of *owe*, and *used* (rhyming with *roost*) is an old d-form of *use*. But since the modern English verbal group developed, the modals have taken on a variety of new meanings, of prophecy, permission, obligation, etc. This book does not describe all their separate meanings, but rather sets out features that they share.

Two of them, *needn't* and *daren't*, are only in common use as modals when they are negative.

(9) You needn't come.
(10) I bet you daren't jump.

The positive of these sentences is not made by omitting *n't*.

As well as modals *needn't* and *daren't*, there are main verbs *need* and *dare* which behave just like any other verbs. In phase they are usually followed by the to-form, and of course they cannot be followed by *n't*. The following sentences show negative groups with main verbs *need* and *dare*, then two incorrect sentences with *need*, and two positive sentences with *need* and *dare*.

(11) You don't need to come.
(12) I bet you won't dare to jump.
(13) *You needn't to see that picture.
(14) *She need have someone talk to her sharply.

(15) You needed to come.
(16) He dared to jump.

Exercise 22.5

Explain why (13) and (14) are incorrect, and correct them.

Polarity

The 'negative particle' or 'bound morpheme' written *n't* can only occur at
the end of an auxiliary verb which is finite. Sometimes an unstressed *not*
is preferred, because many English speakers avoid n't after the sound *[t]*.
Table 22.4 sets out what is perhaps the commonest usage.

n't	not	special forms
wouldn't	may not	mustn't[2]
shouldn't	might not	don't
couldn't	ought not	won't
needn't	(used not)[1]	shan't
daren't	cannot[3]	can't[3]
haven't		
hasn't		
hadn't		
isn't		
aren't		
wasn't		
weren't		

Table 22.4. Negative Forms of the Auxiliary Verbs

1. In the speech of many people this verb changes to a main verb when
   negative: *didn't used*. Nowadays *used not* is rather stilted.
2. Although written without looking irregular, the first written *t* is not
   pronounced *[mʌsnt]*.
3. *cannot* and *can't* are both common.

Exercise 22.6

Go back to the groups that you used to answer Exercises 22.3 and 22.4.
Make all the positive auxiliary verbs negative.

Summary

The characteristic structure of verbal groups is *aux v*. *Aux* stands for auxiliary verb, *v* for main verb. Auxiliary verbs are divided into modal verbs, which must come first in the group, and the verbs *have* and *be*, which have some features of main verbs (e.g. a full range of principal parts) and some of modals (e.g. negative forms).

Main verbs have several principal parts: usually 5 or 6, and concord rules operate in the group so that the ending of a word is part of the choice of the previous word: only the first word in the group has a free choice of ending.

Have and *be* are used in several structural places in the verbal group. Most auxiliary verbs can have a negative form *n't*. *Needn't* and *daren't* are used as modals only in the negative.

SECTION 23: INITIAL SYSTEMS

The systemic choices in the English verb are of two distinct kinds.

(*a*) The contrasts which are shown in the *first word* of the group, no matter whether it is an auxiliary or a main verb. These are called initial systems and are set out below. Present or past tense is an example.
(*b*) The choices of which words shall make up the group, e.g. whether the group is continuous or not. These choices are described in Section 24, and are medial and final systems.

The initial choices are *status* (finiteness), and simple tense.

Finite and non-finite verbs

The name *finite* refers to the relation between a subject and a verb. In many languages, including the ancestors of English, the verb shows concord with the subject, particularly in number. Very little concord remains in modern English, and the exponents of finiteness overlap with those of non-finiteness. The base-form may be either finite or not, and for most verbs in English there is no difference between the d-form and the n-form.

But we are very rarely in doubt in a stretch of English, for syntactic reasons. The base-form, for example, is never the only predicator in a non-finite clause; non-finite predicators are the ing-form and the to-form mostly; very occasionally the n-form. Where the n-form is predicator, there is usually no subject.

Here are some examples:

1. Pleased with the result, the visitors retired to change.
2. Bill wants that book.
3. They will help him load the car.
4. Mr Plumtree ate all the cream cakes.
5. To start the washing-machine, insert 10p.
6. With Madge navigating, they all set out.

Exercise 23.1

Identify each form in the above examples, and discuss its finiteness.

In this analysis, the first word in the verbal group will be labelled x, so that the choices can be discussed without reference to medial and final systems, which introduce words into the group. There is, then, a system of *status* at x as follows: (the symbols f and b deliberately suggest Free and Bound clauses, but the relationship between the clauses and the verbs is not simple).

Terms	Structures	Classes
finite	f	$f:$ s, d, ø, modal verb
non-finite	b	$b:$ t, ŋ, n, ø

System at x: status

Simple Tense

The first word in a verbal group has a special choice of form, as follows:

(*a*) finite group: { s-form / d-form / base }

(*b*) non-finite group: { to-form / ing-form / n-form }

Finite groups. The usual names for the finite choice are *present* and *past*, and since the choice can fall on a simple (one-word) verbal group they are commonly called the *simple* tenses to distinguish them from tenses which require two-word verbal groups and more. In this account we shall use the common names, but only to avoid lots of new terms. Remember there is nothing simple about the *meaning* of these terms.

In English the tense that we call present has very little to do with time. Its time reference usually includes the *moment of utterance*, but to use the present tense is to highlight some other aspect of the meaning of the verb. Here are some examples.

1. I like spinach.
2. Mr Plumtree cycles to work.
3. I accept your offer.
4. My friend needs some advice.
5. This fabric repels water.

Exercise 23.2

Suggest what aspects of the verb meanings are highlighted in the examples above apart from present time.

The tense that we call 'past' has the meaning 'this verb form does not relate to the moment of utterance'. Often there is a reference-point in an adjunct or a bound clause, or implicit in the situation.

Here are some typical uses of the past tense.

(1) I saw him last night.
(2) I lived in London when I was a boy.
(3) Ten years ago a catastrophe occurred.
(4) We wondered if you were all right.
(5) I hoped to see you now.
(6) I knew you'd be here.
(7) If he came, what would you do?

(1)–(3) show the tense in concord with past-time expressions *last night, when I was a boy, ten years ago*. (4)–(6) show a use of the tense in a present-time situation, where its meaning is of some distance from the immediate situation. It is easy to show that a simple reference to a point in the past is not the meaning here: add the word *yesterday* to the beginning of the sentences.

(8) Yesterday we wondered if you were all right.

But the original sentence (4) is either a deferential way of asking how someone is, or a reaction to being told how he is. It is not a report of something that happened.

(9) Yesterday I hoped to see you now.

The original sentence (5) does not at all suggest careful planning of a meeting, but a reaction to, say, finding a colleague busy.

(10) Yesterday I knew you'd be here.

The whole time reference of the sentence is changed. The original (6) does not refer to a point in the past when the speaker knew something. It is an immediate reaction to a situation in present-time.

(11) *If he came yesterday, what would you do?

In a bound clause like this, the so-called 'past' tense does not refer to past time at all, and *yesterday* is an impossible adverb. In (7) the tense suggests that the event (his coming) is unlikely. The same meaning can be seen in (4) and (5).

It is clear from the examples that the word *past* is often misleading in use with this tense, and in this chapter it will be used along with the word *indirect*. The *present/direct* tense, then, refers us if anything to the moment of utterance but its meaning is really free from time at all: the *past/indirect* tense refers us elsewhere. Where the past/indirect tense does refer to past time there must be a reference-point somewhere, or else it will often be poor English. Consider the four sentences of Table 23.1. Class A have no time-adjunct; Class B have one. Class 1 is present and Class 2 is past.

A1	I expect nothing	A2	I expected nothing
B2	I expected nothing last year	B1	I expect nothing tomorrow

Table 23.1. Present and Past Tenses

The left-hand column, A1 and B2, form a contrasting pair of clauses, showing the distinction between present/direct and past/indirect tenses. No time-reference is needed with A1, but *last year* is required with B2.

In the other examples, A2 shows a past/indirect tense without adjunct, and B1 shows a present tense with an adjunct. A2 could only occur within a past-time framework that another sentence had made for it.

B1 is an interesting sentence: clearly the time of expecting is 'now', and not even the adverb *tomorrow* can advance it. Sometimes, however, a verb can be used which forces a future time reference:

(12) I leave for London tomorrow.

(13) He presents the prizes tomorrow.

The meaning of this construction — a present/direct verb with a future time-adjunct — is that all the arrangements have been made. Although the event is in the future, it can be predicted quite confidently, it is as good as happening now.

The wider question of future time-reference is dealt with in Section 24. At this place the important points are the distinction of simple tense, and the virtual necessity of adjuncts for past-time-reference of the past/indirect tense.

The modal verbs are a mixture of past and present forms, from a historical point of view. But they all time themselves from the moment of utterance: they can occur regularly without any other time-reference, and so we conclude that in modern English they are present/direct forms.

The remarks on Simple Tense can now be summed up in a diagram:

Terms	Structures	Classes
present/direct	u	u : s, ø, modal
past/indirect	i	i : d

System at f in Verbal Group Structure. Simple Tense

Exercise 23.3

Classify all the verbs in the following examples as direct or indirect. Consider the form of the first word in the group, and, if necessary, the ending of the second word.

1. I am the manager.
2. That boy hit me just now.
3. We will continue on page 116.
4. Mr Plumtree ought to know.
5. It was a bright, windy day when we set out.
6. Can you see my cuff-link anywhere?
7. I have told you all this before.
8. I hurt myself every time I drive.
9. They're all ready.

10. Madge was using the iron at first.
11. Had anyone noticed the crack before last night?
12. Bill was taught by an expert in his youth.
13. The leading runner is just coming into your picture now.
14. May I leave a little early tonight?
15. There were a few people here earlier on.
16. I've known Mrs Plumtree for years.
17. Madge graduates next July.
18. I hurt myself every time I drove.
19. Who'd drive that car?
20. I told you Bill'd be here.

Exercise 23.4

Some of the examples have a time-expression in them – a word, a phrase or clause. Find all the time-expressions, and say how they relate to the verb tense. Where an example has no time-expression, explain its absence.

Non-finite groups. Here are a few notes on the first word in non-finite verbal groups. There isn't anything to correspond to a *present/past* choice. Non-finite verbs are found in several structural places, set out in Table 23.3.

(*a*) Verbal group (i) initial position (A) where the group is the first predicator of the clause
(B) where the group is part of a phase string
(ii) non-initial
(*b*) Outside verbal group [e.g. noun (*meeting*), conjunction (*considering*), adjective (*puzzling*)]

Table 23.3. Non-finite Verbs

At first we describe only (*a*) (i) (A) – that is, the place where finite verbs can also occur. At the end of the section there are some notes on the other structural places.

The main non-finite forms which occur in (*a*) (i) (A) are the to-form and the ing-form. We shall ignore the others for the present.

A B-clause usually follows the F-clause closely for time-reference, and this fact is particularly true of the non-finite B clauses.

(14) To arrive in time we had to take a taxi.
(15) To arrive in time we must take a taxi.
(16) Watching the opposition closely, he eased the car into the corner.
(17) Watching the opposition closely, he eases the car into the corner.

The timing of the B clause is taken from the F. In both cases the to-form describes a future event, relative to the F, and the ing-form describes an event that overlaps in time with the F.

The contrast shown in (14)–(17) above is the basic initial contrast. It can be found in most non-finite groups, however long. Here are some examples:

(18) Having washed his hands, the surgeon picked up the scalpel.
(19) To have finished in time, we would have had to rush like mad.
(20) Being sworn to secrecy, he would not tell.
(21) To be accepted by the army, he had to pass certain tests.

Notice the concord between F and B clauses. There aren't many complex groups with *to have* initially since the to-form suggests the future and the *have*-form suggests the past. We can set out the initial contrast as a grammatical system because there is a certain amount of free choice and distinctive meaning.

Terms	Structures	Classes
prospective	t	t = to-form of a verb
neutral	ŋ	ŋ = ing-form of a verb

System at X^b. Initial Choice

We now return to the other non-finite forms and the other structural places where non-finite forms can occur.

First of all, in category (*a*) (i) (A) there is an extra choice where the verbal group has only one word. This choice is the n-form of the verb, as in Example (24) below.

(22) Praising the chairman, Mr Sprout said . . .
(23) To praise the chairman, Mr Sprout said . . .
(24) Praised by the chairman, Mr Sprout said . . .

Example (24) is passive and similar in meaning to (25) or (26).

(25) Being praised by the chairman, Mr Sprout said . . .
(26) Having been praised by the chairman, Mr Sprout said . . .

There is no equivalent of this structure among finite groups. It is one of the most important links in the chain which relates verbs and adjectives:

(27) The boys ate hungrily.
(28) The sausages were quickly eaten by hungry mouths.
(29) having been ⎫
             being ⎭ quickly eaten by hungry mouths . . .
(30) quickly eaten by hungry mouths . . .
(31) the quickly-eaten sausages . . .

In this chapter we will not go into details about the n-form of the verb. Our main task is to describe finite forms in F clauses and these are only a few notes.

Other Structural Places (*a*) Where the verbal group is part of a phased string: again the two forms used in almost every case are the *to-* and *ing*-forms (see Section 16).

The time-reference of a verbal group in phase depends on the initial group:

(32) He likes to meet people.
(33) He liked to meet people.

(*b*) Where a verb is not initial in the verbal group: here, we have seen, all the non-finite forms can occur, but the base-form and the n-form are perhaps the commonest.

Exercise 23.5

Pick out each verbal group from the sentences below, and describe all you can about its structure. For the main verb, use the symbol *v*; for a modal verb use *m* and for *have* use *h* and for *be* just use *be*.

Have three rows of symbols:

Row 1 : the distinction at *x* between f and b and the choices of status
and tense
Row 2 : the actual forms of the successive words.
Row 3 : *m, h, be* or *v*.

Example:

He has been sitting there all night.

	has	been	sitting
Initial systems	f, u	b	b
Principal parts	s	n	ŋ
Medial systems	h	be	v

1. Wanting to watch television, Bill cleared the children out of the room.
2. No-one would contemplate a fellow like that.
3. Don't you enjoy bingo?
4. I was being followed, constable.
5. I've been hearing about you, my lad.
6. Released from his contract, Bill can now look around for a better job.
7. Just to have smelt the sea air ought to have cheered him up.
8. Were those people bothering you, madam?

Summary

The first word of a verbal group has choices that are not open to subsequent words, because they concern the relationship of the whole verbal group to surrounding structures. The main one is *status*, which contrasts finite and non-finite forms. The choice *finite* leads to a further system of simple tense, with the traditional choices of present and past.

The present tense form is neutral as regards time, and with adjuncts of future time can give the meaning of fixed arrangements. The past tense requires a time to be specified outside the verb (e.g. in an adjunct) or else it may suggest formality in the present.

Non-finite verbs at P in clause structure carry no relationship to 'real time', but follow a related finite verb in time-reference.

Other non-finite forms are used to mark successive choices in the verbal group (e.g. the *n* form in the passive), or phase structures.

A three-layered notation for verbal groups is proposed, where the first layer shows initial systems; the second the principal parts, and the third the medial choices.

SECTION 24: MEDIAL AND FINAL SYSTEMS

The previous section has dealt with the choices at place x in the verbal group. In this section we consider what words can be chosen elsewhere, and in what order they appear.

First of all, very simple groups can be made with the choice of v only: so that v is in place x, and there is no difference between the first and the last words in the group. *Says, came, singing, hit* are all examples. Towards the end of the last section there is a note about the extra choice among non-finite verbs when v and x coincide. With finite verbs there is more complexity: Consider these examples:

A. *Polarity.* Finite verbal groups choose from this system (Section 23) and the main exponent of negative is the morpheme *n't*. But only verbs that we find as auxiliaries can be followed by *n't*:

(1) He hasn't come.
(2) *He sangn't in the evening.

Sentence (2) is impossible because *sang* is not an auxiliary verb.

B. *Interrogative.* Finite verbal groups choose *interrogative* structures by placing an auxiliary verb in front of the subject.

(3) Has he come?
(4) *Sang he in the evening?

Sentence (4) is again impossible, since *sang* is not an auxiliary verb.

C. *Emphasis.* In English the normal way of emphasising a whole verbal group is to stress the first word, e.g. *hasn't* in (5) and *came* in (7). Stressing other words in the group draws attention to those particular words.

(5) He *hasn't* come.
(6) He hasn't *come*.
(7) He *came*.

Sentence (7) cannot make the contrast shown in (5) versus (6).

The conclusion we must draw is that a main verb can only carry finiteness when the group is positive and unemphatic, and the clause is *declarative*. In other cases the main verb is preceded by *do*, which then occupies place x in structure.

(8) He didn't sing in the evening.
(9) Did he sing in the evening?

(10) He *did* come.
(11) He *came*.
(12) He *didn't* come.
(13) He didn't *come*.

In this usage, *do* is often called an auxiliary verb, and it has many of the characteristics of an auxiliary, or a modal verb. As well as the patterns shown in (8), (9) and (10), there is the important point that no word can go before *do* in the verbal group:

(14) He couldn't come.
(15) *He couldn't do come.
(16) He didn't come.

And also that it cannot be non-finite in front of a main verb.

(17) Having finished work, Bill went to the pub.
(18) *Doing finish work, Bill went to the pub.
(19) Finishing work, Bill went to the pub.

The only purpose of *do* is to occupy place *x* when the finite main verb is restricted in position.

This 'special auxiliary' *do* is quite different from the main verb *do* which is very common, and which occupies place *v*.

(20) I can't do it.
(21) John can't tie the knot—will you do it?
(22) I do that every morning.

Both verbs *do* can be compared in

(23) He didn't do it very well.
(24) *He didn't it.

There is one major difference between the special auxiliary *do* and the other modal verbs: *do* cannot be followed by the auxiliaries *have* and *be*: it can only form verbal groups with a main verb.

(25) He hadn't finished it.
(26) *We didn't have finished it.

We recognise, then that *do* is a word which carries those grammatical systems that a simple main verb cannot carry, in verbal groups *where only a main verb is chosen*. So we describe *do* as a part of what occurs at place *v* in structure, not as one of the modals which occur at place *m* in structure.

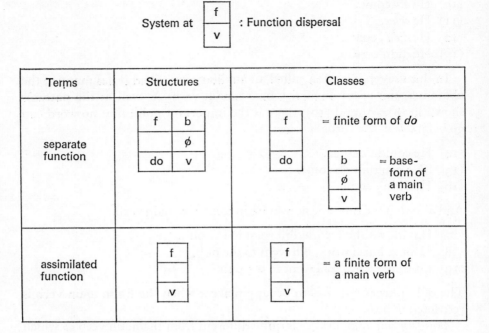

System at [f / v] : Function dispersal

Terms	Structures	Classes
separate function	f b ø do v	f do = finite form of *do* b ø v = base-form of a main verb
assimilated function	f v	f v = a finite form of a main verb

Exercise 24.1

Add the 'special auxiliary' *do* to as many as possible of the verbal groups in these sentences. Replace any auxiliary verb with *do* if you can. If you can not add *do*, give a reason why not.

1. Madge *eats* an awful lot.
2. *Feeling* a little tired, *I used to fall asleep.*
3. *Will* you *help make* the beds?
4. Mr Plumtree *liked to run* for his bus.
5. These cups *chip* easily.
6. It *hasn't been delivered* this morning.
7. That sort of work *won't do.*

Exercise 24.2

On the basis of this section so far, list the main structural characteristics of the 'special modal' *do.*

Medial Systems: Tense

So far we have seen the patterns and choices which occur at the beginning and at the end of verbal groups in English. We know that at the beginning of the groups the structure is:

$$\mathbf{x} \; (\mathbf{b}, \mathbf{b} \ldots)$$

That is to say, the first or only word carries all the systems of *finiteness*, *polarity*, *emphasis* and *simple tense*: and these choices are normally shown in the ending of the word: the other words in the verbal group are non-finite, and their endings are fully decided by the previous choice.

We also know that two classes of word can occur in the group—auxiliaries (with the sub-class modals) and main verbs. Their sequence is:

(modals)   (other auxiliaries)   (main verbs).

Modals must occupy place *x* in structure, but the other verbs can occur at *b*. There are special rules that we have just seen which operate when a main verb is at place *x*, that is, when no auxiliaries are chosen.

In this section we shall look at the 'other auxiliaries', and the choices that they show: *perfect*, *future* and *continuous* tenses, and *voice*. Each of these choices can add a word or more to the group, unlike the simple tenses which are shown in the ending of the first word.

The sequence of these medial systems is:

$$\left\{ \begin{array}{l} \text{perfect} \\ \text{and/or} \\ \text{future} \end{array} \right\} , \quad \text{continuous} , \; \text{passive}$$

And the whole sequence of possible words in the group is:
(modal) (perfect/future) (continuous) (passive) (*v*).

Perfect Tense

We have already seen that the perfect tense is formed by *have* + *n-form*. It is a tense which refers to 'past' time, but not in the same way as the past-indirect tense of Section 23.

The past-indirect tense has to have some reference-point outside the verb. In contrast, the reference-point of the perfect tense depends on the choices at place *x*. If *present-direct* is chosen, along with *perfect*, the perfect tense refers to some time before the moment of speaking. If past-indirect is chosen, along with its reference-point, the perfect tense refers to some time before that reference-point. So the perfect tense is not found with its own timing.

(27) I have passed my exams.
(28) *I have passed my exams in 1962.

(29) I passed my exams in 1962.
(30) I had passed my exams in 1962.

The timing of these tenses has an effect upon their meaning. The past-indirect tense (29) and (30) emphasises the *distance* in time between now and then, suggests that the event is over and done with. The 'present-perfect' tense (27) emphasises the present relevance of a past event, no matter when it was. In Example (27) above, it doesn't matter when the exams were passed—the focus is on the importance of the pass now. In Example (29) we have a simple narrative of what happened several years ago.

(31) I've passed all the necessary exams, so I can take my degree.
(32) I passed some exams in 1962 and then I left university for ever.

The perfect tense is often used, naturally, to refer to the time which has only just passed.

(33) I've done it.
(34) I did that many years ago.
(35) I haven't used a parachute for twenty years, so you must remind me about what to do.
(36) He left about ten minutes ago.

Here are some more examples of the perfect tense, with typical time-expressions.

(37) You haven't worked at all in the last five years.
(38) Yes we have done business with that firm, but not since 1910.
(39) Mr Plumtree has been singing all evening.
(40) Have you ever seen that before?
(41) Bill has come here for a month.

When the choice at *x* is past-indirect and perfect (the 'past-perfect' tense, as it is often called) there has to be some reference-point for the time.

(42) When I last met him he hadn't worked at all in the previous five years.
(43) We had at one time done business with that firm, but not after 1910.
(44) By 10 p.m. yesterday Mr Plumtree had been singing for 3 hours.
(45) Had you ever seen that before I showed you this afternoon?
(46) Last July we got into a jam—Bill had come to stay for a month and then Aunt Margaret turned up with eight children.

We can summarise the perfect tense choice in the following way:

Terms	Structures	Classes
perfect		h: (i) a form of the verb *have* (ii) the next word is an n-form g: is explained in the next few paragraphs
neutral	any other verbal group	

Exercise 24.3

Note the structure of each verb that has appeared in the examples in this section. Use the three-layered notation explained in Section 23 (see page 188). Example:

(30) I *had passed* my exams in 1962.

(the diagonal arrow shows that the *have-form* predicts the n-form of the next word).

(14) he *couldn't come*

Future Timing

This account of the English verb picks out one future tense, the sequence

be going + *to-form*

Some grammars say there is no proper future tense in English, some say that *will* and *shall* form a future tense, and some allow a range of tenses.

First of all, let us look at different ways in English of referring to future *time* (not tense). There are several.

(47) Jane is going to sing.
(48) Jane is about to sing.
(49) Jane will sing tomorrow.
(50) Jane sings tomorrow.
(51) Jane is singing tomorrow.
(52) Jane is to sing tomorrow.

(47) *Jane is going to sing.*

The verb *go* here is used as an auxiliary, and has changed in meaning from the main verb *go*. (See Table 24.1.)

	Present-direct	Past-indirect
auxiliary *go*	Jane is going to sing.	Jane was going to sing yesterday.
main verb *go*	Jane goes five miles to sing.	Jane went five miles to sing yesterday.
aux. + main verb *go*	Jane is going to go to London.	Jane was going to go to London yesterday.

Table 24.1. *go*-forms Contrasted

The meaning of this tense is similar to the perfect tense, but in the future rather than the past. It often occurs without any time-reference, because the *is* shows a present-direct tense. It refers to future time in relation to the moment of speaking, just as the perfect tense does with past time. It often refers to the immediate future.

(48) *Jane is about to sing.*

This form cannot occur with a reference-point: we cannot say (53).

(53) **Jane is about to sing at 6 p.m.*

In that way it also is similar to the perfect tense: but it is restricted to the immediate future.

(49) *Jane will sing tomorrow.*

Will is a modal verb, in the same class as *must, ought, can,* etc. It usually occurs with a reference-point, like the past-indirect tense, and it has a rather 'prophetic' meaning. It suggests that the speaker is so much in control of events that he can say exactly what will happen in the future. It does not relate the future to the moment of speaking.

In that last point, it has similarity with the past-indirect tense, but it is important to notice that past and future reference in English are not symmetrical: *will* structurally is a member of the same class as *can*, *ought*, etc., and its use carries modal meaning as well as time-reference.

be going + *to-form* does not escape modal meaning either; as well as (48) there are (53)–(60).

(53) Jane is ready to sing.
(54) Jane is prone to sing.
(55) Jane is able to sing.
(56) Jane is liable to sing.
(57) Jane is sure to sing.
(58) Jane is certain to sing.
(59) Jane is likely to sing.
(60) Jane is bound to sing.

These examples have some similarity to *PCP* phase (see Section 16) but it is not possible here to go into the detailed classifications. Compare the examples with (61)–(63)

(61) Jane is happy to sing.
(62) Jane is eager to sing.
(63) Jane is delighted to sing.

(50) Jane sings tomorrow.
(51) Jane is singing tomorrow.

These are combinations of simple present tenses and future adjuncts. They make up the meaning of 'arrangements are made for Jane'. (49) *will* mphasises the power of the speaker—he can order events. In contrast, (50) and (51) are examples of present tenses that show neither Jane nor the speaker in control. Decisions have been taken, and the result is that Jane is definitely to sing tomorrow. (47) *be going* is the most neutral in meaning; it neither emphasises nor plays down individual control. It can shade from *Jane has decided to sing* to *Jane can't help starting to sing*.

(52) *Jane is to sing tomorrow.*

Another modal verb—*be* + *t*. Here the notion of Jane being ordered is much stronger than in (50) and (51). It is difficult to say where a 'modal' meaning becomes stronger than a simple 'time' meaning. Nearly all the modal verbs in English imply a time-reference but that time-reference is a minor part of the meaning: with *will* and *shall* it is a considerable part of the meaning; with *be going* it seems to be the major part.

We can summarise the two main ways of referring to future time by relating them to the two main ways of referring to past time. Table 24.2 sets it out.

	Past time	Present time	Future time
Time reference is in verb	Jane has sung	Jane is singing	Jane is going to sing
Time reference is outside verb	Jane sang yesterday		Jane will sing tomorrow

Table 24.2

We must also describe a system of the verbal group which brings *be going* into the group.

Terms	Structures	Classes
future	(m) (h) g . . . ┌──┬──┬──┬──┐ │ │ │ │ b │ ├──┼──┼──┼──┤ │ │ │ │ t │ ├──┼──┼──┼──┤ │(m)│(h)│ g │ . . .│	g: (*a*) a form of the verb *be* (*b*) *going* (*c*) the next word is a *to-form*
neutral	any other verbal group	

The past and future tenses can occur together, in either sequence *gh* or *hg*, though the combinations are not very common.

(53) Bill has been going to mend that plug for six weeks now.

(54) We're going to have eaten far too much by the time this meal's over.

Exercise 24.4

Note the structure of the verbal groups underlined below. Use the three-layered notation, and treat *be + going* as one item, **g**, in the third row, e.g.

1. *Couldn't* Bill *have done* it?
2. It's *going to rain.*
3. I'*d been going to see* that film several times before I eventually managed.
4. Madge *was going to have done* that ages ago.
5. Bill *has* just *phoned.*
6. *Hadn't* you *heard*?
7. Look—he'*s going to tell* that policeman.
8. Mr Plumtree *may be going to faint.*
9. I'*m going to have finished* before dawn.
10. They *must have slipped* off somewhere.

Relative Timing

After the choices of tense have been dealt with, the regular sequence of words in a verbal group allows the so-called *continuous* or *progressive* form. This consists of the verb *be* in one of its forms and the *-ing* form of the next word.

The meaning of this choice is best shown by contrasting examples. The past-indirect forms are the clearest.

(64) What did you do last night?
(65) What were you doing last night?

(64) is a straightforward information question; (65) implies reference to another timed event—perhaps the questioner telephoned without success.

(66) The clock was striking ten when I returned home.
(67) The clock struck ten when I was returning home.

One event is timed by another, and the lexical meanings of the verbs adjust to suit the syntactic meaning. So *return* in (66) means something like *arrive back*, but in (67) it means more like *travel back*. The clause which carries the *be* + *ing* form is placed on a time-stream, and the other clause is timed by it. From examples like (66) and (67) arises the idea that the continuous form refers to uncompleted actions.

(68) You should have looked in last night—we were having a party.
(69) The tomatoes grew rapidly last week.

Presumably the party of (68) stopped at some time; the *be* + *ing* form is used to time the *looking-in*. In (69) there is no implication that the tomatoes have stopped growing this week, or even slowed down their rate of growth; only *last week*, the time boundary, has been completed.

Also, there is the fact that past tense forms do not have direct relevance to the moment of utterance (see Section 23, page 183). As a result of this, combined with the lexical meaning of many verbs, there is often the meaning of 'completed action'. It is suggested here that the contrast between 'completed' and 'uncompleted' actions is not the most general contrast in meaning, but arises from the effect of *relative timing* in conjunction with the range of meaning of several verbs.

The *be + ing* form can be used with an adjunct or B clause that states a duration of time, e.g. *from ten o'clock until two, throughout the afternoon, all the time he got ready*. Such items are more specific as timing devices than the *be + ing* form itself, and provide time limits.

(70) Mr Plumtree was practising from three until seven.

(71) *He was working throughout the afternoon, when Bill arrived.

The last example is starred because *he was working* is 'timed' by the adjunct *throughout the afternoon,* so another item cannot also play this role.

Now let us consider the *present continuous* form with some contrasting examples. In each case the verb form times the *moment of utterance,* and creates by interaction with the lexical meanings of the verbs, quite a range of meaning.

(72) He lives in London.

(73) He is living in London.

Living in this sense is a fairly long-term activity. In the neutral case (72) there is nothing to stop the verb giving that sort of meaning. In (73), however, his living in London is used as a time-frame for the moment of utterance, suggesting a brief stay in London rather than a permanent home.

(74) I walk home, thanks.

(75) I'm walking home, thanks.

In much the same way, the 'habitual' meaning of (74) (*I always walk home*) is contrasted with the 'ad hoc' meaning of (75) (*I've decided to walk home today*).

Where a verb has, in its lexical meaning, major reference to the moment of speaking, the contrast is almost lost.

(76) I feel sick.

(77) I'm feeling sick.

Indeed, there is a class of verb which has a meaning that is only valid *at* the moment of utterance. Verbs of this class, therefore, hardly ever occur in the *be + ing* form.

(78) I see him—over there!

(79) I must be seeing things!

(78) is a momentary experience; (79) suggests that some event has convinced the speaker that his vision is unreliable. But (79) is only acceptable because of the idiom *seeing things*; normally *see* does not occur as a timing verb, nor *hear, believe, know* and many other verbs often called 'verbs of perception'.

Another class of verbs that is not normally used to time other actions is the class that can be called, loosely, *performatives*; verbs where there is no distinction between the action and the word; e.g. *promise, vow, declare*.

(80) I hereby undertake to keep the peace hereafter.

Earlier in this section there are examples of the *be* + *ing* form used with future time-reference. In such cases the moment of utterance is timed by the verb form, suggesting that the event will certainly take place, as if it was actually happening at the moment of speaking. Then the adjunct places the time of the event as some time ahead.

(81) He is singing this evening.

The choice of the *be* + *ing* form can be summarised as follows:

Terms	Structures	Classes
timing		r: *am, is, are, was, were, be,* been plus *-ing* as ending for next word tense : (g) or (h)
neutral	any other verbal group	

Voice

Lastly in the medial systems of English verb, there is the choice of active or passive voice. As with the previous medial systems, there is a neutral choice, called *active*, where no words are added to the group. The mark of *passive* is a form of *to be* followed by the *n*-form of the main verb.

There is a description of the voice system in the Introduction and there is no need to repeat the details here. In brief the effect of the passive choice is to separate the subject of the clause and the *prime mover* of the action referred to. The active choice is neutral here, with the majority of instances contrasting in meaning with the passive.

(82) The story was read well.
(83) The story read well.
(84) Mr Plumtree read the story well.

The traditional contrast is between (82) and (84), but (83) shows the intermediate position that is the subject of much technical debate at the present time. Notice that *by Mr Plumtree* is an optional extra in (82), but does not fit into (83) at all.

The two main effects of the passive choice, then, are

(*a*) to avoid the identification of the prime mover of an action.

(85) Smoking is not permitted in the classrooms.
(86) The specimen was placed in a tinting solution.

The author of official notices is usually anonymous, to allow flexibility in administration; likewise in a scientific paper (86) it is irrelevant who actually did one part of the job.

(*b*) To adjust the emphasis of elements of clause structure by position— with a similar effect to theme changes (Section 12).

(87) I was beaten in the second round (by Fiery Freddie).
(88) The orchestra was conducted by Albert Plumtree.

The point of interest in (87) is the defeat of the speaker, not the name of the victor. So *I* is the subject, and Fiery Freddie is left to the end. In (88) the sentence is a device for naming the conductor; the *by*-phrase is not optional here, because the information that the orchestra was conducted is not new—we assume it was, and may want to know who the conductor was. In this case the end-placement of the main information point allows a slight suspense to build up during the sentence; in (89) the sentence tails off.

(89) Albert Plumtree conducted the orchestra.

Terms	Structures	Classes
passive	(r) p v → n b	r : be + *ing* form of following word p : be + *n* form of following word v : lexical verb
active	any other verbal group	

Exercise 24.5

Here are a number of examples of verb groups for analysis. Note *be + ing* as *r* in the bottom line of the three-layer notation, and passive (*be + n*) as *p*.

1. Bill *talks* too much.
2. *Superseded* by atomic power, the old plant *was sold* as scrap.
3. *Needn't* he *know* how to do the job?
4. It *can't have been processed* too much!
5. *Did* you *do* all that?
6. I *was wanting* that, yes.
7. Mr Plumtree *must have been travelling* very fast.
8. *Being employed* by an agency, I *knew* I *was going to work* in a different office every week.
9. *Talk* of the devil!
10. We'*d finished* in two hours.
11. *Were* you *contacted* about the matter?
12. I *wasn't feeling* well.
13. *Talking* of horses, *does* anyone *know* Lord Snottle?
14. You *wouldn't notice* a little thing like that.
15. He'*ll have been missing* for three months next Sunday.
16. *Having been concerned* in the contract, I *was* naturally *appointed* to the governing committee.
17. *Can't* you *come*?
18. You *used to be being pestered* by salesmen all the time.
19. *Should* we?
20. I'*ll come*.
21. I'*ve been looking* for one like this.
22. *To have been standing* so close to Lord Snottle is an experience I *shall treasure*.
23. He *did come*, didn't he?
24. *Don't* you *need to go* yet?
25. He *hadn't gone* away for a month.

Summary

This section has dealt with the final system of the verb, which describes the choice of the word *do*, when the group is negative, emphatic or discontinuous because the subject of an interrogative clause, or an adjunct, occurs inside the group.

After the selection of *do*, the medial systems are described in some detail. The Tenses are perfect and future. Perfect tense involves the present of *have* and so relates to the moment of speaking, in contrast to the past-indirect form described in the previous section.

Future time-reference can be carried by a variety of forms, but only one of them, *be going to*, has simple reference ahead in time. It is part of a sort of secondary modal system in medial position. Present-direct forms used with future-time adjuncts give the meaning of 'arrangement'.

The continuous form of the verb, the *be + ing* form, is next in sequence. The basic function of this form is to allow one event to be timed by another. Present-direct forms are used to time the moment of utterance.

Last in the set of medial systems is voice. Only a few notes are offered because of the description of voice in the Introduction.

A summary of the choices in the verbal group, then, is as follows:

1. *Initial systems.* These determine the choice of the ending of the first word in the group, but only in the case of *m* is the word actually chosen. Apart from that, the first non-neutral choice among the medial or final systems provides the word.

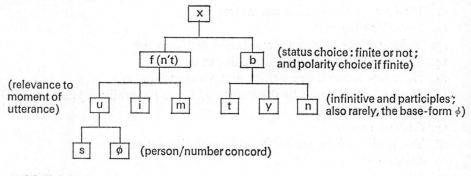

2. Medial Systems

$$(\text{T} \quad \begin{Bmatrix} h \\ g \\ hg \\ gh \end{Bmatrix}) \quad (r) \quad (p) \quad (v)$$

All are optional; these choices supply all the actual words apart from the modals and *do*, in a group. The only sequence variation is between *g* and *h*. Initial systems apply to the first word chosen.

3. Final system

Condition: f = v (i.e. the verbal group is finite but not modal, and all the medial choices are neutral;)

(for carrying negative, interrogative and emphatic choices)

SECTION 25: ADVERBIAL GROUP STRUCTURE

We group together under the general heading of adverbial groups a number of related structures. Much of the patterning is already familiar, because it has been needed in the description of other structures. New terminology for this area of the grammar is kept to a minimum.

In this area we touch the edges of grammar more often than usual. For example, it is often difficult to know whether or not to include an example because of its specialised meaning.

(1) The book's *just in*, Sir.
(2) He's only *just up*; he was out late last night.
(3) That donkey looks *all in* to me.

In in (1) means 'in stock'; *up* in (2) means 'got out of bed and started to dress'; *all in* in (3) means 'exhausted'.

The adverb *in front* looks superficially like a preposition with an object; *in front of the car* would then feature a nominal group *front of the car*, structure *hq*, with *front* as headword. But in this book *in front* and *in front of* are taken as single items, adverb and preposition respectively. The reasons are:

(a) they are fixed forms; *front* cannot be modified without changing the structure; *in the front of the car* is a different place from *in front of the car*!
(b) only a few other items are similar in shape; e.g. *in addition, at first*. We cannot make new items like **in back, *at second* (and *at last* is a separate idiom). For the same reasons, *as soon as* ... is not analysed, though *as quickly as* ... can be; *in spite of the fact that* is all a single item, though here we are on the margins of analysability. Quite a number of common binding and linking adjuncts show traces of derivation from two or more words, though they are not written as single items, e.g. *because* (= by cause) *in case, however, outside, nevertheless*. The language is gradually changing all the time, and some items hover on the edges of grammatical classes.

The main categories of adverbial groups are:

(a) Groups whose headwords are linking and binding elements of structure, often called conjunctions, and interrogative pronouns *when, how, where, why*. Let us call these *grammatical adverbs* to distinguish them from (c).
(b) Groups with an adjective as head.
(c) Groups with a lexical adverb as head.
(d) Groups with a preposition as head.

If the main elements of clause structure are s, p, c, o, a, then we expect a nominal group at s and o; a verbal group at p and an adverbial group at c and a.

(a) linking and binding elements

Exercise 25.1

The following examples illustrate a range of binding adjuncts. Work out which word can occur with which.

1. *Even if* you don't like spinach . . .
2. *Just when* I was leaving . . .
3. *Even though* I spoke severely to him . . .
4. *Right after* we left . . .
5. *Just because* you can't use a corkscrew . . .
6. *Even after* the noise had died away . . .
7. *Just as* John walked in the door . . .
8. *Right before* the clock struck six . . .
9. *Even as* the first enemy troops appeared . . .
10. *Just in case* anyone should hear . . .
11. *Even before* I could stop him . . .

In each case the second word does the job of binding—the first word is optional, and adds shades of meaning. This situation is similar (but not identical) to the structure of nominal groups, so we shall talk of modifier and headword once again.

The following examples show a different structure.

1. *Provided that* the message is delivered . . .
2. *The minute* I get free . . .
3. *Considering* you've only just arrived . . .
4. *Seeing that* it was getting late . . .
5. *Seeing* it's dark now, . . .
6. *Considering that* he's a blooming nuisance . . .
7. *Provided* there's no mistake . . .
8. *The minute that* I sat down . . .

Exercise 25.2

What is the role of the word *that* in the above examples?

Linking adjuncts have already been studied structurally—see Section 8. There it was pointed out that certain of them (e.g. *and, but*) could act as headwords while others (e.g. *therefore, then*) qualified them in *hq* structures.

(*b*) Adjective-head groups

The main lines of this patterning have already been described in the study of nominal group modification (Section 20) and need not be repeated here. Table 25.1 gives some examples with structural markings.

A. Adjective-head	B. Adverb-head
1. His clothes looked *admirable* : h	1. He did the job *neatly* : h
2. That's *quite fast enough* : mhq	2. Madge sang *sweetly enough* : hq
3. It left me *utterly weak* : mh	3. They managed *rather well* : mh
4. Madge seems *very capable indeed* : mhq	4. It was written *very carefully indeed* : mhq
5. They're *as cheap as yours* : mhq	5. I want that table laid *as nicely as you can* : mhq
6. I considered the last candidate *more expert than the others* : mhq	6. She danced *more gracefully than ever* : mhq

Table 25.1

(*c*) Adverb-head groups

In general these closely follow the structure of adjective-head groups, and Table 25.1 shows parallel examples.

Exercise 25.3

From the examples in Table 25.1 derive the general structure of adverb-head and adjective-head groups.

Note that modifiers and qualifiers are closely related to each other; **very carefully enough*, for example, is not acceptable. The *as . . . as*, and *more . . . than* structures can have other clauses or groups as qualifiers.

Here are some more examples of adverb modifiers:

1. I put it *right outside*.
2. The other car is *just in front*.
3. *Far ahead* I could see the mountain.
4. There were books *all round*.
5. Go *straight in*.
6. The world champion was *far in front*.
7. Bill is waiting *just outside*.
8. *Straight ahead*, for Ramsgate, sir.

9. I pushed the knob *right in.*
10. You'll have to climb *right up.*
11. *Just ahead* we saw a brilliant rainbow.
12. He's *right in front* now.
13. The rocket rushed *straight up.*
14. The cave goes *very far in.*
15. *Right ahead* loomed the palace.
16. Sit looking *straight in front*, please.
17. It's *rather far up*, I'm afraid.
18. I turned *right around.*

Exercise 25.4

Work out which modifiers can occur with which adverbs.

These examples are on the boundary between adverbs and the next category of headword, prepositions. They have different modifiers from the rest of the adverbs, and do not have qualifiers. A few, like *far*, can have submodifiers.

Exercise 25.5

Give the structure of the italicized adverbial groups in the examples below. Identify the headword as grammatical adverb, adjective or lexical adverb, and if lexical adverb whether regular (like *neatly*, *well*) or special (like *in front*, *up*).

1. It only moved *a little bit down.*
2. Bill walked *as quickly as he could.*
3. He handled it *very roughly indeed.*
4. *When* is he coming?
5. *Slightly farther* on they met the vicar.
6. He spoke *gently.*
7. *As if* I can help it!
8. *Very probably* Madge has just slept in.
9. He managed *better than ever before.*
10. The hurricane came *terribly close.*
11. I moved over *so that* Madge could sit down.
12. Bill found the chair *exceptionally hard.*
13. We talked *as quietly as possible.*
14. I'll come *just as soon as* I can.
15. *But then* what's to be done?
16. Put it *right here.*
17. He was blue *all over!*

18. *Just below,* Bill could see the mouth of the cave.
19. She sang *more sweetly than the others did.*
20. *Even when* I spoke to him . . .
21. It went off *tremendously well.*
22. The stick appeared *long enough.*

(*d*) Prepositional groups.

Structures consisting of an adverbial group and a nominal group have been referred to previously, in Section 18, page 148. The adverbial group has the structure (*m*)*h*, and the headword is called a preposition. The nominal group has unrestricted structure, and is usually called an object, to echo the term object in clause structure. It is useful to think of prepositions as 'transitive adverbs', requiring a nominal to complete the structure.

The rules of position that govern relative pronouns are more powerful than the preposition-object rules. Consider (1)–(4) below.

(1) The Palace Yard, in which stands the statue of Ptolemy, is accessible from the road.
(2) A second difficulty, which I shall deal with in the next chapter, is the cost of travel in this area.
(3) Go back to the square that you have just come from.
(4) That's not the place we went to.

Exercise 25.6

(*a*) Identify free, bound and rankshifted clauses in the examples above.
(*b*) Identify all the prepositions and their object if present. Note particularly any where the object does not follow directly on the preposition.

The key to this exercise shows that a relative pronoun must occur early in the clause, whether or not it is *governed* by a preposition. Formal English, as in Example (1), puts the preposition to the front also, but the positions in (2) are probably the commonest, in present-day written and spoken English. A problem for the grammarian arises in (3), because *that* cannot occur in the normal place for the object of a preposition; (5) is unacceptable.

(5) *Go back to the square from that you have just come.

There is no relative pronoun at all in (4), so the preposition has no object.

The general structure of prepositional groups, then, is (*m*) *ho*; but when the prepositional group is an adjunct in the clause, and when the adjunct is the element of structure that shows binding or rankshifting in the clause, there is an alternative discontinuous structure (o) ... $(m)h$. In this structure the object may be *that*, or may not be there at all.

Prepositions have modifiers of a class that we have already met. Here are some examples:

1. You'll find the box *just under the table.*
2. That chair's *rather near the fire*, don't you think?
3. We live *very near the sea.*
4. It's *just over the hill.*
5. She looks *just like her mother.*
6. I sent the letter *straight up to Headquarters.*
7. It was *for all the world like Venice.*
8. It's *rather like mine.*
9. Go *right inside* the house immediately.
10. She dashed *straight round the corner.*
11. His books were littered *all over the bedroom.*
12. The ball rolled *far under the sofa.*

Exercise 25.7

Make a list of the modifiers in the above examples.

Exercise 25.8

At the beginning of this section, there is a note about adverbs and prepositions that contain more than one word, and yet form a single grammatical item. In the following examples, find all the prepositions. What is *just* in no. 10? Note any similarities of structure in the prepositions.

1. In addition to his other work, Mr Plumtree heads the local steel board.
2. I'd never have got there but for Madge's help.
3. Due to a legacy, we are able to redecorate the entire premises.
4. We went out of politeness.
5. All celebrations are cancelled owing to our recent bereavement.
6. Get out of my way!
7. Don't expect me to dress up, on top of all this.
8. He'll never finish it, in spite of what he says.
9. We found out some nasty facts in the course of our investigation.
10. Just because of you, I have to do all this!
11. Move nearer to the fire.
12. I'll give up to £7.50 for that vase.
13. Apart from the climbing, I love ski-ing.
14. By reason of negligence, we have lost several customers.

Table 25.2, page 211, shows contrasting arrangements of adverbial groups in clauses. Many clause adjuncts consist of one adverbial group, but some more complex relationships occur. The prepositional group shows combination with a nominal group, and Column A of Table 25.2 shows combinations of two adverbial groups, making up one adjunct. In Column B the two adjuncts are independent of each other. Study the difference in meaning.

A	B
1. *From here home* you're on your own.	1. *From here, all the way,* you're on your own.
2. *Down here in Margate* the crowds are milling on the beach.	2. *Over there, in Margate,* the crowds are milling on the beach.
3. He's *out in the garden,* I suppose.	3. He's *out, in the garden* I suppose.
4. Mr Plumtree was indisposed *from January to June.*	4. Mr Plumtree had been indisposed *since January, until last week.*
5. You'll find it *through there in the cupboard.*	5. You'll find it *through there, in the cupboard.*

Table 25.2. Adverbial Group Combinations

Phrasal Verbs

Some combinations of verbal and adverbial groups cause problems both to the grammarian and to the learner of English.

   6) Will you please *let* me *through*?
   (7) A person I didn't know *let* us *in*.
   (8) Bill *let* me *down*.
   (9) When Mr Plumtree starts a thing, he never *lets up* until it's done.
   (10) Did you *let on* about the present for Madge?

Examples (6) and (7) show *let* in one of its normal meanings, followed by a common adverb. (8) also can be understood in that way, but it has another meaning, similar to (11)

(11) I was relying on Bill to do something, and he didn't do it.

In Examples (9) and (10), *let* is used without an object, but with *up* and *on* following. This structure does not normally occur with *let*, and in both cases gives a new meaning: *let up* means, very roughly, 'stop', and *let on* means 'disclose', also roughly.

   A combination *PA* which produces a new meaning is called a *phrasal verb*, like *let down, let up, let on.*

Exercise 25.9

Here are some italicized examples of phrasal verbs, and each one's meaning is paraphrased below the examples. Pick out the paraphrase for each verb.

1. The party *came off* very well.
2. Are you *having* me *on* about the snow?
3. I can't *make out* your writing.
4. These cousins of ours are forever *falling out*.
5. Our annual dinner has had to be *put off* again.
6. Will you please *look over* these notes to make sure that they're accurate?
7. The advance party *set out* at ten.
8. The Government is threatening to *take over* several more sectors of private industry.
9. Just look who's *turned up*!
10. Bill *went down* with flu last week.

Paraphrases

a. postponed
b. assume control of
c. decipher, read
d. appeared
e. took place
f. quarrelling
g. quickly examine
h. took ill
i. deceiving
j. started on a journey

These are clear cases of new meanings. However, many *PA* combinations are not so clear, and we must examine some of them. Consider the following examples:

(12) *Eat up* your dinner!
(13) You'll have to *fill* that hole *in* with sand.
(14) I *found out* how she does it.
(15) It's time to *finish off* your work now.
(16) Let me just *read* it *through* quickly.
(17) In (12) to (17), the adverbs can be *left out*.

The adverbs are not structurally necessary, and the verbs do not have a different meaning without them. The function of the adverbs is to emphasise the completion of the verb's meaning. (12) without *up* means 'carry on eating' rather than 'eat *all* your dinner', and so on. (14) and (17) are more specialised, and (18) still more.

(18) Please fill in Form P. 72.

It is important to notice that (12) to (18) are still phrasal verbs, not very different from the previous examples. There are clusters of *PA* combinations which range from fairly clear new meanings to ordinary combinations, e.g. (19)

(19) Let me just $\left\{\begin{array}{l}\text{read}\\\text{look}\\\text{go}\\\text{read}\\\text{look}\\\text{go}\end{array}\right\}$ $\left\{\begin{array}{l}\text{over}\\\\\\\text{through}\end{array}\right\}$ that article right now.

There is not much difference in meaning among all six of the *PA* combinations, yet *look over* seems to give a new meaning, while *read through* does not.

Phrasal verbs are idioms, and are related to other idioms. The closest relatives are *PAA* structures like *set out for, put up with*, which are discussed later in this section. But in a number of cases, one or more nominal groups are associated frequently with the verbal and adverbial groups. The commonest is *it*:

(20) They quarrelled, but made it up the same evening.
(21) Come off it—that's completely wrong!
(22) She isn't really upset—she's just putting it on for your benefit.

Note

Some fixed phrases contain structures of this kind, but they can only be mentioned here; *run to seed*, for example, meaning 'deteriorate', and *look down your nose at* someone, meaning 'despise'.

Some words in every day English are only found in idiomatic uses—e.g. *spick and span, hale and hearty, at loggerheads, on tenterhooks*. They are usually historical survivals, or specialised terms that have broadened their meaning. Here are some examples of verbs in phrasal verb combinations.

(23) Here's a little milk to eke out the cream.
(24) You can depend on that firm for good service.

(25) They trumped up a few accusations against me, but none of them could be proved.

(26) I don't know how he plucked up enough courage.

Now we turn to the grammatical classification of phrasal verbs. Most of the examples so far have shown adverbs at A; the other main type has prepositional groups at A. In the next few paragraphs, we shall distinguish the *PA* (adverb) structures from the *PA* (preposition) ones, and then treat them separately.

The two main distinguishing features of *PA* (adverb) phrasal verbs are:

(*a*) The adverb is stressed in speech; the preposition is only stressed for contrastive emphasis.

(*b*) Here is an ambiguous sentence

(27) Can you look over the garage?

This example could be analysed *PAO*, involving the phrasal verb *look over* = 'examine'. Alternatively, it could be *PA*, with *over the garage* a prepositional group, and no phrasal verb meaning at all; like 'over the top of the garage'. But (28) can only have the phrasal verb interpretation

(28) Can you look the garage over.

The structure is *POA*. In general, then, nominal groups associated with *PA* (adverb) phrasal verbs can occur in *POA* or *PAO* sequence. But there are two important exceptions to this statement, brought out by (29) and (30).

(29) *The government is threatening to *take over* them.

(30) *The government is threatening to *take* several more sectors of private industry, only recently returned to investors after the June recession and consequent change of plans *over*.

(29) shows that a personal pronoun object must occur before A, and we have met many examples of this sequence. (30) shows that a long and complicated object normally follows the adverb, so that P and A are not more than a few words away from each other.

Exercise 25.10

Make notes on the examples below as follows:
(*a*) is there a *PA* structure
    (i) that gives a new meaning?
    (ii) in which an adverb emphasises the completion of the verb's meaning?
    (iii) in which the verb is mainly confined to phrasal verb usage?
    (iv) in which the *PA* structure has a fixed object?

(*b*) is the Adjunct   (i) an adverbial group?
　　　　　　　　(ii) a prepositional group?

1. The ground opened, and swallowed up the whole village.
2. Please look after this small matter for me.
3. Many people went through this gate today.
4. We were egged on by the applause of thousands.
5. I'll have it out with Smithers in the morning.
6. I came to in a small dark cell.
7. Madge chose beans, but Bill plumped for artichokes.
8. They called it off because of the snow.
9. I won't stand for any more of this!

Phrasal verbs with adverbs

The previous examples show that these verbs can be transitive or intransitive (e.g. *He looked it over, it came off*). The regular transitivity of the verb does not matter; *look* is usually intransitive.
　　Some phrasal verbs are confined to the imperative form of the verb.

(31) Come on!
(32) Hurry up!
(33) Look out!
(34) Look here!

(31) and (32) are similar in meaning, and (32) is an example of category (*a*ii) in exercise 25.10 above. (33) is a warning of a possible accident, and (34) means, roughly, 'pay attention!'

Phrasal verbs with prepositions

The preposition, of course, usually has an object following it. (35) and (36) show that the verb also can be transitive (*POA*) or intransitive (*PA*)

(35) I took you for a policeman.
(36) I took to him right away.

(35) means 'I thought, wrongly, that you were a policeman', and (36) means 'I liked him as soon as I met him'.

PAA structures

(37) Let's *set out for home* now.
(38) The people from London *look down on us*, I'm afraid.
(39) Mr Plumtree won't *put up with this* for long.

The first adjunct has an adverb, and the second is a prepositional group. (37) is related to (40) (and see sentence 7 of Exercise 25.9).

(40) They set out bravely to face the eternal ice.

but this is not a regular correspondence; there are several phrasal verbs *put up* (see (41)–(43)) but none of them has the meaning of (39): 'tolerate'.

(41) My bank put up the money. (= 'advanced')
(42) Can you put up at your aunt's in Burnley? (= 'stay', 'board')
(43) Who put you up to that trick? (= 'told you about')

(43) is a *PAA* phrasal verb *put up to*.

Exercise 25.11

Here are some more examples of the structures described in the last few pages. Describe them according to the categories of Exercise 25.10 but add the following:

(c) is the verb (i) transitive?
                  (ii) intransitive?
(d) is the verb imperative?

In examples of PA_1A_2, treat A_1 and A_2 separately in (b).

1. I like to keep in with my neighbours.
2. Could you sort out this tangle for me, please?
3. Don't rely on a lift on that road.
4. Do you think she'll pull through after such a serious illness?
5. The aircraft took off on time but met strong headwinds.
6. May I speak to Mr Plumtree, please?
7. After the announcement, we had to fend off dozens of enquiries.
8. Steady on there now!
9. Jot these addresses down please, Miss Plumtree.
10. I don't believe their story; I bet they made it all up.
11. We'll have to see about a little celebration, then.
12. Watch out—here's trouble coming.
13. Madge and I don't eat out a lot.
14. The train started off with a jerk.
15. Look after these glasses for me, will you?
16. Everyone standing around was roped in to help.
17. Bill saw an eagle high up.
18. I told them off and no mistake.
19. We'll have to fall back on our savings.
20. Has the water soaked in yet?

Key to Exercises

Exercise 1.1

1. FB statement
2. BF command
3. FB command
4. FB question

Exercise 1.2

No.	Sentence structure	Clause boundary	Sentence action
1	FB	rain/when	statement
2	FB	plane/the	statement
3	FB	off/since	question
4	FB	fire/in	statement
5	FB	in/whenever	command

Exercise 1.3

Example: *go if you can*: FB command

Exercise 2.1

1. When I left, / it was pouring with rain.
2. The minute I got my luggage through the customs, / I dashed for the plane.
3. Since you don't like it, / should I leave it off?
4. In case he falls over, / you'd better watch that fire.
5. Whenever you want to, / just pop in.

Exercise 2.2

No.	Boundary (a)	Reversed clauses (b)	Structure (c)
1	not/we	We'll have to invite him, whether he'll come or not.	FB
2	concession/provided	Provided that you . . . years, you are entitled . . . concession.	BF
3	her/however	However much . . . cries, don't go up to her.	BF
4	asleep/immediately	Immediately he . . . supper, he fell asleep	BF
5	expense/I'm	I'm a . . . delay, while I . . . expense	FB
6	on/even	Even though . . . out, he carried on	BF
7	mind/Mr	Mr Plumtree . . . pipe as if . . . on his mind.	FB
8	off/I	I just . . . myself until the plane took off.	FB
9	it/as	As soon as you can, buy it.	BF
10	flowers/seeing	Seeing everyone . . . sweets, we brought flowers.	BF
11	met/some	Some little progress . . . made since we last met.	FB
12	in/before	Before you . . . Robinson he jumped in.	BF
13	late/let's	Let's take a taxi since it's so late.	FB
14	takes/I	I intend . . . tonight, no matter how long it takes.	FB
15	round/after	After we'd finished supper he came round.	BF

Exercise 2.3
whether (or not), provided that, however (much), immediately, while, even though, as if, until, as soon as, seeing, since, before, since no matter how (long), after.

Exercise 3.1
which, by which, into which, where, who, from whom, when, whose (voice)

Exercise 3.2 (examples only)
in, after, through, of, to, under, across, behind, before, in front of, underneath, on, up.
Note: In formal written English you will find, e.g.
(a) *in the presence of whom* (the event occurred)
(b) *to whose unfailing and generous munificence* (we are often indebted)
(c) *the full extent of which* (is as yet unknown)
But in everyday speech even *in which* is less common than *which . . . in.*
(d) we stopped at a small hut, in which he kept his stuff.
(e) we stopped at a small hut, which he kept his stuff in.
   (e) is more common than (d) in informal conversation. (a), (b) and (c) have no informal equivalent.

Exercise 3.3
1. *Otello*
2. Harrogate
3. my new colleague
4. no particular referent
5. A series of pilot experiments

6. the drive towards economy of operation
7. after ten o'clock
8. my father
9. no particular referent
10. Mr Plumtree

Exercise 4.1
1. FB cont.
2. B cont. F
3. F
4. FB add.
5. FB cont.
6. FB cont. (this type of B clause is explained in Section 7)

The F clauses of this exercise are the same as the B clauses of column (B) of Fig. 4.1.

Exercise 4.2
9. If he can manage, I'll slip off. $B^{cont}.F$
10. Whether . . . things, he'll manage somehow. $B^{cont}.F$
11. If he . . . first, I'll cheer and cheer. $B^{cont}.F$
12. Whether anyone . . . or not, keep . . . still. $B^{cont}.F$

Exercise 4.3

BF	Restriction
1. He would lift the thing, I thought.	*never*
2. He was very rich, they believed.	*no-one*
3. You're getting married, you told me.	*don't* + imp.
4. The radio could be mended, he was sure.	*wasn't* + int.
5. He's staying the weekend, you can say.	*needn't* + deny
6. He should watch himself, I warned him.	*just*
7. The letter had gone astray, I assumed.	*only*
8. He was coming, Bill knew.	*if*

Exercise 4.4

Structure	Reversibility
1. FB	reversible
2. FB	*that*
3. FB	*didn't* + just
4. FB	*whether* + imp.
5. FB	reversible
6. FB	*that*
7. FB	*merely*
8. FB	*that*

Exercise 4.5

assume	find (out)	mention	say	whisper
be (sure)	hear	notice	see	yell
believe	imagine	observe	shout	
deny	inform	promise	tell	
expect	insist	remind	think	
feel	know	report	warn	

Exercise 4.6 (No key.)

Exercise 4.7

why	what	which (bus)
how	when	where
who		

Exercise 4.8

This verb	can be followed by a B rep. clause starting with				
	no binder	that	if/whether	wh-	Notes
assume	✓	✓	N	N	It is difficult to say 'yes'
be (sure)	✓	✓	N	N	or 'no' in some of the
believe	✓	✓	x	x	cases, and this table is
deny	✓	✓	x	x	offered as a fairly safe
expect	✓	✓	x	x	guide to usage
feel	✓	✓	x	N	✓ = likely to occur freely
find (out)	✓	✓	✓	✓	
hear	✓	✓	✓	✓	x = very unlikely to occur
imagine	✓	✓	N	N	N = only likely if F clause
inform	✓	✓	✓	✓	is negative
inquire	x	x	✓	x	+ = interesting borderline
insist	✓	✓	x	x	examples
know	✓	✓	✓	✓	Consider the sentence
mention	✓	✓	x	✓	(a) He'll shout if she
notice	✓	✓	✓	✓	arrives.
observe	✓	✓	x	✓	With structure FB cont.
plead	x	x	x	x	this sentence tells us
promise	✓	✓	x	N	what a shout will signify,
remind	+	✓	x	✓	but it does not tell us
report	x	✓	✓	x	what he will actually
					shout.
say	✓	✓	✓	✓	A structure B cont. F
see	✓	✓	✓	✓	would give a similar
					meaning.
shout	x	✓	+	✓	(b) If she arrives he'll
					shout.
tell	✓	✓	✓	✓	But sentence (a) can
think	✓	✓	N	N	also be labelled FB rep.
warn	✓	✓	x	✓	and with this structure
whisper	✓	✓	+	✓	it tells us that he will
yell	x	✓	+	✓	actually shout
					something like 'she's
					arrived !'
					A B rep. F structure is
					now not possible.

Exercise 5.1 (Part key.)

selection: clause REP.; *binder* none; *structure* BF:

example: It was a long journey, he warned us.

selection: clause CONT.; *binder* by the time; *structure* FB:

example: We were very late by the time we had made a big picnic lunch.

Exercise 6.1

(*a*) and, but, however, nevertheless, then, therefore, thus.

(*b*) cont. clauses. It is unlikely that any other sort of clause would split an F at this place. The linkers are only loosely attached to any clause.

Exercise 6.2

(*a*) among the guests, at our newest retail store, at seven-thirty, in Athens, in London, in this company, last summer, later on in the day, never, often during the night, quickly, tonight.

(*b*) set (i) has cont. clauses; set (ii) has add. clauses.

Exercise 6.3

1. Where you can shop in the most modern and tasteful surroundings, you will find yourself buying rather more than you intended.
2. I was abroad when we had all that rain.
5. Where the light has exceptional clarity—as, for example, in Athens—you get wonderful photographs.
3. Where they make cutlery, there are to be found the remains of England's traditional craftsmanship.
5. We'll go out when Bill arrives home.

Exercise 6.4

1. I	4. I	7. II (ii)
2. III (ii)	5. II (i)	8. III (i)
3. II (ii)	6. III (i)	9. II (ii)
		10. III (ii)

Exercise 6.5

The B clauses are reported

1. split after A	4. split within P
2. split after A	5. split after S
3. split after S	

Exercise 6.6

Then, you see, he ran upstairs

(a) sentence structure F; clause structure A^LA^LS P A

   you see is a signal for a response

(b) sentence structure B [F]; clause structure B: A^LS P A

                                          F: S P

   'you must understand that afterwards he ran upstairs.'

Exercise 6.7

No.	(a) Structure	(b) B-type	(c) F [B] Breakdown
1	F[B]	cont.	II
2	F[B]	add.	III
3	B[F]	rep.	
4	F		
5	F[B]	cont.	I
6	F[B]	add.	II
7	B[F]	rep.	
8	F[B]	cont.	III
9	F		

Exercise 7.1

dashing	driven
having got	to get
feeling	to wash
having been disappointed	to be

  The B clauses are all contingent

Exercise 7.2

after, before, *by*, *for*, if, *on*, though, while, *with*, *without*.
(Italicized items are P-binders only.)

1. *after* We went home quickly after we had been to the pictures.
2. *before* Before you fit the legs on, apply a coat of varnish.
3. *if* You must move on if a policeman tells you.
4. *though* Though he was very tired, Bill soldiered on.
5. *while* The aircraft landed while we were there.

Exercise 7.3

No.	Subject	Predicator	P-binder
1		-ing	with
2		-ing	after
3	+S	-ing	
4		-ing	before
5	+S	to	for
6		-ing	on
7	+S	-ing	
8		-ing	while
9		to	
10	+S	-ing	
11		-ing	for
12		-n	if
13		-n	though
14	+S	to	without
15		-ing	by
16	+S	to	for

Exercise 7.4 (No key.)

Exercise 7.5
1. III   4. II
2. III   5. III
3. I   6. I

Exercise 7.6
(a) the binders are almost the same as 4.7, but *whether* is also used in this exercise, and *why* is not
(b) BF: nos. 5, 7.

Exercise 8.1
and, but, nevertheless, *or*, then, however, therefore. *Without linker*: 6, 9, 11, 17.

Exercise 8.2

A^+ A^L
and   however
but   perhaps
or   nevertheless
               therefore

Exercise 8.3

Linker	Fixed initial position in structure A	Links structures below clause rank B	Allows branching C
and, but, or	√	√	√
yet	√	X	X
for	√	—	—
so	X	—	—
however, nevertheless, perhaps, etc.	—	—	—

Exercise 8.4 (No key.)

Key 9

No.	(a)	(b)	(ci)	(cii)	(ciii)	(d)	(e)
1	FB	S	that A^B	rep.	2		
2	F[B]	S	P-bound	cont.	2	III	
3	BF	S	A^B although	cont.	2		
4	F[B]B	Q	A^B once	cont.	2	I	list, unbranched
			A^B that	rep.	2		
5	F[B]	S	S^B who	add.	2	III	
6	BF	S		rep.	2		
7	F[B]	S	P-bound	cont.	2	II	
8	FBFF	S	A^B if	cont.	2		so...linked and...list, branched after S
9	FB	C	A^B once	cont.	2		
10	F[B]	S	P-bound	cont.	2	II	linked
11	FB	Q	A^B when	cont.	2		
12	BFB	C	A^B if	cont.	2		
			A^B unless	cont.	2		
13	F[B]	S	A^B if	cont.	2	I	list, unbranched
14	B[F]	S		rep.	2	II	
15	F[B]	S	A^B unless	cont.	2	I	linked
16	FB	Q	A^B that	rep.	2		
17	FBB	S	P-bound A^B	cont.	2		
18	F[B]	C	when A^B	cont.	2	II	
19	FBBB	S	A^B that	rep.	2		
			A^B whenever	cont.	3		
			A^B where	cont.	4		
20	FB	S	A^B where	add.	2		
21	FBB	Q	A^B that	rep.	2		
			A^B just because	cont.	3		
22	FB	S		rep.	2		
23	F[B]	S	S^B who	add.	2	III	
24	F[BB]BF	S	A^B when	cont.	2	I	linked (in the end)
			O^B what	rep.	3		linked (however)
				rep.	2		
25	F[B]	S	A^B when	cont.	2	I	linked
26	FF	S					contact
27	FB	C	G^B that	rep.	2		
28	FBF	S	A^B if	cont.	2		contact

Exercise 10.1
Nos. 7, 8 and 16 are special types of utterance; none of the four categories exactly fits them.

1. response
2. response
3. statement
4. question
5. statement
6. statement
7. *greeting*
8. *exclamation*
9. response
10. question

11. statement   17. statement
12. statement   18. statement
13. statement   19. response
14. command   20. statement
15. question   21. statement
16. *greeting*

Exercise 10.2

1. Agreement to a statement, question or command.
2. Acceptance of a command: 'I shall do it at once, Sir.'
3. An informal statement like 'Falmouth is a nice place', but the main emphasis on *a nice place*, and practically none on Falmouth (the usual intonation would be 13).
4. 'what are you going to do about me?'
5. A statement, as found in newspaper headlines. 'There were scenes of horror at a fatal accident.'
6. A statement, as found in the title of a book. 'This book contains the poetical works of Thomas Chatterton.'
7. A greeting—it cannot be paraphrased, but is just what people say on meeting in the evening, when they are fairly formal with each other.
8. An exclamation; again it cannot be paraphrased closely: it shows surprise, perhaps, and anxiety.
9. A response; 'it was a pleasure, my friend'.
10. Mr Plumtree has been mentioned. 'Why should it be Mr Plumtree?'
11. A shop front might have this notice. 'This is J. Squid's shop, and he is a high-class fishmonger.'
12. The statement of the announcer at a boxing match. Similar to no. 3 ('Bill Blood of Barnsley is on my right') but the boxer's name will be heavily stressed.
13. An introduction; 'Dr Plumtree, I'd like you to meet Miss Wiggins'.
14. 'You will move forward at once.'
15. A question that picks out a name from something that has been said. 'I'm surprised that you mention *his* name.'
16. A greeting.
17. A notice in a shop window. 'Giant size Rinso costs 19p.'
18. The beginning of a notice about a house; found in a house-agent's publicity. 'We have a desirable modern villa for sale in the Newton district.'
19. A very strong refusal. 'I certainly won't do it.'
20. The beginning of a dictionary entry. 'The word *longanimity* can be pronounced in two ways (details given). It is a rare noun.'
21. A greeting.

Exercise 10.3

1. interrogative P[S]
2. interrogative P[S] Wh-word, but not subject
3. imperative P
4. declarative SP

5. interrogative SP Wh-word subject
6. imperative P
7. declarative P verb is not imperative
8. interrogative P[S] Wh-word, but not subject
9. moodless A
10. imperative P
11. declarative SP
12. interrogative P [S]
13. declarative P verb is not imperative
14. imperative P
15. imperative P

Exercise 10.4

am	had	ought
are	has	shall
can	have	should
could	is	was
did	may	were
do	might	will
does	must	would

Note: Most of these words can occur with the negative *n't*.

Exercise 10.5

1. *Come* is not an auxiliary, and so cannot come before S in an interrogative clause. *Did he come?*
2. *Threw* is not an auxiliary, and so cannot come before S in this kind of response. *So did Bill.*
3. A PS structure can follow quoted speech, but hardly ever precedes it. *'Why?' asked Mr Plumtree.*
4. In APS structures S cannot be a pronoun. *Here they come.*
5. The adjunct in APS structures is not usually a *quality* adverb like *brightly*. *The moon shone brightly that night* or *Brightly the moon shone last night.*
6. S cannot be a pronoun, just as 4. *Over there it rises.*
7. PS declarative must have a preceding adjunct. *In Trafalgar Square stands a statue of Lord Nelson.*

Exercise 10.6

No.	SP sequence	Mood	Contextual type	Remarks
1	SP	interrogative	question	Wh-word subject
2	APS	declarative	statement	Place-adjunct
3	—	moodless	response	
4(a)	Voc. P	imperative	command	*Ladies* is probably vocative though the sentence is
(b)	SP	declarative	statement	ambiguous
5	Paux. S	interrogative	question	P aux. = *be* as main verb
6	—	moodless	statement	
7	P[S]	interrogative	question	
8	APS	declarative	statement	Place adjunct thematic. Note *there* is stressed and so is not the neutral subject *there* of no. 13.
9	P	declarative	statement	P = *been*, which is not base-form.
10(i)	P[S]	interrogative	question	quoted speech.
(ii)	PS	declarative	statement	following quoted speech. P is reporting verb.
11	P[S]	interrogative	question	wh-word thematic, but not subject.
12	P	imperative	command	P = base-form
13	Paux. S	interrogative	question	P aux. = *have*. Subject = neutral (unstressed) *there*.
14(i)	SP	declarative	statement	
(ii)	P	declarative	statement	branched structure; P is not base-form.
15	AP [S]	declarative	statement	A = A neg. thematic, which forces P[S] structure in clause.

Exercise 11.1

1. won't he?
2. shoudn't I?
3. hasn't it?
4. mustn't they?
5. aren't you?

Exercise 11.2

1. might he
2. is there
3. hasn't it
4. don't they (*isn't he* is not correct here since *he's coming* is a B rep. clause)
5. won't you
6. didn't I
7. do I
8. can't you
9. shouldn't he
10. is it
11. did he
12. weren't they
13. aren't I
14. ought it
15. won't you

Exercise 11.3

1. mightn't he
2. isn't there
3. has it
4. do they
5. will you
6. did I
7. don't I
8. can you
9. should he
10. isn't it
11. didn't he
12. were they
13. am I
14. oughtn't it

Exercise 11.4

3. so it has
4. so they do
5. so I will
6. so you did
8. so I can
9. so he should
12. so they were
13. so you are

Exercise 11.5

These are just examples of correct responses; any subject can be chosen.

1. Neither might I
3. So has Bill's
5. So will plenty of other people
6. So did Madge
7. Neither do I
8. So can all my friends
9. So should the chairman
11. Neither did the girl
12. So were the ones on the next table
13. So am I
14. Neither ought anything else

Exercise 11.6

(The choice of *yes* or *no* is arbitrary.)

1. Yes, he does
2. No, there isn't
3. Yes, it has
4. Yes, they do
5. Yes, I will
6. Yes, I did
7. No, I can't
8. Yes, he should
9. No, it isn't
10. No, he didn't
11. Yes, they were
12. No, I'm not

Exercise 11.7

1. Mr Plumtree: vocative tag
2. did he: copy tag
   so did I: new subject response
3. Bill will: gloss tag
   Madge: vocative tag
   will you: checking tag
4. an old man with a cup: gloss tag
5. lady: vocative tag
   so it can: restatement response

Exercise 11.8

From A sentences to B sentences:
   omit *it, be, that*
From B sentences to C sentences:
   move initial Adjunct to the other end of the clause.

Exercise 11.9
1. *it*-theme, with *the pearl* object.
2. FB rep.; P-bound clause, binder *what*.
3. Rankshifted subject *where we go for holidays*.
4. *it*-theme, with Adjunct *next year*; also a checking tag *isn't it*.
5. Adjunct theme *over there*.
6. FB rep. with *it* (compare *To see you is lovely*).
7. tag theme *Bill*, relating to Subject *he*.
8. it-theme with *the dog* subject.
9. FB rep. with *it* (compare *That Mr Plumtree has another engagement is unfortunate*).

Exercise 12.1
(*a*) These words are binding and listing adjuncts.

Listing adjuncts (A⁺)	*Binding adjuncts* (Aᴮ)
and	when
or	if
but	whether
	notwithstanding the fact that

(*b*) A listing adjunct precedes a binding adjunct.
(when he's tired) *and when* he's lonely
(Bill didn't say whether they'd go the short cut) *or whether* they might stay the night somewhere.

Exercise 12.2
These are linking adjuncts (Aᴸ). Examples of them in other positions:
1 (*a*) We, furthermore, must be perpetually aware of the competitive nature of the enterprise.
  (*b*) We must, furthermore, be perpetually aware of the competitive nature of the enterprise.
  (*c*) We must be, furthermore, perpetually aware of the competitive nature of the enterprise.
  (*d*) We must be perpetually aware, furthermore, of the competitive nature of the enterprise.
  (*e*) We must be perpetually aware of the competitive nature of the enterprise, furthermore.

2 (*a*) There's also the question of money.
  (*b*) There's the question, also, of money.
  (*c*) There's the question of money also.

3 (*a*) Why, then, did you bother phoning?
  (*b*) Why did you then bother phoning?
  (*c*) Why did you bother then phoning?
  (*d*) Why did you bother phoning, then?

4 (*a*) That, after all, sounded good at one time.
  (*b*) That sounded good, after all, at one time.
  (*c*) That sounded good at one time, after all.

5 (*a*) Bill, as a matter of fact, couldn't find the key.
  (*b*) Bill couldn't, as a matter of fact, find the key.
  (*c*) Bill couldn't find the key, as a matter of fact.

Exercise 12.3

These are the most likely sequences, but not the only possible ones.

1. We went home *in the morning.*
2. You'll find a pillar box and a phone box *at the end of the street.*
3. He got to know us quite well, *in time.*
4. He picked his way *carefully* among the sharp stones.
5. When we continued the debate *after ten* . . .
6. However, he was able to tell his story *between periods of pain.*
7. I have *seldom* listened to such poppycock.

Exercise 12.4

1. I need big nails, not these little ones.
2. I don't like as big a meal as that, really.
3. On the other hand, we can take table linen easily.
4. . . . and there is mince.
5. He'll recognise any aircraft you care to mention, first time.
6. Put chairs over here (tables down the corridor, please).

Exercise 12.5

1. Subject of bound adding clause.
2. Object of bound contingent clause.
3. Object of preposition *on* which is adjunct in bound reported clause.
4. A^B in bound reported clause.

Exercise 12.6

1. C	6. A^S	Where the *wh-word* is in the
2. O	7. Object of preposition	subject, the word-sequence is
3. A^G	8. A^G	SP; otherwise it is P[S] or
4. S	9. A	Paux S.
5. A^G	10. S	

Exercise 12.7

1. *nevertheless*: minor
   can you: neutral
2. *F clause*
   thus: minor
   five weeks hence: A-theme
   B clause
   in England: A-theme
3. *I*: neutral
4. *therefore*: minor
   early this morning: A-theme

5. *B clause*
   All of a sudden: A-theme
   F clause
   Bill-neutral
6. come: neutral
7. *F clause*
   who: (subject) *wh*-theme
   B clause
   next Tuesday: neutral
8. *his last chance*: O-theme

9. *B clause*
   after all this: A-theme
   F clause
   in Africa: A-theme
   how: *wh*-theme
10. *Will you*: neutral
11. *what*: *wh*-theme
12. *tomorrow*: A-theme
    what: *wh*-theme
13. *Your latest consignment*: O-theme
    however: minor
14. *F clause*
    Mr Plumtree: neutral
    B clause
    who is: neutral

15. *B clause*
    the very next day: A-theme
    F clause
    we: neutral
16. *Madge*: O-theme
17. *it*: neutral
    (but note contrastive *where*)
18. *whatever*: *wh*-theme
19. *calmly and skilfully*: A-theme
20. *F clause*
    How: *wh*-theme
    B clause
    you: neutral

Exercise 12.8
(13) it-theme; A
(14) it-theme; S
(15) it-theme; O
(16) it-theme; O (preposition)

Exercise 12.9
1. *last Friday*: major A-theme (checking tag isn't thematic)
2. *Are you*: neutral
3. *Now*: minor link theme
   Mr Plumtree: S-tag theme
4. *Madge*: major neutral theme (contrastive *wh*)
5. *Doris*: minor vocative theme
   Bill: major *it-S* theme
6. *whose party*: major *it-O* theme (prepositional object, contrastive *wh*)
7. *the dog*: major S-tag
8. *around here*: it-A theme
9. *Sir John*: minor vocative theme.
   last night: A-theme
   at what time: thematic *wh* (adjunct)
10. *I*: major neutral theme.

Exercise 13.1
1. In-P (P [A])
2. In-P (one-word P)
3. SAP (special emphasis on *mentioned*)
4. (a) In-P
   (b) Post-P
5. Post-P
6. SAP
7. In-P
8. (a) In-P (one-word P)
   (b) Post-P
9. A-theme

10. Post-P
11. SAP
12. In-P (one-word P)
13. In-P
14. In-P
15. SAP (special emphasis on *terrified*)
16. In-P (one-word P)
17. Post-P
18. In-P
19. In-P (one-word P)
20. A-theme

Exercise 13.2

In-P		Post-P	
always	nearly	last week	later
ever	never	at night	noisily
hardly	only	before	now
just	quite	by then	tonight
merely	rather	for a walk	to school
	usually		

Exercise 13.3

A. 1. never, scarcely, hardly, merely, rather, nearly, almost, usually, just, quite, only, ever.

2. still, always, often, already.

B. 1. quickly, quietly, noisily, willingly, later.

2. at home, in the kitchen, here, there, tonight, now, on Tuesday, last week, for a walk, before, at night, by then, to school.

not normally theme: just, only, merely, rather, almost, nearly.

(I) means 'only on new Tone group'

	In-P	Post-P	Notes	
never	√		P[S] when theme	⎫
scarcely	√	I	″ ″ ″	
hardly	√	I	″ ″ ″	
merely	√	I	″ ″ ″	
rather	√	I		
nearly	√	I		Class
almost	√	I		A1
usually	√	I		
just	√			
quite	√			
only	√			
ever	√	I		⎭
still	√	√	In-P is natural position	⎫
always	√	√	″ ″ ″ ″	A2
often	√	√	″ ″ ″ ″	
already	√	√	″ ″ ″ ″	⎭
quickly	√	√	Post-P is natural position	⎫
quietly	√	√	″ ″ ″ ″	
noisily	√	√	″ ″ ″ ″	B1
willingly	√	√	″ ″ ″ ″	
later	√	√	″ ″ ″ ″	⎭
at home		√		⎫
in the kitchen		√		
here		√		
there		√		
tonight		√		
now		√		
on Tuesday		√		B2
last week		√		
for a walk		√		
before		√		
at night		√		
by then		√		
to school		√		⎭

Exercise 13.4

1. *Easily* means 'as if it was easy'.
2. The sentence means 'it is easy for me to manage that', and *easily* in this meaning is never theme.
3. 'The chairman spoke in a definite manner, firmly'—Class B.
4. 'I'm sure that the chairman spoke'—Class A.

Exercise 13.5

(a)

place	*manner*	*time*
at the office	unexpectedly	yesterday
		at half past two.

(b) 1. Mr Plumtree lived happily before the war.
    2. Mr Plumtree lived here happily.
    3. Mr Plumtree lived here before the war.
    4. Mr Plumtree lived here happily before the war.

(c) z = place; Y = manner; x = time.

Exercise 13.6

place	*manner*	*time*
across the room	by himself	at 23.27
on the table	by train	last night
to me	by yourself	tomorrow
to Scotland	with a smile	yesterday

Exercise 13.7

place	*manner*	*time*
at home	quickly	on Tuesday
here	quietly	tonight
in the kitchen	willingly	
there		

Exercise 14.1

Objects: Nos. 3, 6, 7, 10, 11, 14. Complements: Nos. 1, 2, 8, 12, 15.
Adjuncts: Nos. 4, 5, 9, 13.

Exercise 14.2

N.B. other pronouns may be used, e.g. *this*, *one*.

(a) 3. it   10. him
    6. them   11. them
    7. it   14. them

(b) e.g. 1. important   (c) 4. daily
          12. very unhappy   5. eventually
          15. customary   13. quite soon

Exercise 14.3

1. *Them* is object in the clause, and so names other people than *the older boys*.
2. *a happy family* is complement in the clause, as we can see by trying to replace it by (*a*) an adjective group; (*b*) a pronominal group.
   (*a*) They stayed *very happy*.
   (*b*) *They stayed *us*.
3. (i) *visit* usually has an object
   (ii) *every week* is adjunct in the clause, although it is a nominal group. It can readily be replaced by an adverbial group or a prepositional group.
   (*a*) my cousins visit *often*
   (*b*) my cousins visit *on Fridays*
4. *reasonable* is complement and so the structure is *PC*, which is rare with P in the imperative. It is really a request to Dad to stop being unreasonable.
5. A moodless clause, structure *ZZ*. It is clearly related to the *SPC* clause
                          Bill is a good chap.
6. *Normally* is adjunct in the structure *SPCA*. We interpret it as meaning 'at normal times', 'on occasions'. We do not think of it as a qualitative adjunct 'in a normal fashion' as in
                     Madge spoke quite normally
   Our interpretation arises from the tendency of *PC* structures not to contain qualitative adjuncts.
7. The verb *prove* is rather like *turn*: it can occur with many, but not all, adjectival groups.
   (*a*) *the dress proved red   (*c*) *Bill proved unhappy
   (*b*) the weather proved cloudy   (*d*) his injuries proved fatal
8. Technically, this clause is ambiguous, though meaning (ii) below is the one we would normally assume.
   (i) Bill was tired by almost any effort.
   (ii) We didn't go out because Bill felt tired.
9. The verb *sit* does not occur with a complement except in a few clichés, like this one, and *sit tight*.

Exercise 14.4

1. B *cont.*	6. B *cont.*	11. B *cont.*	16. A
2. O	7. C	12. C	17. C
3. O	8. B *cont.*	13. A	18. B *cont.*
4. C	9. C	14. O	19. B *add.*
5. C	10. C	15. B *cont.*	20. C

Exercise 15.1

Verb	Class	Indirect and direct object	Direct object only	Indirect object only	Notes
allow wish	a a	11 13			Between the extremes of classes (a) and (b) there is a lot of variation;
bring finish grant	b b b	7 9 15	16 5 4		grant is far closer to class (a) than bring, and bring is closer than finish. Finish is only rarely used with a double object.
ask promise	c c	1 12	(6) (8)	10 3	Sentences 6 and 8 are not a very common type, and ask and promise are reporting verbs.
pay	d	2	14	17	pay is on a borderline, like feed. In I paid him it is doubtful if him should be analysed as the indirect object.

Exercise 15.2

1. SPOC (C-S or perhaps C-O)
2. SPOO
3. SPOC (C-O)
4. SPOO
5. SPOC (C-O)
6. SPOC (C-O)
7. SPOC (C-O or perhaps C-S)
8. SPOO
9. SPOO
10. SPOC (C-O)

Note: Notice the difference in meaning of the *find* verbs. No. 5 is the usual meaning of *find*, but no. 3 is more like *we decided that he was irresponsible*. No. 5, of course, is ambiguous, as it could be interpreted as the same structure as no. 8.

Exercise 15.3

1. O^I
2. O^D
3. O^D
4. C (cliché)
5. A
6. S
7. O^D
8. C
9. O^I
10. O^D
11. O^I
12. O^D
13. O^D
14. O^D
15. O^I
16. C
17. O^I
18. C

Exercise 16.1

(a) agree   mean   (b) remember   expect
    remember   expect   bear   choose
    bear   choose   refuse   begin
    refuse   pretend   deserve
    deserve   begin

Note: *mean* is not in the (b) list although *I mean you* occurs. This point cannot be discussed in full here, but note that *you* must be stressed. Pronoun objects do not have to meet this restriction. (See also *say.*)

Exercise 16.2

(a) bear   ask   (b) bear
    mean   teach   mean
    expect   tell   expect
    choose   command   choose
    find   think   ask

Exercise 16.3

1. PP;   2. PP;   3. P O/s P;   4. PP;   5. PP;
like occurs in both types of phase.

Exercise 16.4

manage; continue; remember; like; try; can't bear.

Exercise 16.5

remember; fancy; keep; like; can't bear.

Exercise 16.6

(a) 1. S P O/s P A   (b) 4. PP (P)   (d) all except *make*
    2. P O/s P A   6. P O/s P (Pto)
    3. P [SA] O/s P A   8. P O/s P (P Ø)
    4. S P P O
    5. S P O/s P A   (c) 1. feel
    6. S P O/s P O A   2. make
    7. S P O/s P A   3. see
    8. P [S] O/s P O Voc.   5. notice
                                 7. hear

Exercise 16.7

I am very happy to introduce . . .   I am happy for you to introduce . . .
He seemed rather sorry to leave.
Bill was extremely lucky to escape.

                                          The stranger was anxious for me to
                                          communicate . . .
Are you quite content to settle . . .   Are you content for me to settle?

Exercise 17.1

1. q (rankshift)	6. A, S, O, S
2. o, o	7. *Madge's* m; *Madge's uncle*: O/s; *last night*: A
3. S, q, O	8. m, S A
4. O, o	9. S
5. O	10. o

Exercise 17.2

shape	boy	groceries	we	Madge's	friend's	he
statue	age	house	you	uncle	mother	station
hours	tie	week	John	night	way	

Exercise 17.3

1. that	4. the, the	7. Madge's, last
2. the	5. the	8. my best friend's, my best, this
3. a, his own	6. next	10. the

Exercise 17.4

1. cows, milk, they	4. that, you, it	7. we, several
2. we	5. anyone, tennis	8. beer, you
3. he	6. Bill	9. walking
		10. I, meetings

Exercise 17.5

1. Nurse (proper)
2. Walsall (common)
3. Shakespeare (common)
4. Captain (proper)
5. Uncle (proper)
6. John Smith's (common)

(b) 1. Do you want to be a nurse?
2. Walsall is in the West Midlands.
3. Most people have heard of Shakespeare.
4. We must pick a captain.
5. That man is my wife's uncle.
6. Isn't it awful to be called John Smith?

Exercise 17.6

1. (iv) *one or two* is an idiom meaning *just a few*.
2. (iii); 3. (iii); 4. (i), (ii); 5. (iii); 6. (ii), (ii);
7. (iv) *one . . . another* form a pattern of contrast like *this . . . that*.

Exercise 17.7

1. one; 2. ones (possibly *one*); 3. ones; 4. one; 5. ones . . .

Exercise 17.8

(a)		(b)		(c)	
1.	dh, eh	1.	hq, h	1.	h
2.	hq, xh	2.	hq	2.	h, h, h,
3.	dohq, eh	3.	hq	3.	h
4.	dhq	4.	hq		
5.	dh	5.	hq		
6.	hq, deh	6.	hq		
7.	dh	7.	hq		
8.	eh, dh	8.	hq		
9.	deh	9.	hq		

Exercise 17.9

1. dhq (common)
2. h (proper)
3. oeh (common)
4. oh (common)
5. dhq (common)
6. h (proper)
7. h (proper)
8. ohq (common)
9. dhq (common), h (proper), dh (common)
10. dh (pronoun)
11. dh (common) [h otherwise adjective]
12. dh (common), deh (common)
13. deh (common)
14. hq (pronoun)
15. hq (pronoun)
16. h (common)
17. dhq (common)
18. hq (pronoun)
19. dhq (common) [h usually proper]
20. dh (pronoun)

Exercise 18.1

	A	B		A	B
1.	place	Lake Lebro	2.	Anyone	I
	we	which			brother-in-law
	holiday	spot		who	who
	year	year		himself	
	village			doctor	doctor
	mountains	mountains			
3.	man	Sir William Plumtree	4.	I	I
	whom	whom		spinach	hot-pot
	I	I		that	which
	voice			mush	mutton
	yours	that			potatoes
5.		I	6.	I	I
	remarks	remark		season	April
	speaker	I		flowers	flowers
		heat			
		moment			

Exercise 18.2

1. clause. r/s. s	5. group. r/s. d	9. clause. r/s. q
2. clause. r/s. q	6. clause. r/s. q	10. clause. r/s. q
3. clause. r/s. q	7. clause. r/s. s	11. clause. not r/s. B *add.*
4. clause. not r/s. B *add.*	8. group. r/s. d	12. clause. r/s. q

Exercise 18.3

	(a)	(b)			(a)	(b)
1. a week	q	Nom. Gp.	7. approaching		q	vbl. Gp.
2. the same length	q	Nom. Gp.	8. what he thinks		s	clause
3. no rankshift			9. you saw		q	clause
4. no rankshift			10. to read		q	vbl. Gp.
5. the next day	q	Nom. Gp.	11. Bill's		d	Nom. Gp.
6. occasionally	q	Adv. Gp.	12. he said		q	clause

6. occasionally (but if you interpret it as if *occasionally* can occur as theme or at the end of the clause, it is an adjunct and there is no rankshift)

	(a)	(b)
13. recommended	q	vbl. Gp.
14. in a green suit	q	prep. Gp.
15. people's	d	nom. Gp.

Exercise 19.1

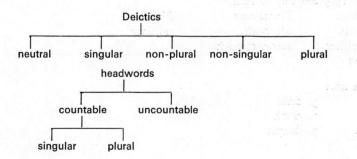

	Deictics	Headwords
neutral	singular A, EACH, ANOTHER	countable—singular COW
THE	non-plural THAT, THIS	uncountable FURNITURE
HIS		
THEIR	non-singular ENOUGH, SOME	countable—plural COWS
	plural BOTH, THESE, THOSE	

Deictics
— neutral — singular — non-plural — non-singular — plural

headwords
— countable — uncountable

countable
— singular — plural

Exercise 19.2

some (unstressed)	:	general.	**all some trouble* **all some songs*
a	:	general.	(*you are all a great trouble to me* is a different structure, where *all* is qualifier of *you*, as in *you all are . . .*)
enough	:	general.	**all enough cabbage* **all enough chocolates*
another	:	general.	**all another wood*
each	:	general.	**all each coffee*
both	:	general.	**all both coffees*
that	:	specific.	*all that wheel*
his	:	specific.	*all his obvious virtues*
their	:	specific.	*all their troubles*
the	:	specific.	*all the woods*
these	:	specific.	*all these cabbages*
this	:	specific.	*all this money*
those	:	specific.	*all those soldiers*

NUMBER

neutral : specific;   singular : general;   non-plural : specific; non-singular : general;   plural : mixed.

Exercise 19.3

General	Specific
all	Bill's
any	my
every	
no	

Exercise 19.4

Total	Partial
each	some
both	enough
all	another
every	any
no	a

Exercise 19.5 See key to 19.4.

Singular noun	Plural noun	Neutral
every, each, neither, either, a, another	all, both, some, enough	no, any

Exercise 20.1

1. deh
2. doh
3. denh
4. doeh
5. dnh
6. donh
7. doenh

Exercise 20.2

1. onh, dh
2. doenh
3. onh
4. oeh, dh
5. dnh
6. denh
7. deh, dh
8. eh
9. doh, deh
10. dnh

Exercise 20.3

1. $s^{t}e^{a}h$
2. $d\ s^{c}e^{a}e^{b}h\ q^{s}$
3. $o^{c}e^{a}e^{b}h$, dnh
4. $d\ e^{a}s\ e^{b}h$
5. $d\ s^{t}e^{a}h$
6. $d\ o^{c}e^{b}n\ h$, $d\ s^{c}e^{a}h\ q^{s}$
7. dnh, dnh
8. $d\ s\ e^{b}h$, dnh, $d\ e^{b}n\ h$
9. $s^{t}e^{a}h$, $d\ e^{a}h$
10. $d\ s^{s}e^{a}h$, dnh

Exercise 20.4

1. a small house
　a red house
　a suburban house
2. a small suburban house
3. a very red house
4. a very suburban house
5. a very small red suburban house

Exercise 20.5

1. $d\ s^{t}e^{a}e^{c}h$
2. $d\ e^{c}h$
3. $o\ e^{c}e^{c}h$
4. $d\ e^{c}h$, dnh
5. $d\ e^{a}e^{c}h$
6. $e^{c}h$
7. $d\ e^{a}e^{c}h$
8. $d\ s\ e^{b}e^{c}h$ (or $d\ e^{a}e^{b}e^{c}h$, but much less likely)
9. $e^{c}h$
10. $d\ e^{a}e^{b}e^{c}h$

Exercise 21.1

```
 T    S
instruction-manual
 T
holder
 T    (S)
coal-merchants
 T
foundation
 T  (S) (T)
buffet-car service
 T   S   T
radio-control facilities
 T   S   T
car-battery filler
```

```
   S      S
chrome kitchen fittings
 S   S   T
Latin grammar texts
  S    S
Worthing cantilever
 T
bridge
 S   S   T
factory lightning strike
 S   S   T
ebony desk calendar
```

```
 T    S    T
army trials-driver
 T    T   (S)
Latin word-count
  S    T
transistor radio-set
 S    T
police patrol-car
 S    T   (S)
pocket address-book
```

Exercise 21.2

1. C
2. A
3. D (snsh)
4. A
5. A
6. C
7. B
8. A
9. B
10. A
11. B
12. C
13. A
14. D (nnsh)
15. D (nsnh)
16. A
17. B
18. A

Exercise 21.3

e^a^: 3. 4. 5. 7. 9. 10. 11. 12. 13. 14. 15.   e^c^: 1. 2. 6. 8.

Exercise 21.4

e^a^: 2. 4. 5. 7. 10. 11.   e^c^: 1. 3. 6. 8. 9. 12.

Exercise 22.1

	(a)	(b)		(a)	(b)
1.	has gone	gone	6. is	is
2.	works	works	7. should be being questioned	questioned
3.	might have fallen	fallen	8. see	see
4.	can't be spoken	spoken	9. is needed	needed
5.	do want	want	10. used to be praised	praised

Exercise 22.2

might takes the base of the next word
can't takes the base of the next word
be often takes the n-form of the next word
do takes the base of the next word
should takes the base of the next word
used takes the to-form of the next word

Exercise 22.3

1. could have gone
   (*could have to go* is not included because it is a phase structure of two verbal groups)
2. must wash
3. have slept
   had slept
4. is to drive   was to drive   5. To sit   is
   is driving   was driving   sitting   was
   is going to drive   was going to drive   6. does . . . like
   is driven   was driven   did . . . like

Exercise 22.4

1. needn't run
2. ought to have arrived
3. 'll be coming
   'll be going to come
   (*come* has no passive)
4. may be announced
   (*by the headmaster* shows that this example is a passive)
5. used to fish
6. shall speak

Auxiliaries

has have; might; can't; do; should; be being is to be; used; ought; must; needn't; 'll, shall; may

Exercise 22.5

(13) is incorrect because *needn't* must be a modal and so must be followed by the base-form *see*

You needn't see that picture

Another solution is to convert *needn't* to *don't need*

You don't need to see that picture

(14) is incorrect because *need* is not a modal and so should be the s-form of the main verb *needs*; also the base-form *have* must be changed to *to have* for the correct phase concord.

She needs to have someone talk to her sharply

Exercise 22.6

couldn't; mustn't; haven't; hadn't; isn't; wasn't; doesn't; didn't; ought not; won't; may not; didn't used; shan't.

Exercise 23.1

1. *pleased*: n-form or d-form. There is no subject, so it is non-finite n-form.
   retired: n-form or d-form. Subject present, so d-form.
2. *wants*: s-form. always finite (must have subject).
3. *will help*: modal (always finite) and base-form, here is concord with modal.
   load: base-form, phase with *help* (see Section 16).
4. *ate*: d-form, always finite.
5. *to start*: to-form, always non-finite
   insert: base-form; no subject, imperative.
6. *navigating*: ing-form, always finite
   set: base-form or d-form of this verb: subject present so ambiguously finite *base* (like *come*) or d-form (*came*).

Exercise 23.2

1. a settled state of affairs; now, and for some time past and future.
2. his habit is to cycle, but there is no suggestion that he is at present cycling.
3. the verb here does a job—that of accepting. Once the sentence is spoken, the deal is made. The moment of accepting is the moment of uttering the words (like the moment of marrying, nominating, etc.).
4. present time is probably relevant here because of the urgency of the verb *need*—but it can readily be interpreted like no. 1—as a regular state of affairs, not connected with the immediate present.
5. an inherent quality in the fabric; hardly anything to do with time.

Exercise 23.3

1. *am* direct
2. *hit* indirect (but ambiguous with direct form in this verb)
3. *will* (modal) direct
4. *ought* (modal) direct
5. *was* indirect
   set indirect (but ambiguous with direct form in this verb)
6. *can* (modal) direct
7. *have* present

8. *hurt* direct (but ambiguous)
   drive direct
9. *'re* direct
10. *was* indirect
11. *had* indirect
12. *was* indirect
13. *is* direct
14. *may* direct

15. *were* indirect
16. *'ve* direct
17. *graduates* direct
18. *hurt* indirect (but ambiguous)
    drove indirect
19. *'d* (modal) direct
20. *told* indirect

Exercise 23.4

1. direct: settled state
2. *just now*: immediate past time
3. modal
4. modal
5. *when we set out*: timing of indirect
6. modal
7. *before*: *have* is a present form but relates to past events
8. *every time I drive*: statement of habit
9. direct: present time reference is assumed
10. *at first*: timing of indirect
11. *before last night*: timing of indirect

12. *in his youth*: timing of indirect
13. *now*: actual moment of utterance
14. modal
15. *earlier on*: timing of indirect
16. *for years*: *have* is a present form but relates to past events
17. *next July*: direct; timed in the future
18. *every time I drove*: timing of indirect
19. modal
20. indirect but refers to the present —the sentence in its common meaning is occasioned by Bill being there.

Exercise 23.5

1.

wanting	to watch	cleared
b	b	f, i
ŋ	t	d
v	v	v

2.

would	contemplate
f	b
ø	ø
m	v

3.

don't	enjoy
f, u	b
øneg	ø
m*	v

4.

was	being	followed
f, i	b	b
d	ŋ	n
be	be	v

m* do is treated separately in Section 24.

5.

've	been	hearing
f, u	b	b
ø	n	ŋ
h	be	v

6.

Released	can	look
b	f	b
n	ø	ø
v	m	v

7.

to have	smelt
b	b
t	n
h	v

ought	to have	cheered
f	b	b
ø	t	n
m	h	v

8.

were	bothering
f, i	b
d	ŋ
be	v

Exercise 24.1

1. . . . *does eat* . . .: emphasis
2. . . . *feeling* . . .: *do* is never non-finite as an auxiliary
   . . . *did used* . . .: emphasis: rare among educated speakers, but shows that *used* does not have all the characteristics of a modal.
3. . . . *will* . . . *help make*: *do* never before non-finite or auxiliaries
4. . . . *did like to run*: emphasis
5. . . . *do chip* . . .: emphasis
6. . . . *hasn't been delivered* . . .: not before auxiliary
7. . . . *won't do* . . .: not before auxiliary

Exercise 24.2

1. *do* as non-final word, at place *v* can occur only when *x* and *v* coincide. So no auxiliaries precede or follow *do*.
2. It is used when the verbal group has only made a single choice, but where there are syntactic reasons for requiring a two-word group—for interrogative, negative and emphatic verbal groups.

Exercise 24.3

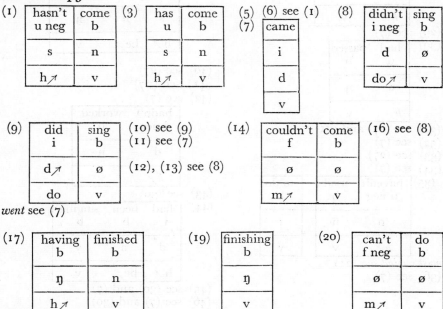

(1)

hasn't	come
u neg	b
s	n
h↗	v

(3)

has	come
u	b
s	n
h↗	v

(5)
(7)

(6) see (1)

came
i
d
v

(8)

didn't	sing
i neg	b
d	ø
do↗	v

(9)

did	sing
i	b
d↗	ø
do	v

went see (7)

(10) see (9)
(11) see (7)

(12), (13) see (8)

(14)

couldn't	come
f	b
ø	ø
m↗	v

(16) see (8)

(17)

having	finished
b	b
ŋ	n
h↗	v

went see (7)

(19)

finishing
b
ŋ
v

(20)

can't	do
f neg	b
ø	ø
m↗	v

(21)

can't	tie
will	do
f	b
ø	ø
m↗	v

see (20)   (22)

do
u
ø
v

(23) see (8)   (25)

hadn't	finished
i neg	b
d	n
h	v

(Exercise 24.1 examples)

1.

eats
u
s
v

2. see (19)

used to fall	
f	b
ø	t
m↗	v

3. will help. see (21)

make
b
ø
phase

4. see (7)

to run
b
t
phase

5. see (22)

6. hasn't been delivered

u neg	b	b
s	n ↗	n
h↗	be	v

(pass)

7. see (20)

(Exercise 24.3 cont)

(27)

have	passed
u	b
ø	
h↗	v

(29) see (7)

(30)

had	passed
u	b
d	n
h↗	v

(31) see (27) and (21)
(32) see (7)
(33) see (27)
(34) see (7)

(35)

haven't	used		to do
u neg	b		b
ø	n		t
h↗	v		v

must remind see (21)
(36) see (7)

(37) see (35)
(38) see (27)
(39)

has	been	singing
u	b	b
s	n	ŋ
h↗	be↗	v

(40) see (27)
(41) see (27)
(42) see (7)

hadn't	worked
i neg	b
d	n
h↗	v

(43) see (30)
(44)

had	been	singing
i	b	b
d	n	y
h↗	be↗	v

(45) see (30) and (7)
(46) see (7) and (30)

Exercise 24.4

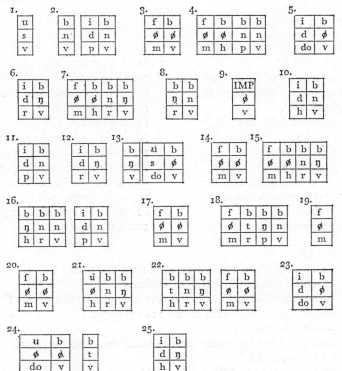

Exercise 24.5

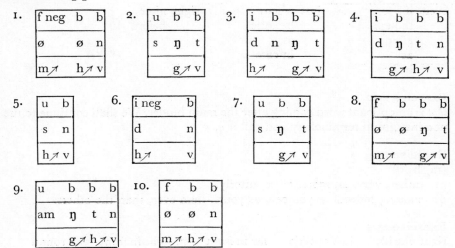

Exercise 25.1

even	if	just	when	right	after
	though		because		before
	after		as		
	as		in case		
	before				

Exercise 25.2

that is an optional word coming after the main binder. We shall continue to use nominal group terminology and call it *q*.

Exercise 25.3

(m) h (q)

m: rather, very, as, more, quite, utterly.

q: enough, indeed, as you can, as yours, than ever, than the others.

Exercise 25.4

right	outside	just	outside	far	in front	straight	in front	all	round
	in front		in front		ahead		ahead		
	ahead		ahead		in		in		
	around				up		up		
	in								
	up								

Exercise 25.5

1. m h; lexical adv.; special
2. m h q; lexical adv.; regular
3. m h q; lexical adv.; regular
4. h; gram. adv.
5. m h; lexical adv.; special
6. h; lexical adv.; regular
7. m h; gram. adv.
8. m h; lexical adv.; regular
9. m h q; lexical adv.; regular (*better* as comparative is symbolised *m h*)
10. m h; adjective
11. h q; gram. adv.
12. m h; adjective
13. m h q; lexical adv.; regular
14. m h; gram. adv.
15. h q; gram. adv.
16. m h; lexical adv.; special
17. m h; lexical adv.; special
18. m h; lexical adv.; special
19. m h q; lexical adv.; regular
20. m h; gram. adv.
21. m h; lexical adv.; regular
22. h q; adjective

Exercise 25.6

(a) (1) The Palace Yard . . . is accessible from the road   F
       in which stands the statue of Ptolemy   B *add.*

   (2) A second difficulty . . . is the cost of travel in this area   F
       which I shall deal with in the next chapter   B *add.*

   (3) whole sentence   F
       that you have just come from: rankshifted q to *the square*

   (4) whole sentence F
       we went to: rankshifted q to *the place*.

(b) (1) *in which; of Ptolemy; from the road*
   (2) *with—which* at beginning of clause; *in the next chapter; in this area*
   (3) *to the square that you have just come from*
       from—that at beginning of clause
   (4) *to*—no object present.

Exercise 25.7
just   rather   very   straight   for all the world   right   all   far

Exercise 25.8
1. in addition to	8. in spite of
2. but for	9. in the course of
3. due to	10. because of (*just* is a modifier)
4. out of	11. nearer to
5. owing to	12. up to
6. out of	for
7. on top of	13. apart from
	14. by reason of

The compound prepositions end in a word which is commonly found on its own as a preposition—*to, for, of, from.* Those with three or more words have a preposition also as their first word.

Exercise 25.9
1. e	6. g	Notice that *set* (no. 7) is normally transitive, and *look*
2. i	7. j	(no. 6) is normally intransitive. Here the phrasal verb
3. c	8. b	usage gives them extra syntactic possibilities, as well as
4. f	9. d	new meaning.
5. a	10. h	

Exercise 25.10
1. a ii, b i (swallowed it up)	6. a i, b i
2. a i, b ii	7. a iii, b ii
3. b i (no phrasal verb)	8. a i, b i
4. a iii, b i	9. a i, b ii
5. a iv, b i	

Exercise 25.11
1. PAA. a i, b i, b ii, c ii
2. a ii, b i, c i
3. a iii, b ii, c i, d (but not restricted to imperatives)
4. a i, b i, c i
5. a i, b i, c i
6. not phrasal verb usage (b ii, c i)
7. a iii, b i, c ii
8. a i, b i, c i, d

9. a iii, b i, c ii, d (but not restricted to imperatives)
10. a iv, b i, c i
11. a i, b ii, c ii
12. a ii, b i, c ii, d
13. a i, b i, c ii
14. a ii, b i, c ii
15. a i, b ii, c i, d (but not restricted to imperatives)
16. a iii, b i, c ii (but not passive also, so can be transitive when active)
17. not phrasal verb usage (b i, ci)
18. a i, b i, c i
19. PAA. a i, b i, b ii, c ii
20. a ii, b i, c ii

Selective Glossary

The number of new terms in this book have been kept as low as possible and many traditional terms are used, usually in their best-known meanings. But it may be useful until all the terms become quite familiar, to have quick access to a note on their meanings. The glossary also functions as an index, giving section and page references to full text discussions of the terms.

It is not designed as a general glossary of English grammatical terminology, and concentrates on the terms that are frequently used in this book.

Add(ing)
A class of *bound* clauses, sometimes called *non-defining relative* clauses. They usually start with a relative pronoun, e.g. *who, which*. They indicate extra optional details of meaning and normally refer to an *antecedent* in the clause they are bound to. (Section 3).

Addressee
The person spoken to, or written to, in an act of verbal communication. See *speaker*. (Introduction, page 2).

Adjectival Group, or adjective–head group
A group whose headword is an adjective. Cannot be subject of a clause, but is regularly complement. (Sections 14 and 15)

example:

	m	h	q
She is	*very*	*sweet*	*indeed*.

See Table 25.1 for relations with adverb-head groups.

Adjective
A word class chiefly occurring:
(*a*) as headword of adjectival group, standing as complement in the clause (Table 25.1)
(*b*) as modifier of a noun headword of nominal group (Section 20).

Adjunct
An element of clause structure, symbol A.
Its main exponents are:
(*a*) Lexical Adjuncts
   (i) adverb-head groups, e.g. *very faintly*
   (ii) preposition-head groups, e.g. *in Italy*
   (iii) nominal groups, e.g. *the next day* in *I returned the next day*
(*b*) Grammatical Adjuncts
   Linking and binding elements in the clause (e.g. *and, but, when, that*)
use the same symbol, as also responses like *yes, no*.

Section 25 analyses adverbial groups. Sections 12 and 13 discuss the positioning of adjuncts in the clause, because they are very mobile, and structures ASP, SAP, SP[A], SPA are all found.

Grammatical adjuncts are discussed throughout Chapter 1, but particularly Fig. 8.1 and Section 9.

Adverbial Group (Section 25)
One of the three group types in English (see also nominal and verbal groups). Subdivided into prepositional, adverb-head and adjective-head.

Affected Entity (E)
The name used here for one of the categories of deep grammar, explained in the Introduction, page 7. Its closest parallel in surface grammar is the direct object.

Agree(ment) (with)
Concord; where one choice determines another. For example in the nominal group *another boy* the two words choose each other; **other boy*, **another boys* are both wrong, and *other boys* means 'more than one other boy'. The deictic and the noun agree in number, that is they are in number concord with each other.

See also **the boy sing*. Either *boy* or *sing* must have an *s* to make the structure grammatical.

the boy sings: singular, one boy
the boys sing: plural, more than one boy.

Antecedent
A nominal group to which a B[add] clause refers. In everyday English it is not necessary for every B[add] clause to have an antecedent—see Section 3.

Apposition
A very general term in traditional grammar to indicate various relationships, e.g.

my friend Bill . . .
we Europeans . . .
Lord Snooks . . .
The river Thames . . .
the notion that we should vote . . .
Then he arrived, my uncle, . . .

See *gloss tags* in Section 11, rankshifted clauses in Section 18, and some discussion in Section 14, around fig. 14.4.

Article
The traditional name given to *a* (indefinite article) and *the* (definite article).

In Section 17 and particularly Section 19 they are described as typical examples of *deictics*.

Auxiliary Verb
Any verb which can be used in front of the main verb of a verbal group. Usually the list comprises modal verbs, *have* and *be*. In this book a few others, e.g. *going* (*to*) are included. Auxiliaries feature all over the grammar, and are dealt with particularly in Section 22, and the beginning of Section 24.

Base (form of the verb)
The verb without any endings and without *to* in front, e.g. *come*, *see*.

See notes to Table 22.1.

Binder
A general term for the element in clause structure that shows that a clause is bound. Usually it is an adjunct (symbol A[B]), e.g. *when, as soon as, why*, but it can be subject or object (S[B], O[B]) like *who, which*. The range is shown in Section 9.

Bound Clause
(Often called subordinate or dependent.) A clause whose structure does not affect the contextual function of the sentence (i.e. statement, question, command or response). There are three main types: contingent, adding and reported. Most of Chapter 1 is about bound clauses.

Branching
A feature of some co-ordinate structures; see Section 8.
branched
Mr Plumtree likes fish and eats some every day.
unbranched
Mr Plumtree likes fish, and he eats some every day.

Cardinal (numeral)
One, two, three etc. Section 20 refers.

Case
Traditionally the cases of nouns and some other words are different forms that the words take according to their syntactic function, e.g. subject, prepositional object, vocative. In modern English the personal pronouns still show the remnants of a case system, e.g. *he* (subject), *him* (non-subject); *my* (modifier), *mine* (headword), *myself* (reflexive meaning).

Recently, the notion of case in deep structure has been developed. The various categories of deep structure illustrated in the Introduction, M, E, I are considered 'cases' of nominal groups in relation to P, and these deep cases remain the same whatever the surface structure.

Category
A very general term for the classifications made by a grammar. See Introduction, page 4.

Checking Tag
Section 11. Example:
Apples taste nice, don't they?

Class
A list of grammatical items defined by one or more syntactic criteria, i.e. arising from terms in systemic choice. The list may be one-member only, e.g. *the, 's,* or indefinitely large, e.g. common noun. See Introduction, page 13.

Clause
One of the ranks of English grammar, lying between *sentence* and *group.* The main additions to clause structure in this book—Chapter 2—are:
(*a*) to admit clauses with non-finite predicators, or no predicators at all, because of the syntactic function of the items. See Section 7.
(*b*) to allow more than one predicator in the clause—see phase (Section 16) and tags (Section 11).

Cliché
A frequent co-occurrence of words which follows the general pattern of grammatical rules but needs a special note on its meaning, e.g. *fall ill, blue blood.* See also *idiom.*

Collective
Fig. 19.3. In this book the term roughly refers to a singular noun occurring with a plural verb. *The committee have met.*

Command
An utterance that shows expectation of an action, whether verbal or not. Contrasted in Section 1 with *statement, question* and *response.*

Common Noun

A word that can form the headword of a full nominal group; in particular one that can be preceded by a deictic (e.g. *the*). Chapter 3 deals with nominal groups, and Section 17 distinguishes common nouns.

Comparative

A type of submodification of adjective—see Fig. 20.2. There are two forms:

(a) suffix *-er*, e.g. *nicer* (most words of one or two syllables)

(b) submodifier *more*, e.g. *more energetic* (some two syllable words and all with three or more).

Complement

An adjective-head group or nominal group substitute, in a dependent relationship with the predicator. (Section 14).

Componence

One of the three types of grammatical evidence (the other two are *meaning* and *syntax*). The internal structure of a grammatical item. The three types of evidence are discussed in various places: see Sections 1 and 5 for example.

Concord

See *Agreement*.

Constituent

Part of a structure which has its own coherent structure, or is a morpheme. This is a very general term used many times in the book.

E.g. in the clause *my friend/went/to London* the constituents of the clause are as marked, so that there is no constituent *friend went* or *went to*.

Contact

See Section 8.

Cont(ingent)

One of the three classes of bound clause (see also *adding* and *reported*). Similar to the traditional class of adverbial clause but including also clauses without finite predicators. See Sections 2, 3 and 7.

Continuous

A verb form *be* + *ing-form*. See Section 23.

Co-ordinate

A structure which is related to but not subordinate to another. Typically beginning with *and*; other linkers as shown in Section 8. See also *branching*.

Copula

The verb *be* when it is the main verb of a verbal group.

Copy (tag)

Section 11.

Example: *He's going to cause a fuss, is he?*

Countable

A feature of some common nouns. They have two forms, singular and plural, like *boy/boys* and the singular can occur with *a* as deictic. Section 19.

Declarative

See *mood*, and Sections 1 and 10.

Deep (grammar)

A recent development in grammatical theory is the distinction between *deep* and *surface* grammar. The Introduction gives a very brief illustration. The surface structure of an utterance is held to be no more than an indication of the deep structure, which is derived by

(a) making general statements to cover many examples which

might have quite different surface structures.

(*b*) making particular rules to relate the 'deep' statements of (*a*) to the surface structures.

The grammar in this book ignores the distinction between deep and surface, but chooses the level of abstraction for each description on practical criteria. Each stage in depth adds complexity to the grammar, and the justification of that complexity (in terms of eventual simplifications) is not easy.

Defining (relative clause)
This kind of clause is analysed as a rankshifted qualifier to a nominal group, and is thus quite different from a non-defining relative clause (see *adding*). A defining structure has the meaning of selection. Example: *Many people* I TALKED TO *were tourists.* Of the general set 'people' there is a subset 'people I talked to' identified. See Section 18.

Degree
A traditional term to describe the sort of meaning given by submodifiers *very, more, most.* See fig. 20.2.

Deictic
An important class of modifier of the nominal group, also called *determiner.* Typical examples *the, this, that, my, his, John's, a, each, all, every, some.* Fairly fully treated in Section 19.

Delicacy
Introduction 14. Example: If the class of bound clauses is divided into three sub-classes, these sub-classes are more delicate than the whole class. If among the contingent clauses there is a distinction between 'P-bound' and 'P-finite', this gives rise to a still more delicate classification.

Demonstrative Pronouns:
this that these those
See fig. 17.2, and Sections 17 and 19 for the syntax of these words.

Depth
Recursive subordination—see Section 8.

Direct (tense)
See Present-Direct.

Direct Object
Section 15 distinguishes direct and indirect objects. The part of the introduction on deep grammar is also relevant.

Double Transitivity
Of a verb: capable of occurring with two *objects,* one *direct* and one *indirect.* Of a clause: contains the elements O^I and O^D.

Dual
A special form, in between singular and plural, for indicating two of anything. There are traces in modern English (*between, both, the other, neither, the more interesting picture*), but the meaning of 'twoness' is not respected.

Element
Each symbol of a structural formula denotes an element of the structure. So the first sentence of this entry has the structure F, i.e. a one-element, or simple structure. The free clause has the structure SPC. This is a three-element structure of subject, predicator and complement. See Introduction.

Ethic Dative
See Section 15.

Exponent
Example: *Mr Plumtree wanted an apple.* This is a sentence, structure F. The exponent of F is *Mr Plumtree wanted*

an apple. F is a free clause structure SPO; the exponent of S is *Mr Plumtree*, of P is *wanted* and of O is *an apple*. O is a nominal group structure dh and the exponent of d is *an*, of h is *apple*. See Introduction, page 4.

Finite
A clause whose predicator is finite is potentially a free clause. The distinction between finite and non-finite runs through this grammar. The forms are listed in Section 22 and explained on page 175.

Foot
In phonology, a unit that contains one stressed syllable. It starts at the onset of one stressed syllable and continues until the onset of the next. See page 16 and Volume 2 of this course.

Free (clause)
A clause that can determine the contextual type of a sentence. See Section 1.

Future
Time reference in the verb is treated in Section 24. Some modern grammars regard English as having no future tense at all, but in this account the form *be going to* is described as a tense.

General
A class of deictic (Section 19) that does not involve identification of the referent(s) of the nominal group:
a, some, all, both, enough, another, each, every, no, neither, any
the other class is *specific*.

Global (nominal group)
A nominal group without *d* or *o*. See Section 19.

Gloss (Tag)
See Section 11.

Govern
The grammatical relationship between a verb, or a preposition, and its *object*.
Bill threw an apple to Madge
an apple is governed by *threw* and *Madge* is governed by *to*.

Group
One of the ranks of English grammar, lying in between *word* and *clause*. There are three types of group, *nominal, verbal* and *adverbial*. Chapters 3 and 4 describe groups, and the relation of group to the other ranks is described on page 12 of the Introduction.

Headword
In nominal groups, the word which is both lexically and grammatically most important. Lexically it names a set, and the *modifiers* and *qualifiers* select within that set. Thus *five red houses in my street*.

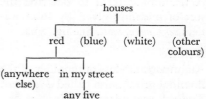

Grammatically the headword is essential (to the structure) in the case of countable nouns, because it carries the number-choice.

Section 25 shows groups with adverbs and adjectives as headwords.

Idiom
A structure where the general rules of grammar do not apply. Grammar states broad rules that apply to large

classes of words, but there is a contrary principle in language, a tendency to fix phrases and give them unique meanings.

Example: *at* + Nominal Group (*at my house*, etc.)

this is a general grammatical structure.

at home is restricted (*school/ play/rest*)

but still grammatical.

at loggerheads is unique, meaning *opposed*,

and so is an idiom.

Imperative

A finite use of the *base* form of the verb, which does not allow a grammatical subject. The basis of commands in English—dealt with in the mood system in Section 10. See also Section 1.

Indirect (tense)

See Past-Indirect.

Indirect Object

See also the part of the Introduction on Deep Grammar. In this treatment of English the term *indirect object* is used only for nominal groups, and not prepositional groups. Consequently:

(*a*) I gave her the book   SPO^{IO}D
(*b*) I gave the book to her   SPOA

Section 15 explains this point in more detail.

Infinitive

The form of the verb preceded by *to*, e.g. *to go*. This form contrasts with *go* (base form) *going, gone*, the non-finite forms of the verb. See *finite*, and Section 22. Note particularly in this grammar the distinction between *infinitive* and *non-finite*.

Inflection

The changes made at the ends of words to indicate such things as *number, degree, finiteness*. Very little remains in modern English, and what there is is described in this grammar in the chapters on group structure. See *concord* and *case*.

In-P

A structural position in the clause, described in Section 13. If P has both an auxiliary and a main verb, In-P is the position after the auxiliary. For a one-word P, In-P is the position immediately before P.

Interested Party (I)

The name used here for one of the categories of deep grammar, explained in the Introduction page 7. Its closest parallel in surface grammar is the indirect object.

Interrogative

See *mood*, and Sections 1 and 10.

IT-theme

When a clause, e.g.
John gave Bill the book yesterday is rearranged by a structure beginning with *it*,
It was yesterday that John gave Bill the book
It was John that gave Bill the book yesterday
It was Bill that John gave the book to yesterday
It was the book that John gave Bill yesterday
See fig. 11.4.

Item

This is a general term in grammatical description, used for any individual morpheme, word, group, clause or sentence. See page 12 of the Introduction.

Lexical Adjunct
See Adjunct.

Linkage
A type of co-ordination. Section 8.

Linker
Co-ordinating adjuncts of two main types:
A^+ 'lister'—*and, but, or*
A^L (sometimes called 'sentence adverb' or 'sentence-linker') *however, in that case, consequently*, etc.
See Section 8.

Main Verb
The final word in a verbal group is usually one with lexical meaning; so in *will have come*, the auxiliaries *will* and *have* are mainly grammatical operators, and *come* is the main verb.

Manner
A traditional category of adverb, applied in this grammar to adjuncts (page 101). Contrasted with place, time and sometimes frequency.

Marked
A very general term in linguistics, contrasting with *unmarked*. Typical uses:
(*a*) marked = prominent because unusual, e.g. a marked sequence of clauses in a sentence, with bound clauses coming before free ones.
(*b*) marked = showing in its form an indication of its structure, as against unmarked, whose form is neutral. For example, a few countable nouns, like *sheep*, are not marked for number.

Mass (noun)
= uncountable noun
See the discussion of number in Section 19.

Meaning
One of the most difficult words in linguistics. Here it refers to our intuitive sense of similarity and difference among utterances. In Section 5 it is contrasted with two other types of evidence, *componence* and *syntax*. Meaning, the most difficult to support with evidence, is the most important sensation of language, and the whole of linguistics is an attempt to record faithfully the relationship between the physical facts of language and the meaning that we perceive in it.

Medium
The raw material of language in the physical world—the channel of communication. The two main media for human language are sound waves (speech) and visual symbols (writing)—but there are many minor variations.
    The medium puts limitations on what can be transmitted, and thereby affects the structure of language. For example, the fact that sound waves die away very quickly, while visual symbols are much longer-lived, affects the structure of speech and writing. See Introduction, page 2.

Minor Theme
When the first thematic element in a clause is a linker (A^L) like *therefore*, capable of occurring in many different places in sentence structure without affecting its surroundings, this is called minor theme. See Section 12.

Mixed Mood (sentence)
A sentence which contains F clauses in more than one mood, e.g. *We're going to have a drink—would you like one?* See Section 1.

Modal Verbs

A sub-class of auxiliary verbs with considerable meaningful contrasts: one of the distinctive features of modern English. They crop up throughout this book, but particularly in Section 22. Their meaning is basically to qualify the assertive power of utterances, so that instead of *Bill likes fish* there is *Bill might like fish* or *Bill would like fish* (if . . .) or *Bill ought to like fish*. *Will* and *shall* are modal verbs rather than markers of tense.

Modifier (m)

This word is used in group structure in a very particular meaning; briefly it is a category for items occurring before the *headword*, e.g. deictics, numerals, adjectives. Items occurring after the headword are called *qualifiers* (q). See Section 17.

Moment of Utterance

The actual time at which one speaks or writes something. It is a useful concept in studying the verbal group in English, since the tenses are more easily seen in relation to the moment of utterance than to abstract models of time. See Sections 23 and 24.

Mood

The arrangement of subject and predicator in a clause. Used to distinguish free and bound clauses in Section 1, it is fully discussed in Section 10. Briefly, the four moods of F clauses are:

Dec.(larative): SP
Int.(errogative): P[S]
Imp.(erative):   P (no S)
Moodless: (no P)

Moodless Clause

See *mood*.

Morpheme

The lowest rank in the grammar; the indivisible unit. If you divide a morpheme, you find you are in the area of phonology, but not grammar. The word *socks* divides into two morphemes, *sock* and *s*, but *sock* does not sub-divide in the grammar. Analysis into *s* and *ock* is a phonological analysis of the syllable, since neither *ock* nor this *s* is a morpheme.

Negative

See *polarity*.

Neutral Theme

Where the first choice in a clause is mood (i.e. S or P). See Section 12.

n-forms

The 'past participle' of the verb; in most English verbs it is the same as the finite past tense.

He liked me
He has liked me
Liked by all his friends, . . .

But in some common verbs there are separate forms

Bill stole the spoons
Bill has stolen the spoons
Stolen by Bill, the spoons . . .

See fig. 22.1.

Nominal Group

Chapter 3
A structure with a noun or pronoun as headword, and optional modifiers and qualifiers.

Nominalised

Section 16, page 125.

Non-Defining

(or non-restrictive)
See *relative clause*.

Noun

The typical headword of a nominal group—Section 17.

Noun Clause

A traditional term for a clause thought to substitute for a noun. There were two types.

(a) *What I did was right.* The clause *What I did* is subject of the whole clause, and is described here as a case of rankshift (Section 18).

(b) *I said that I was coming. That I was coming* is described here as a reported clause (Section 4).

Number

A system of the (countable) noun, the deictic, and the present tense of the finite verb. Each is slightly different, giving rise to several categories of number in the nominal group (see page 150), and the *collective* use of the noun (page 153).

Object

Clause objects—see Sections 14 and 15. Prepositional objects—Section 25. This term is used in a traditional way to name a nominal group that forms a structure of mutual dependence with a predicator or a preposition, e.g. I want *a hat*, Bill went to *the pictures*. See *direct* and *indirect*.

One

This word has several functions, mentioned in various places in the grammar.

(a) numeral   *One book is enough*

(b) personal pronoun   *One can do what one likes*

(here meaning is neutral among the three persons, but the tone of the English is pompous, and most people in conversation would say, *You can do what you like*).

(c) as a substitute for any countable noun   *The big ones are on the table*

Note that *ones* is an acceptable form,

and that the group is not just *h*, but has to be modified or qualified.

One-way

A communication situation where one person or group is permanently speaker/writer. (E.g. a lecture, printed book.) See Introduction page 3.

Ordinal

first, second, third, etc. (Section 20).

O-theme

See *Theme*.

Participle (present and past)

Traditional term for some uses of the *-ing* form and the *n* form (see fig. 22.1 for the verb terminology of this book).

Partitive

See Section 19.

Passive

A Predicator with structure . . . *be n-form:* Voice (active and passive) is discussed in several places in the grammar. See Introduction, page 9 (comparison with *complement* structures) and Section 23, page 188.

Past-Indirect

The 'simple past tense' of most English grammars, here coupled with the word *indirect*—for reasons see *present-direct*. See Section 23.

P-Bound

A clause whose Predicator is non-finite. See Section 7.

Perfect (tense)

Traditionally a verb form *have + n-form*, e.g. *I have arrived*.

Performative verbs

Verbs whose utterance is a performance of their meaning, e.g. *I declare him elected* is a declaration. *I appoint you Chairman* is an actual appointment.

Phase
The selection of second and subsequent predicators in the structure of a single clause, e.g. *I would like you* TO LEAVE. Fully set out in Section 16.

Phrasal Verb
A grammatical and lexical association between a verb and either a preposition or a common adverb.
I won't go into the details (go into)
He puts a song over very well (put over)
More examples and discussion, in Section 25.

Phrase
A common linguistic term for a structure comprising more than one word, but less than a clause. It has specialised uses in modern grammars, and some confusing uses outside linguistics (e.g. 'a German phrase book'). This book avoids the term.

Pivot (P)
The name here for the verb category of deep grammar, explained in the Introduction, page 7.

Place
A traditional category of adverb, applied in this grammar to adjuncts. Contrasted with manner, time and sometimes frequency. See Section 13.

Polarity
A system of the verbal group (Section 21) and also reflected in the clause by adjuncts such as *never*. Important in the description of *tags* (Section 11) and adjunct position (Section 13) Terms: *positive, negative*.

Positive
See *Polarity*.

Possessive
The form of a nominal group ending with *'s* or *s'* or the corresponding form for pronouns, e.g. *his, their, theirs*. See Section 19.

Post-P
A structural position in the clause, meaning 'after the predicator'—described in Section 13.

Pre-Deictic
The first of two deictics in a nominal group (e.g. in *all my friends, all* is pre-deictic). This structure is developed in *partitives*. See Section 19.

Prepositional Group
A sub-class of Adverbial group, commonly exponent of A in clause structure or Q in nominal group structure. Some discussion late in Section 1; a note at the end of Section 18; structural description, Section 25.

Present-Direct
The 'simple present tense' in most grammars. Here it is coupled with the word *direct* to indicate
(*a*) that present time is a misleading meaning for this tense.
(*b*) that the contrast between direct reference to the moment of utterance, and indirect reference is more important.
See Section 23.

Pretonic
In phonology, the patterns of intonation in a tone group that precede the tonic syllable. The pretonics and tones of English are fully set out in Volume 2 of this course.

Prime Mover (M)
The name used here for a category of deep grammar, explained in the Introduction, page 7. Its closest

parallel in surface grammar is the subject of an active transitive clause.

Progressive
= continuous
See Section 24.

Pronoun
A word which can occur as headword in a restricted nominal group—fig. 17.2.
The word *one* is different—see separate entry.

Proper Noun
Section 17. A noun that cannot be modified or qualified by anything selective or identifying.

Proposition
One part of a two-part clause structure; the other part is the *tag*.
e.g. *he's happy,   isn't he*
    PROPOSITION   TAG
Section 11 is all about two-part clause structures.

Qualifier (q)
With *modifier* and *headword*, makes up the full structural possibilities of nominal groups. Items occurring after the headword are qualifiers, and it is notable in English that they are most frequently prepositional groups or rankshifted clauses (Section 18). Adverb-head and adjective-head groups also have MHQ structures (Section 25) and show a limited range of qualifiers.

Qualitative
Established term for adjectives that indicate qualities. In the grammar a syntactic criterion identifies them, namely ability to be regularly submodified by, e.g. *very*. See Section 20.

Question
An utterance that shows expectation of a particular verbal response.

Contrasted in Section 1 with *command*, *statement* and *response*.

Quoted Speech
Where one utterance is quoted inside another. In writing we use inverted commas (' ') to indicate quotes; in speech there are no obvious clues. Contrasted with *report* structures where the syntax of the reported clause fits in with the surrounding syntax. Effects on *mood*—Section 12. Section 7 shows report structures, but quoted speech is not discussed in any detail in this book.

Rank
A unit in grammar which is in a special relationship with other units. Any structure is composed of one or more instances of the rank next below. See Introduction, fig. 0.5.

Rankshift
Section 18.
An important concept in this grammar. The elementary structure of this description of English supposes five ranks (sentence, clause, group, word, morpheme) related as set out in the Introduction, fig. 0.5. Each item at a rank is made up of items from the unit next below.

Rankshift is the exception to this last statement. It is possible in certain clear and restricted circumstances for higher-ranked items to be shifted into a lower structure, as in this nominal group;
The house that I'm going to buy is not built yet.
The clause *that I'm going to buy* is a qualifier of **house**, within the nominal group that is subject to the whole clause.

Recursive

A syntactic pattern which can be repeated indefinitely without making an ungrammatical item. This is an important area of study in modern grammars, and languages are rich in recursive patterning. One of the simplest is listing

I want beer and wine and whisky and gin . . .

But there are many others

He is a big, ugly, stupid, cowardly, lazy horse (Section 20)

I want to see you help him find it (Section 20)

The crane jib pulley tension arm bearing has fractured (Section 21)

Reference (system of deictics)

Terms: specific and general

Typical specific deictics: *the, this, my, John's*

Typical general deictics: *a, another, each, no*

Referent

A general term for the item referred to by a pronoun or deictic. See also *antecedent*.

Reflexive

A type of pronoun reference. The personal pronouns each have a reflexive form: *myself, himself*, etc.

Bill and Tom were playing soldiers. Bill waved a spear at Tom and hurt $\begin{cases} \text{him} (= \text{Tom}) \\ \text{himself} (= \text{Bill}) \end{cases}$

See Section 14.

Relative Clause

Traditional term for clauses which relate closely to nouns. Divide into two types:

(*a*) defining (or restrictive). See *defining* and Section 18.

(*b*) non-defining (or non-restrictive). Here named *bound adding clauses*, described in Section 3.

Although both types of relative clause can look the same, their structural relations are so different that the term *relative clause* is avoided in this book as much as possible.

Relative Timing

A system to account for the meaning of the verbal group structure (*be + ing*). Otherwise called *continuous tense* or aspect. See Section 24.

Report (also Reported, Reporting)

A structure formed by a reporting clause (which has a reporting verb like *say, tell, think* in it) and a reported clause bound to it. One type of noun clause of traditional grammar. Some detail in Section 4 and subsequent sections in Chapter 1.

Response

An utterance that does not initiate any response or action. See Section 1.

Restatement Response

Formed from any positive statement by the formula

so + pronoun + auxiliary

e.g. *Madge is writing*

    So she is

See Section 11.

Restrictive

A type of relative clause—see *defining*.

Rheme

The remainder of a clause when the theme has been identified. Some modern grammarians are taking a great interest in 'theme-and-rheme' analysis, but it is not developed here. *Rheme* is only used in the tag structures around fig. 11.4.

Scaled, Scaling
The system of arranging degree sub-modifiers in nominal groups. Terms: simple, tempering, comparative, superlative. See Section 20.

Selectivity
A system of the nominal group set out in Section 19. A selective group includes *d* or *o* in the modifier, while a *global* group does not.

Seminegatives
A class of adjuncts, e.g. *hardly, scarcely*, which have their own patterning in *checking tags* (Section 11) and in the position of adjuncts (Section 13).

Sentence
The highest unit of grammar, and the smallest unit of discourse. The distinction between sentence and clause is carefully maintained in this grammar, even though many clauses are, or could be, simple sentences. So it is not said of sentences that they have subjects, nor of clauses that they are statements. See Introduction and Chapter 1.

Sentence-Adverb; Sentence-Linker
See Section 8. Adjuncts like *however, perhaps*.

Silent Stress
In English phonology, it is assumed that stresses occur at roughly equal intervals of time. Usually this is evident from the occurrence of a stressed syllable, but occasionally the gap between stressed syllables is about twice the usual, and it is held that a foot with a silent stress must be indicated by the gap.
Some examples of the grammatical function of a silent stress are in

Section 8. See also Volume 2 of this course.

Simple (tense)
A verbal group which consists of just one word.

Situation
The non-linguistic objects events and ideas that are relevant to the understanding of an utterance. See Section 1.

Specific
A class of deictic (Section 19) that involves the identification of the referent(s) of the nominal group.
the this that there those, my, his, her, our, your, their,
all rankshifted possessive groups at D, e.g. *Bill's*. The other class is *general*.

S-Tag Theme
See page 94.

Statement
An utterance that initiates a general, not a particular, response. Contrasted in Section 1 with *question, command* and *response*.

Status
The system that distinguishes between finite and non-finite verbs in English (see page 181).

Structure
A grammatical statement is expressed in symbols which have great generality. For example there is an indefinitely large number of clauses, but only a few different clause structures, like SPC, ASP, made up of combinations of even fewer *elements* of structure, like S.

Subclassifiers
A classifier of a classifier in nominal group structure, e.g. in *wing-nut*

cutter, wing is a subclassifier of the classifier *nut*.

Subject (S)
That element of a clause which can set up number concord relationships with the predicator. Also the unmarked theme of the clause, and, with P, the indicator of the mood of a clause.

Subject Clauses
See page 62.

Submodifier
A modifier of a modifier; particularly in the nominal group, e.g. in a *very nice party*, *very* is a submodifier of the modifier *nice*. See Section 19.

Subordinate
A general linguistic term for a relationship of unequal status between grammatical items, bound—free, dependent—independent, modifier —head, qualifier—head, are all examples (subordinate item first). See also *co-ordinate*.

Subqualifier
A qualifier of a qualifier or modifier —in nominal group structures. See Sections 19 and 20.

Superlative
A type of submodification of adjectives. See fig. 20.2 and the entry under *comparative*.

Surface
See *deep*, and Introduction, page 4.

Syntax
The use of the terms 'syntax' and 'grammar' is variable in modern linguistics. In this book the only attempt to pin down the words is in the use of *syntax* for the external structural relations of an item, contrasting with *componence* (e.g. Section 5).

System
One of the central concepts of this approach to grammar. A system is an arrangement of structural patterns according to small sets of mutually exclusive, meaningful choices. Discussion in the Introduction, page 12.

Tag
One part of a two-part clause structure. The other part is the *proposition*. The most typical example is the question-tag, e.g.

It's late,	*isn't it?*
proposition	tag

Section 11 is all about Tags.

Tempering
Parallel with *comparative* and *superlative* degree—the submodification of adjectives by words like *very, quite, awfully*. See fig. 20.2.

Term
One choice in a system, e.g. *singular* and *plural* may be two terms in a system of *number*. See fig. 0.6.

Theme
(Section 12)
The theme of a clause is the element selected to be in the initial position, and therefore gaining some prominence. When no element is specially selected S comes first and is regarded as unmarked theme. Any variation on this pattern bringing C, A, O, or an extra S to the front of the clause is described as *marked* theme.

For example where the first element in a clause is an adjunct, it is called *thematic* unless it is an adjunct like A+ or A^B that must come first. In the case of A^L it is called *minor theme*, and a second, major, theme is chosen.

Time (adjunct)
A traditional adverb category, contrasting with place, manner and frequency. See Section 13.

Tone (Group), Tonic (Syllable)
In phonology, the *tone group* carries meaningful intonation patterns. Each tone group is made up of one or more *feet*, and one of the feet (usually the last) is called the *tonic foot* because it contains the *tonic syllable*. The tonic syllable carries the main contrast of intonation, and is the most prominent syllable in the tone group. There are a few notes on intonation at the end of the Introduction, and Volume 2 of this course deals with it in detail.

Transitive
Of a verb: capable of occurring with an object, as P in SPO.

Of a clause: contains the element O.

Transitivity is a fundamental notion in grammar; Sections 14 and 15 are concerned with it, but *phase* structures (Sections 16) and report structures (Section 4) and phrasal verbs (Section 25) also deal with aspects of transitivity.

Two-Part Clause
See Section 11.

Two-Way
A communication situation when no one person or group is permanently speaker/writer. See also *one-way*. An ordinary conversation is two-way, and there are several situations in between completely one-way and completely two-way discourse; e.g. a discussion with a chairman, the correspondence column of a newspaper.

Uncountable
A class of noun that cannot occur with a singular deictic (e.g. *a, an*) or the numeral *one*. Also called *mass* nouns. See Section 19.

Unit
A carrier of grammatical patterns—any of the five *ranks*.

Unmarked
In systemic contrast with *marked*.

Verbal Group
A structure made up of verbs: auxiliary and main verbs. Sections 22, 23 and 24 refer.

Vocative
A tag structure (Section 11) where the addressee is named.

Wh-groups
A small set of groups containing items that start with the letters *wh-*, e.g. *which, who, whose book, why*. They have several grammatical roles
(*a*) interrogative pronouns
(*b*) reported clause binders
(*c*) adding clause binders (not *what*, not often *when*)
There are separate theme statements in Section 12 for *wh*-groups.

Some wh-words have limited occurrence; *what* is never an adding clause binder; the items with *-ever* are restricted, etc. One word, *how* is frequently in this set without having initial *w*.